THE PREDATOR AND VARMINT HUNTER'S GUIDEBOOK

D0916705

BY PATRICK MEITIN

Published by

Krause Publications, a division of F+W Media, Inc.
5225 Joerns Drive, Suite 2 • Stevens Point, WI 54481
715-445-2214 • 888-457-2873
www.krausebooks.com

**To order books or other products, call toll-free 1-855-864-2579
or visit us online at www.krausebooks.com**

Cover photography by Ralph Hensley/windigoimages.com

ISBN-13: 9781440248504
ISBN-10: 1440248508

Designed by Molly Rauss and Tom Nelsen
Edited by Brian Lovett and Chris Berens
Printed in China

10 9 8 7 6 5 4 3 2 1

DEDICATION

For my father, who rekindled my passion for varmint shooting, tack-driving firearms and precision reloading on a grand scale after a long absence. And, of course, my loving wife, who puts up with all my scattered gear and long absences.

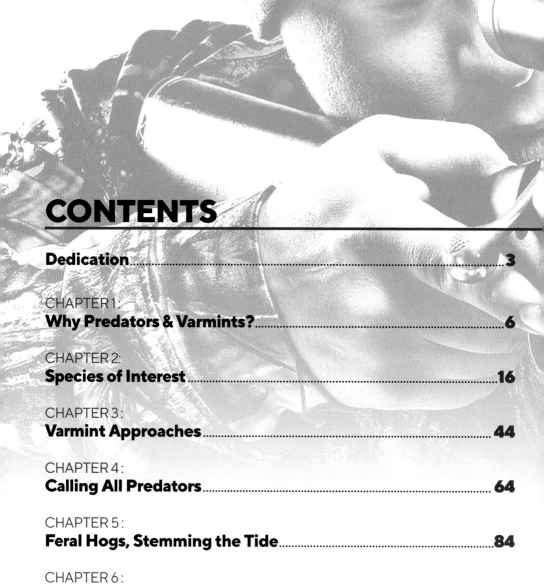

CONTENTS

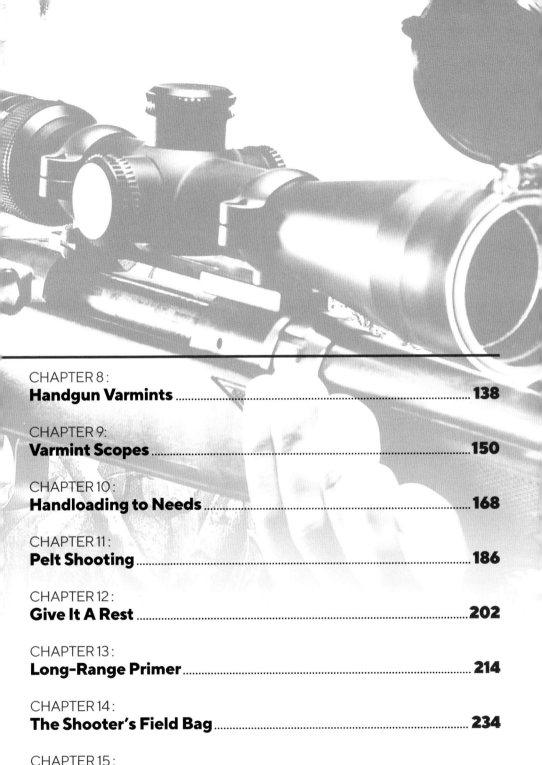

⊕ Chapter 1
Why Predators & Varmints?

Born and raised in the West and close to open spaces, I began hunting early, tagging my first rifle mule deer when 10 or 11 and my first elk at 14 (with my own handloads). Because of this early initiation, the transition into muzzleloaders and then serious bowhunting was a predictable progression. By the time I graduated high school, I'd forsaken big-game hunting with rifles, becoming a dyed-in-the-wool bowhunter in my late teens and not shooting a big-game animal with rifle for more than 25 years. Yet I maintained a full arsenal of rifles and handguns and continued avidly handloading, forever seeking more accurate loads for every firearm I owned. This had everything to do with varmints and, to a larger extent, predator hunting, as I never have seen a coyote I didn't desperately want to shoot. Despite bowhunting as the cornerstone to my big-game journey, I never lost my fascination with firearms and their use in pursuing small varmints and predators.

Varmint is a term tossed about loosely, with many inclined to include any small-game species. The official definition is an American-English colloquialism of vermin, representing animals that are considered a nuisance to man, and/or unprotected by game laws. Further, varmints are animals widely believed to spread disease or inclined to destroy crops, livestock or other private property. Strictly speaking, varmints do not include common small-game species such as cottontail rabbits, snowshoe hares or tree squirrels, though those species often exhibit pest-like behavior — just ask the backyard gardener or bird-feeder enthusiast. These popular small-game animals are rightly official game in most states in addition to providing excellent table fare. There is also the designation of predator — including foxes, bobcats and coyotes — and these are often afforded seasons, but also frequently considered vermin.

So, licensing and/or season restrictions are no sure demarcation between varmint and genuine small-game or furbearer status, as many states require permits to shoot even nongame species. Idaho, for example, requires a hunting license to shoot ground squirrels (definite vermin) and coyotes (known livestock

LEFT: *There is no better way to get a youngster hooked on shooting than through small varmint shooting. The nonstop action keeps short attention spans from wandering and beats videos games any day. Scott Haugen photo.*

The author enjoys varmint shooting as much for the time he spends with his father as the shooting itself. This kind of quality time is difficult to find in these hectic times, even while big-game hunting.

killers), and Oregon requires hunting licenses for varmints on public but not private lands. Colorado requires a hunting license for varmints such as marmots or prairie dogs (and rattlesnakes) and has instituted highly defined seasons — the sure mark of a blue state. Texas, despite exploding populations of invasive feral hogs and resulting depredation, requires nonresidents to purchase a nongame license even while hunting private lands that Texas Parks and Wildlife invests zero resources to maintain. This, of course, says as much of the bureaucrats' lust for revenue as it does management concerns.

And let's get something straight from the beginning: I'm the farthest thing from a conquer-the-wilderness, Manifest Destiny type who believes every corner of North America must be made comfortable for livestock at the expense of all other living creatures. There is a balance to everything, even varmints and predators, and besides, if an animal is going to be eliminated from the landscape, it isn't going to be by my bullets but rather a landowner's poison. And for our purposes, just to keep things tidy, varmint will specify smaller rodents and birds meeting the aforementioned definitions, and predator will mean common furbearing fauna such as foxes, bobcats and coyotes.

So the legitimate question becomes, why all the fuss about varmints and predators? The easy answer is that varmint shooting and predator hunting (calling usually) is just plain fun. The more involved answer is that varmints, predators and nongame species offer a fun, relaxing, rewarding and extremely affordable way for average blue-collar sportsmen (and ladies) to more thoroughly enjoy the shooting sports. And let's be frank: Although we might work under the mantle of pest elimination, we shoot not with the veniality of day traders but the zeal of children devouring ice cream.

Another harsh reality: Big-game hunting has become increasingly expensive with each decade. Quality big-game property has grown progressively more difficult to access, mostly because of the bane of the modern hunting lease and well-heeled hunters' willingness to pay top dollar to keep prime habitats to themselves. Even in areas with abundant public lands, top-quality big-game licenses in proven trophy areas are secured only through low-odds lottery drawings after accumulating the correct number of preference points or by purchasing expensive landowner tags. It's easy for the average working man to feel left out.

Varmint and predator hunting allow easier access to private lands (by helping thin destructive pests), year-round seasons for many species and fewer regulations and permit requirements — in short, the ability for a serious firearms enthusiast to stay engaged and sated. Interestingly, even varmints go only to the highest bidder in select locations, and guided varmint shoots and lodges are now more common than ever. But in the bigger picture, varmints are still largely wide open to those willing to do their homework.

....

More private ground is locked up each year because of hunting leases or landowners fearful of a litigious society. Helping eliminate vermin can help a shooter get his foot in the door and gain access to prime private properties.

For many, varmint shooting and predator hunting offer welcome off-season sport. Here in northern Idaho, for example, after the last general big-game season passes in early December, there's nothing to look forward to but a long, tedious winter of ice-fishing (no thanks), snowmobiling (can't afford it) or skiing (over it). Predator calling becomes my way of avoiding the creeping shack nasties, getting me out of the house and busy with something challenging and rewarding that sometimes actually pays for itself via the raw-fur trade. In New Mexico, when winter doldrums got me down, there was productive predator calling in the offing, but for an uncomplicated, carefree afternoon stroll, it was difficult to beat jackrabbit hunting.

In fact, superfluous jackrabbits (and prairie dogs) are what I honed my rifle-shooting skills on while young and building big-game ambitions. I was lucky to work on large ranches during summer vacations, bucking hay for 10 cents a bale, or traversing large ranchlands pitching hay to starving cows and checking watering tanks during drought months, years before I earned an official driver's license. A rifle of some sort invariably rode along. Throughout my formative years, I treated my .243 Win. Remington 700 ADL like a .22 Long Rifle, handloading 100 rounds of Sierra 60-grain hollow-points at a time and shooting every one of them at jacks, prairie dogs or occasional thirteen-lined ground squirrels while making ranch rounds. Another landowner, an alfalfa farmer I worked for sporadically, supplied a friend and me bricks of .22 LR shells, a farm pickup and 10-cent-each bounty for jacks, encouraging nighttime spotlighting on his sprawling alfalfa fields. We regularly filled pickup beds with dead hares.

The raw-fur market also hit all-time highs while I was in middle and high school, spawning an intense interest in predator calling that persists today. A $30 to $60 coyote and $50 gray fox (late '70s through '80s prices) was big money for a teenager — a $200 to $400 bobcat akin to winning a lottery. By the time I'd earned

For many serious hunters, predator calling fills those long gaps between the end of fall big-game seasons and beginning of seasons for spring turkeys and bears. Predator calling can also pay for itself when fur prices are healthy.

a driver's license at 15, I bought my own car and insurance, and owned only the best rifles, scopes and other sporting equipment, all financed with fur money.

Varmints and predators offer the ultimate big-game preparation. The tendency in varmint shooting is for ever-greater challenges — running or longer shots, and smaller targets or handguns. After all, unlike big game, in which a wounded animal spells disaster, imperfect hits on smaller varmints translate into sure kills 98 percent of the time; a hit-or-miss proposition. A big-game season can hinge on one trigger pull. The best varmint shoots include hundreds of shots fired daily. Breath and trigger control, wind, doping trajectories and better understanding cartridge capabilities become second nature.

A lot of firearms loonies out there couldn't care less about big-game hunting but love varmint shooting. This normally hinges on the opportunity for lots of shooting with minimal license requirements and regulations — and expenses.

Varmint and predator shooting takes the edge off. I mean, when you can snipe a woodchuck, prairie dog or ground squirrel with regularity at 200, 300 or 400 yards, hitting big game at any reasonable range seems like child's play. It was no mistake I used that .243 Win. to tag many elk and mule deer while still attending high school. Varmints had ingrained prerequisite shooting skills and absolute confidence.

Meanwhile, you're helping control unwanted or harmful pests. Those nighttime spotlighting missions for alfalfa-raiding jackrabbits weren't just for amusement (though we had a hoot while doing it). Ten black-tailed jackrabbits consume as much alfalfa annually as a cow. Multiply that by pickup-beds of jacks and you can imagine the damage inflicted on a farmer's cash crop. Likewise, during those droughty years of my eastern New Mexico youth, cattle were having a difficult time surviving. Abundant jackrabbits only compounded the problem. Interestingly, the Western jackrabbit seems to thrive during drought conditions, likely because more of its prolific young surviving during hot, dry conditions.

Woodchucks, prairie dogs and ground squirrels, because of their proclivity for digging, have become enemies of most agricultural producers. Not only does their extensive burrowing and tunneling threaten livestock and farm equipment, but the vegetation they consume and clear away from burrow entrances to better view approaching danger adds up quickly when they're congregated in large colonies. Ground squirrels are especially notorious for undermining roads, which cave away during wet winter months, and breaching livestock-pond dams, which then require costly repairs.

With feral hogs, you're entering a unique realm of destruction. Wild boars, as I like to call them, ravage agricultural fields, push holes through woven fences, root and wallow in livestock pastures, undermine or pollute stock tanks and chew through waterlines, and generally compete with native species such as deer, turkeys and quail for food. In Texas, where deer leases are big business, off-season hog hunts can be arranged for affordable daily fees, prices dependant on how much of a nuisance hogs are at the time and lodging facilities provided. I've never hunted Texas free — aside from the generosity of friends — but have enjoyed productive hog hunts (say, five to seven hogs per diem) for $50 to $100 daily fees. Likely because Texas has little public land, there seems to be an unwritten law among Texas landowners that no gratis hunting be allowed.

In eastern Oregon, where we enjoy our most productive high-volume ground squirrel shooting, you'll find the highest concentrations around and across irrigated hay and alfalfa fields. Outlying areas harbor these Belding's "sage rats," but irrigated crop circles have artificially inflated their numbers, so a young or cut field can resemble the migrating herds of Africa's Serengeti in miniature. Shoot 400 or 500 rats one day, leaving a field looking like a battle scene from a Sylvester Stallone movie, convinced you've made a considerable dent, and you'll return the next morning to find the fallen have disappeared (ground squirrels greedily eat one another) and been replaced by fresh volunteers. There seems to be no end to them. They're a bane to farmers if a great boon to the rifleman. I mean, where else can you effortlessly burn 1,000 rounds of .22 LR and centerfire ammo in a weekend? It's the epitome of varmint shooting ecstasy; a howling good time, while also honing shooting

Varmints and predators have traditionally meant species such as prairie dogs, ground squirrels, groundhogs, coyotes and foxes. Today, that includes invasive feral hogs, which seem to be appearing in new areas annually.

skills to a razor's edge. And landowners love you for it — provided you avoid shooting holes in irrigation pipes and machinery.

Which is another huge benefit of simple varmint shooting: I can name many properties where I've easily gained permission to shoot varmints or predators but where game-bird and/or big-game hunting was restricted or came only at a hefty price. I've enjoyed open access to ranches where I could call coyotes any time, but hunting the desert mule deer sharing the same ground was forbidden. I recall knocking on Montana doors, begging trespass permission. The answer was usually an unapologetic no, until I pointed out I only wanted to snipe a few prairie dogs, upon which I was welcomed with open arms, ranchers often taking time out of their busy day to lead me to productive pastures they wanted thinned. Our shooting property in eastern Oregon was accessed only because of destructive ground squirrels, but the abundant upland birds and big game were strictly off limits. And so the story goes in too many places to relate here.

Also, because prime varmint and predator seasons generally occur during off-seasons —ground squirrels and prairie dogs in spring and early summer, the predators in late winter — you disturb no one, namely big-game hunters paying to hunt a piece of real estate or enjoy a guided hunt.

I've also observed through the years that varmint/predator shooting gets my foot in the door initially, and a prolonged relationship with a landowner who observes courteous and reliable behavior often leads to eventual

invitations to hunt big game or game birds. This means closing gates behind you, picking up after yourself, avoiding shooting equipment or creating ruts in wet fields or roads, and, well, you know, exercising basic common sense. It doesn't hurt to drop in and show a rancher a couple of dead coyotes once in a while, remember them at Christmas with a bottle of hooch or brick of .22 shells, or offering a cold beer and pausing to chat a while when you run into them in the field. Farmers and ranchers often live isolated, solitary

Whether plinking with an auto-loading .22 Long Rifle within 100 yards or sniping at long range, small varmints such as these Belding's ground squirrels hone shooting skills and better prepare you for big-game hunting.

lives, so chewing the fat is generally welcomed. Just remember to say, "Yes sir," and, "No sir," look them in the eye while speaking, and take your hat off before entering their house or addressing the missus. Rural residents still appreciate such old-fashioned gestures, even if the rest of the world has abandoned basic manners.

After many years of shooting "rats" on that eastern Oregon spread, my father has become genuine friends with the landowner, allowing me to shirttail into the deal. We have run of the place and are welcomed to hook up to his electricity and water while camping. He stops by camp to share a beer and see how we've done. He recently offered a pronghorn landowner tag in a state where such tags are highly coveted. Only because of ground squirrel shooting did this cozy relationship develop.

For the gun-loony shooter, varmint hunting offers it all. If you like to shoot guns of all kinds and burn a lot of powder, varmint shooting and predator hunting allows that opportunity, providing abundant targets and shooting volume big-game hunters never experience. Generous off-season opportunities and plenty of shooting ultimately lead to more finely honed shooting skills, whether that means shooting jackrabbits offhand at reasonable ranges with rimfire rifles or pistols, or pushing the envelope of centerfire range capabilities from a portable bench among a colony of copious prairie dogs or ground squirrels. This confidence follows you into big-game arenas, though interestingly, many shooting enthusiasts I know shoot only varmints, leaving big game to those with more ambition or thicker wallets.

While you're enjoying all this shooting fun, you're also doing your part to thin destructive pests or predators that cost landowners money or damage habitats for more desirable game species. This dynamic opens doors to further hunting opportunity, igniting lasting relationships with landowners who provide a place to shoot for years to come — and just maybe future upland-bird or big-game invitations.

⊕ Chapter 2
Species of Interest

Varmint shooting has become increasingly popular across the country as shooters seek something more readily available than modern big-game hunting. This has resulted in some areas near municipalities being shot out, but good shooting is still available. Fred Eichler photo.

Varmint shooting includes many species of opportunity, largely dependent on region. My old friend the late Jim Dougherty, a pioneer in predator calling, aggressively defended backyard bird feeders against invasive starlings, sniping them with an air rifle from his office window. I recall an early gun writer spinning tales of men visiting Northeastern landfills after nightfall, directing vehicle headlights into heaped rubbish and shooting a seemingly inexhaustible supply of scurrying rats with .22 LR rifles. Sounds like great fun to me.

There are no rules here. The Western varmint shooter has it especially good from the variety standpoint. Maybe the East was once like this, but sprawling

LEFT: *One of the wonderful things about varmint and predator shooting is the wide variety of species available across the country. The author shot these black-tailed prairie dogs in West Texas at the end of a long road trip including dozens of species.*

Woodchucks are the quintessential Eastern varmint species. Strongholds such as the Northeast have become more problematic because of burgeoning human populations, but the Upper Midwest has stepped in as the new hotspot.

suburbia has diminished varmint habitats and target species to just a few — not that Eastern varmint shooters take their sport any less seriously. Still, varmint shooting usually involves targeting one species by seeking landscapes those critters frequent most reliably.

Today, the best varmint shooting — and easiest private-land access — is generally farthest from cities and towns. That's not because landowners close to town don't want varmints exterminated. It's just that varmint shooting has become so popular that readily accessible areas can become quickly shot out. Sadly, landowners near major metropolitan areas are also more likely to have had negative experiences with the public and become reluctant to allow trespass rights.

Planning varmint shoots starts with choosing species readily available in your region, learning what habitats they prefer and seeking settings where shooting is permitted or access easily gained. Productive varmint shooting requires plenty of up-front investigation, but when you discover a hotspot, you'll generally have it mostly to yourself into the foreseeable future. Dedicated varmint shooters continually keep an ear to the ground. Wildlife conservation biologists can be great sources of information. I once located a ground squirrel hotspot by chatting up a state-forest employee who complained of the squirrels chewing replanted seedlings.

Woodchucks, the Original Eastern Varmint

Varmint shooting isn't supposed to be complicated. Isolate a species of interest, find

Woodchuck Range

David Kelly, Frank Gallant and Nick Gallant, left to right, take their woodchuck hunting seriously, investing in precision rifles and scopes for long-range shooting. Their skill is evident in this photo of a successful morning's shoot. David Kelly photo.

private land you can access or open public land, and have at it. Here's some food for thought.

As a gun-crazy youngster and voracious reader of outdoor literature, I relished the tales of long-range Eastern woodchuck shooting that were *de rigueur* in the hunting magazines of my youth. It was precision shooting, careful reloading, specialized rifles and cartridges, and honed shooting skills wrapped into one. Though I'd shot mule deer and elk, I wanted badly to someday travel East to enjoy this exacting pastime. Woodchucks, or groundhogs, likely sparked varmint shooting passions in many other riflemen. Northeastern woodchuck fields aren't what they once were, nor do you see a lot written about them today. White-tailed deer now dominate sporting-journal print space.

The woodchuck still inhabits most of its original range, but encroaching civilization has made so much of it off limits to shooting — if not for fear of ricocheting bullets, then the suburbanite's aversion to jarring rifle cracks.

The real solution, as with any modern varmint shooting, is to venture farther afield. Western New York and the Catskill areas harbor good populations of woodchucks where shooting bothers no one. The upper Midwest is likely a better destination today, with varminteers quietly enjoying woodchuck shooting far from traditional Northeast shooting grounds.

Woodchucks, derived from the Cree Indian word wuchak, are found in pastures, meadows, fallow fields and woodlands across Canada south into Virginia and northern Alabama, west into eastern Kansas and northeastern North Dakota, and across the northern part of the country into east-central Alaska and British Columbia. The 16.5- to 34.25-inch-tall, grizzled-brown-to-reddish-black woodchuck wears a brushy tail, short legs and predominant white incisors. It weighs 4.5 to 14 pounds. The woodchuck's 8- to 12-inch mounded burrow openings belie its presence.

Prairie Dog Ranges

Woodchucks are active throughout the day, but especially early mornings and late afternoons. They seldom venture far from their burrows, though they have been known to climb trees for a better vantage. They subsist on vegetation such as grass, clover, alfalfa and plantains but raid farm crops when available to pack on winter fat for hibernation. The latter often puts them at odds with farmers, though moderate woodchuck numbers are beneficial to soil health. When alarmed, woodchucks produce sharp whistles followed by softer whistles while fleeing and peeking from burrows.

Woodchucks emerge in early spring (Feb. 2 is Groundhog Day, according to traditional wives' tales, or later in northern habitats). Males immediately began seeking a mate, and young are

The two major species of prairie dogs, black- and white-tailed, are easily distinguished by black (upper left) and white- tipped tails (upper right). Black-tails live largely on the eastern side of the Rockies, and white-tails inhibit the western slopes.

born in April or May, dispersing at 2 months old. Woodchuck meat is said to be excellent eating.

Prairie Dogs, the Ideal Long-Range Target

What woodchucks are to Eastern varmint shooters, prairie dogs are to Western riflemen. They might represent varmint shooting's most ideal target, living in wide-open, flat-to-rolling, low-nap habitats where they remain highly visible.

Most prairie dogs remain active year-round, save the nastiest portions of winter, when they retire to their burrows and let things blow over. Their size — 14 to 16.25 (black-tailed) or 13.5 to 14.75 (white-tailed) inches tall and a portly 1.9 to 3 pounds (black-tailed) or 1.5 to 2.5 pounds (white-tailed) — makes them ideal for stretching long-range capabilities. They're incredibly prolific

Prairie dogs make the ideal varmint shooter's target. They are hugely prolific, generally considered a nuisance by landowners and remain topside nearly year-round, unlike ground squirrels, which go underground when the weather turns hot.

The author and his father discovered these prairie dogs on wide-open public lands in western Wyoming by exploring oil-field roads in an ulra-remote area. The West's public lands offer nearly unlimited opportunity for varmint/predator shooting.

in prime habitats, with north-central and eastern Montana and almost all of Wyoming offering the most reliable shooting, the fewest (if any) restrictions and abundant public lands. Other than these hotspots, good shooting can be found in isolated pockets throughout their range.

The black-tailed prairie dog enjoys the widest distribution, inhabiting short-grass prairies in northern and eastern Montana and southwestern North Dakota, south to northwestern Texas, eastern and southern New Mexico and extreme southeastern Arizona. It has a pinkish-brown back and light-hued underbelly, its slim tail black tipped, as per its label. White-tailed prairie dogs, and the related Gunnison's subspecies (western Wyoming, northwestern Colorado and northeastern Utah) are slightly darker, with a lighter belly and white-tipped tail. The endangered Utah prairie dog of south-central Utah is protected.

Black-tailed prairie dogs construct conical-shaped entrance mounds of hard-packed earth, usually a foot high to prevent burrow flooding and provide sentry points above entrance holes. White-tailed mounds are generally less conspicuous and seldom hard packed. Instead of inhabiting short-grass prairies,

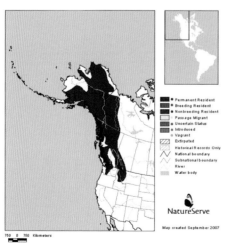

Hoary Marmot Range

white-tails thrive in sagebrush plains at higher, cooler elevations with their range centered in northeastern Utah, northwestern Colorado and western Wyoming.

Prairie dogs often sleep during hot summer middays, and are most active during mornings and evenings, though some action is normally available all day in even the hottest weather. Overcast days sometimes offer wide-open summer shooting. Gregarious black-tails are often found in towns of several thousand animals covering more than 100 acres. They rarely venture far from burrow safety, often pausing at a lateral passage 3 to 5 inches below the surface to listen for danger, with their tunnels dropping as much as 14 feet deep, where separate nesting and toilet chambers are located. Their diet usually consists of green vegetation and only occasionally insects such as grasshoppers.

Prairie dogs are highly vocal. Their double-noted staccato calls consist of distinctive chirps followed by a wheeze and tail flicking. This sounds the general alarm. A wheezing, whistling yip signals all is clear.

Prairie dogs remain on the hit lists of most ranchers because 250 dogs consume as much grass daily as a 1,000-pound cow (in addition to their burrowing), though they are important to prairie health in moderate numbers, so they should never be shot to extinction. Native American tribes relied on prairie dogs as a food source.

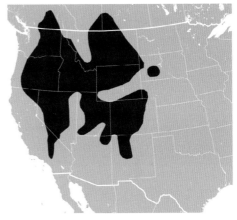

Western "Rockchucks"

The so-called rockchuck is actually a marmot, inhabiting rocky areas and talus slopes in mountainous or foothill regions of the West. Of the two most common species, yellow-bellied and hoary marmot, the former is most widespread, ranging from British Columbia and southern Alberta south through eastern California, west to Colorado and northern New Mexico, and north into Montana, at elevations from 6,000 to 12,000 feet. The hoary marmot is found in identical habitats but only in far northern Washington, Idaho and western Montana, north into Canada and eastern Alaska.

Yellow-bellied marmots typically have yellowish-brown bodies and yellowish bellies. They also have whitish spots between their eyes and brushy tails. They stand 18.5 to 28 inches tall and weigh 5 to 10 pounds.

When not immediately in evidence, marmots' 8- to 9-inch burrows with fans

Yellow-Bellied Marmot Range

....

Rockchunks, more accurately yellow-bellied marmots, are found in various rocky habitats, from high-elevation mountains to high-desert lava flows.

Marmots, often called rockchunks locally, are most commonly found at high elevations, such as the Colorado high country, where the author encountered this one. Colorado has seasons and license requirements, so check regulations before shooting.

of packed earth betray their presence. Burrows are typically located beneath rock piles, in crevices or other rocky shelter. When alarmed, they scurry to their burrows and chirp or whistle their displeasure.

Marmots feed on many kinds of greenery, putting on fat to sustain them from August or October through February or March. A litter of about five young is born soon after re-emergence. Yellow-bellied marmots are common hosts to the tick associated with Rocky Mountain spotted fever, so handle with care.

The slightly larger hoary marmots (often known as "whistlers") are silver-gray above with brownish rumps and white-hued bellies, providing excellent camouflage in their rocky, lichen-covered habitats. They measure 17.75 to 32 inches tall and weigh 8 to 20 pounds. Its habits closely mirror those of its more southerly cousin, hibernating October through February and mating soon after emergence to produce four to five young a month later. Its shrill alarm whistle is louder than the yellow-bellied, providing its nickname. Native tribes have long consumed its flesh.

Colorado and its Rocky Mountain habitat is an obvious hotspot, though seasons are included and licenses required. Southeastern Idaho offers excellent opportunities at lower elevations and the edges of vast lava flows adjacent to irrigated farming. Though really, any high-elevation habitat in the Rocky Mountain West offers potential. Related Alaska, Olympic (far western Washington) and Vancouver (Island) marmots are generally not hunted.

Ground Squirrels: Prolific Western Shooting

I could guess the number of ground squirrel subspecies, but let's just say there are many. A more important factor to varmint shooters is whether a ground squirrel species congregates in numbers dense enough to warrant serious efforts, though many — such as the thirteen-lined ground squirrel of my youth — pop up often enough to provide targets of opportunity while pursuing other species.

All ground squirrels exhibit relatively universal habits, such as producing sharp, high-frequency whistles that often give away their presence and location, to their yearly cycle of summertime estivation (a form of hibernation in response to hot temperatures), which continues through winter hibernation. Ground squirreling

Examples of locally important species include:

- **Washington:** found in isolated if sometimes-dense populations in central Washington, where substantial public ground is sparse.
- **Mexican:** found only in southwestern Texas.
- **Franklin's:** found from the Dakotas eastward to the upper Midwest, but only occasionally in dense colonies.

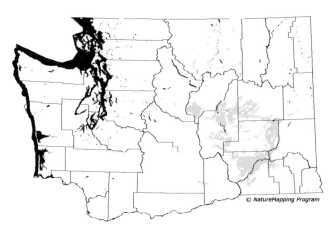

Washington Ground Squirrel Range

Mexian Ground Squirrel Range

is best from the onset of the first sustained spring days; March or April in most ranges, through early June. They're aggressive burrowers with hardy appetites, which make them scorned by most landowners. Vegetation constitutes most of the ground squirrel's diet, though they will consume insects, small rodents and birds, and occasionally, each other. They fight and kill one another in contention for prime nesting burrows. Locally, they are often called gophers or rats.

To serious varmint shooters, ground squirrels that habitually form dense colonies are species of interest, and of those, only a few are widespread enough to interest

- **Unita:** found in far eastern Idaho and western Wyoming and south into a narrow strip along Utah's high mountains.
- **Spotted:** located along Colorado's Front Range into New Mexico and western Texas, but seldom massing.
- **Thirteen-lined:** inhabit all of the Great Plains, but are a solitary or low-density species.

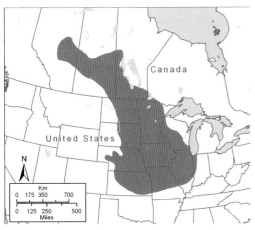

Franklin's Ground Squirrel Range

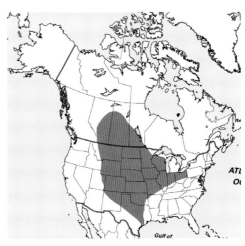

Thirteen-lined Ground Squirrel Range

anyone but regional shooters.

The species I'll highlight no doubt reveal my regional bias, but they're worth prolonged road trips for those seeking high-volume shooting.

Townsend's ground squirrels are relatively widespread and frequently offer fine shooting. They are plain gray above, tinged pinkish with light bellies. They stand 6.75 to 10.75 inches tall and weigh maybe .75 pound. They prefer open sagebrush habitats, often with adjacent rock edges, found in south-central Washington, eastern Oregon, extreme northeastern and southwestern California, most of Nevada and the far-western tier of Idaho. They commonly form large colonies and are most active from April (earlier in Washington) through early June, with their summer estivation beginning in mid-June to July and continuing through winter hibernation.

Richardson's ground squirrels are common on short-grass and sage prairies in locations as varied as northwestern Colorado and western Wyoming and into the Dakotas. They often congregate for high-volume shooting.

Richardson's ground squirrels appear in colonies only in ideal habitats of open short-grass and sage prairie with readily available food and water. I have enjoyed steady shooting in remote areas of western Wyoming and northwestern Colorado, for example. They are gray to yellowish-gray above, tinged with brown or buff and some-what molted with pale bellies. They stand 9.75 to 14 inches tall and weigh up to 1 pound. They range from southern Alberta, Saskatchewan and Manitoba south into northeastern Idaho, northern and central Montana, southwestern Wyoming, northwestern Colorado, northeastern South Dakota and extreme western Minnesota, with an isolated patch in northern Nevada and southwestern Idaho.

They're sometimes called "picket pin" for their habit of standing erect to survey their surroundings. Another handle is "flickertail," which derives from its tail-flicking habits while producing shrill whistles.

Belding's ground squirrels offer some of the densest high-volume sport of the species, commonly congregating in vast colonies. The

Richardson's Ground Squirrel Range

gray-washed, 10- to 11.75-inch, 8- to 12-ounce "sage rat" typically inhabits abandoned agricultural fields, ranch-road edges and other areas where vegetation is thin. They also thrive in rocky areas, but they're typically thickest around hay and alfalfa fields, or along creek banks, where they often undermine irrigation efforts.

Belding's Ground Squirrel Range

They inhabit eastern Oregon, southwestern Idaho, northeastern California, extreme northwestern Utah and northern Nevada. Their habit of standing tall and conducting mating rituals above ground (unusual for ground squirrels) makes them vulnerable targets. Belding's typically remain above ground longer than other smaller species. Males are first to go into hibernation, and young of the year remain topside into July or early August, with females following in September. Males can live three to four years, females four to six years, while producing three to eight young annually.

The tiny Belding's ground squirrel doesn't enjoy the largest range of species (eastern Oregon, northeastern California and northern Nevada), but the squirrels converge in massive colonies and provide high-volume shooting worth traveling for.

Columbian Ground Squirrel Range

Columbian ground squirrel range is limited to the alpine meadows and 5- to 10-year-old clear-cuts, semiarid grasslands and mountainous brushy areas of southeastern British Columbia and southwestern Alberta, south into northeastern Oregon, Idaho's Panhandle and northwestern Montana. But it's also one of the largest ground squirrel species, standing 13 to 16 inches high and weighing up to 1.75 pounds. Because of their

Species of Interest : 29

mountainous habitat, Columbians are attractive to long-range enthusiasts, as older clear-cuts often reveal squirrels perched on hollow stumps to gain a vantage. Many burrows are located at the bases of those stumps. They're grayish mixed with black above, with indistinct buff spotting and rusty-brown faces, feet and bellies. Males invariably emerge before females, often when snowdrifts still dot the landscape, usually early April after three to four days of 50-degree temperatures. Late April and early

May generally offer the most profitable shooting, though Columbians can often be found into late June at higher elevations. Columbians normally move underground by early July or when daily temperatures top 90 degrees. A more pressing seasonal dilemma is vegetation growth as the season matures, meaning you can hear the whistling calls of squirrels but cannot see them. The best shooting occurs when vegetation is still flattened by winter snows.

California Ground Squirrel Range

Californias are likely the sport's most popular ground squirrel, as they're available to the large population centers of the Golden State. They range from central Washington south into western Oregon and most of California, and occasionally western Nevada. They're large, brownish rodents with buff flecking and distinctly brushy tails, standing 14 to 19.75 inches tall and weighing up to 1.5 pounds — one of the largest ground squirrels. They prefer open areas, including rocky outcrops and slash/stump piles near orchards, fields, pastures and sparsely wooded hillsides.

They're active all day and form loose colonies, though when spooked, they retreat into only their own burrow, even if it's farther away. It's most common for burrows to open beneath logs, tree bases or rocks, though Californias will burrow in open areas when necessary. Burrows are used for years by successive occupants. California ground squirrels will climb trees for a better view, though they prefer *terra firma*. They hibernate from November through February, providing one of the longest ground squirrel shooting seasons. Beware: California species can harbor fleas

RIGHT: *The Columbian ground squirrel enjoys a fairly restricted range, mostly in Idaho's Panhandle and western Montana, but offers the opportunity for extreme long-range shooting in challenging mountain terrain.*

that carry bubonic plague, and lead-free bullets might be required in certain areas.

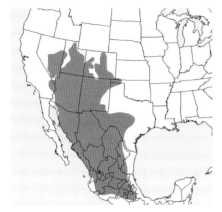

Rock Squirrel Range

Rock Squirrels in Other Places

Though technically ground squirrels, rock squirrels are often discovered in trees, when available. Rock squirrels are also larger than other ground squirrels — about 17 to 21 inches tall and up to 1.75 pounds. They wear grayish-brown and distinctly molted pelts with a light-hued belly and brushy tail. To my eye, they closely resemble the California ground squirrel. They can produce two litters of young per year, so they're often prolific in isolated spots. As the name implies, rocky areas are their preferred habitat. In many areas of the Southwest, I find colonies in isolated rock outcrops in relatively open country, though extensive rimrock and cliffy areas are usually their preferred coverts. They're most likely to be found early and late in the day and are often active year-round in warmer climates or sunny days, though they hibernate in the northern reaches of their range, which stretches from extreme southern Nevada, eastern Utah across Colorado, through the panhandle of Oklahoma, skimming the West Texas border and then encompassing the Trans-Pecos region, Arizona and New Mexico.

They produce sharp but short and sometimes quavering whistles followed by low-pitched trills. Look for them where acorns, cactus, agave, pine nuts, mesquite seeds and wild currants are abundant.

. . . .

RIGHT: *Rock squirrels, technically a ground squirrel, are one of the largest of the species and thrive in rocky places, mostly in the Southwest. They resemble a California ground squirrel, including molted markings and a large, bushy tail.*

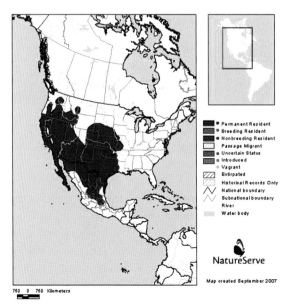

Permanent Resident
Breeding Resident
Nonbreeding Resident
Passage Migrant
Uncertain Status
Introduced
Vagrant
Extirpated
Historical Records Only
National boundary
Subnational boundary
River
Water body

NatureServe

Map created September 2007

750   0   750 Kilometers

Black-tailed Jackrabbit Range

Their diet makes them quite edible, especially when young.

Jackrabbit Bonanza

Four jackrabbit species inhabit North America: the widespread black-tailed and white-tailed, plus white-sided and antelope jackrabbits. Of these, only black- and white-tailed varieties interest varmint shooters.

The white-sided is found only in New Mexico's extreme southern Hidalgo County, and the antelope in south-central Arizona and extreme southwestern New Mexico. Both are protected. Black- and white-tailed jacks are generally afforded the fewest, if any, regulations.

The black-tailed jack is a large hare identified by a dominant black stripe down the top of its tail and large ears up to 5 inches long. It measures 18.25 to 24.75 inches long and weighs 4 to 8 pounds. The black-tailed jack prefers barren areas, prairies, meadows, cultivated fields and sometimes brushy flats and hollows, largely in the West, from West Texas and California in the south, to central Washington and the Dakotas in the north. Black-tails often create distinctive trails between feeding and loafing areas and bedding and dusting dishes beneath cover.

Jackrabbit young are born fully haired with their eyes open. On warm days, you'll find jacks by glassing shady spots beneath scattered brush and sometimes farm or ranch debris or equipment. They often feed in loose social groups, consuming many kinds of plants, but they're partial to alfalfa.

During winter, they'll consume woody or dried vegetation, and often burrow into haystacks while seeking cover and food, much to ranchers' chagrin. The jack uses camouflage and stillness to

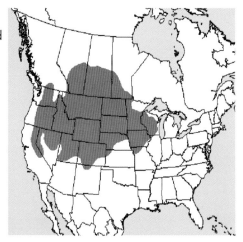

White-tailed Jackrabbit Range

elude danger, using its large ears to detect approaching predators. When flushed, jacks cover ground in 5- to 10-foot bounds, rarely walking, and can push 30 to 35 mph in 20-foot leaps when alarmed. Every fourth or fifth jump, they vault high into the air to get a better view. They also flash the white underside of their tails and occasionally thump their large rear feet as warning signals to nearby jacks.

Jacks normally pause after a short distance to see if they're still being pursued. Black-tail jacks breed year-round but most frequently during milder seasons, producing one to four litters of one to eight young, making them quite prolific. Mothers keep their distance from natal nests by day, arriving during night to nurse young, which can feed themselves within a month.

White-tailed jackrabbits, as you might guess, wear a white tail and lighter overall hue, often turning completely white during winter in northern portions of their range. Their ears are shorter — 4.5 inches maximum — with larger bodies, measuring 22.25 to 25.75 inches and weighing 5.75 to 9.5 pounds. White-

BELOW: *Jackrabbits offer plenty of off-season sport for firearms shooters, being extremely prolific in many habitats and a decided pest for farmers raising irrigated alfalfa. The Southwest generally offers the best shooting.*

tails prefer barren, grazed or cultivated ground and grasslands from eastern Washington and northeastern California eastward through Minnesota, Iowa and Kansas, southward through Utah and Colorado. Traveling in 12- to 20-foot leaps, white-tails can maintain speeds up to 36 mph with spurts of up to 45 mph.

Males fight viciously during the April and early-May breeding season. One to six young are born a month later and can forage for themselves in three to four weeks. Summer forage consists of grasses, clover and other green vegetation. Twigs, buds and dried vegetation get them through winter. White-tailed jacks make excellent table fare, versus black-tails, which are generally not eaten.

Concentrated jackrabbits are normally found in or near irrigated alfalfa fields, though I've enjoyed sustained shooting in sandy desert areas. Southern and eastern New Mexico farm and ranchland invariably offer high-volume black-tail shooting, with the best white-tail shooting occurring in southwestern Wyoming, at least from my experiences.

Jack populations — like other prey species — peak and trough locally season to season, so don't give up on a spot because of a slow year. In my experience, black-tails seem to do best during the hottest, driest years. In my book, jackrabbits offer one of the most fun and challenging long-range targets in varmintdom — a bias no doubt formed during youth, as they provided the impetus to my shooting obsessions.

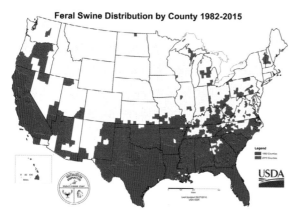

Feral Swine Distribution by County 1982-2015

Feral Hogs Abound

Hunting Hogs

Hunting feral hogs helped keep me in meat while attending university in West Texas in the late 1980s and early '90s. Hogs were relatively scarce then, and tagging one was an event. Twenty-some years later, those coverts are filthy with hogs, and killing many a day is common.

You'll hear much talk of pure European boar blood. I've read seemingly reliable reports of imported European boars, including an 1893 importation of 50 Black Forest, Germany, boars to the Blue Mountains of New Hampshire; 1910 and 1912 imports to North Carolina near the Tennessee border; a 1925 influx near Monterey, California.

Those imports invariably escaped confining reserves. But many more domesticated swine have escaped

RIGHT: *It's safe to say feral hogs have joined the varmint class, as the invasive species continues to spread and reap destruction on agricultural crops and native wildlife. With some exceptions, they can generally be hunted with few restrictions.*

The Scott and Tiffany Haugen family traveled to Florida to enjoy a family hunting outing. The results speak for themselves. Liberal (or no) limits makes hog hunting a welcome off-season sport. Scott Haugen photo.

confinement through the centuries, and lineage muddles quickly. Pure European blood is still believed to exist in North Carolina, Tennessee and parts of California, but it seems like a stretch. I've killed genuine Russian boars in France and far eastern Russia, and have seen nothing remotely resembling the hogs in this nation. North America harbors feral pigs, plain and simple, though I find the wild boar label more romantic.

I'd bet most hunters, no matter where they live, have hog hunting available within a day's drive. These might prove highly scattered, secret or barely established herds — or a full-out invasion — but they're there, all right. Keep your ears open, as you never know where they'll pop up next. Rooting is their most obvious sign; tilled-up soil along field edges and creek beds. They also leave mud rubs 1.5 to 2 feet up tree boles near water. Wallows are also conspicuous and often indicate approximate size. Their cloven tracks are more rounded and splayed than those of deer, with their dewclaw marks usually evident.

Prime coverts include impenetrable swamp, riparian zones or brushy terrain where water is abundant. Hogs must have daily water to survive, especially during summer. However, they will ilk out a living in seemingly unfruitful habitats, as they're resourceful foragers. I recall gutting a fat-laden West Texas summer sow living in drought-bitten habitat off the rocky Caprock. Her belly was stuffed with grasshoppers. I once killed a Texas Edwards Plateau boar that was killing and eating sheep — the rancher's desperation the only reason I gained access to that prime property.

Wild boars move freely during daytime only where left undisturbed — private lands with limited hunting pressure or areas too nasty-thick to encourage casual exploration. The seasonal aspect of human traffic often makes summer best for daytime movement, despite the heat. An average Texas deer lease, for example, sees little summertime human activity. Those willing to brave ticks, chiggers, humidity and heat-stroke temperatures can enjoy awesome success. Apply the smallest amount of pressure, and the largest hogs, especially old boars, quickly turn vampirish. However, as you shall see in a later chapter, there are ways of dealing with these uncooperative characters.

The undisputed hunting loadstones in hogdom remain California, Texas and Florida — states that not incidentally received the first influxes of non-native pigs during Spanish adventures and colonialism. The Deep South has come on strong, though as I've mentioned, wild boars might show up just about anywhere today. Do your part. Kill more hogs. Because in the immortal words of Vincent Vega (Pulp Fiction), "Bacon tastes good. Pork chops taste good."

Common Predators

To many, the word varmint connotes predators — namely coyotes, but also foxes and bobcats. Coyotes earn their varmint label by taking the occasional newborn calf and especially smaller lambs, foxes from stealing chickens, and bobcats because they're especially hard on desirable game birds such as turkeys, pheasants and quail. America's small predators are common from coast to coast, making them popular targets, usually in conjunction with calling ploys.

Once a Western concern, coyotes (derived from Mexico's Nahuatl Indian word coyotl) have spread steadily eastward, even invading Newfoundland Island, where they were never found historically, by traipsing across frozen sea one cold winter (despite global warming). I grew up pursuing coyotes in the West. More recently, I've shot them in Alabama, Illinois and upstate New York. The label wily coyote is apt, as they prove intelligent and cunning

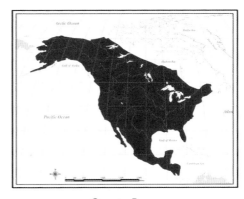

Coyote Range

Once strictly a Western concern, the adaptable coyote has quickly spread from coast to coast -- bad news for wildlife managers, great news for serious predator callers, as coyotes are the epitome of the sport.

adversaries capable of learning from experience.

Coyotes hunt in small groups or pairs, using sight, hearing and especially their keen sense of smell to locate food. They often chase larger prey species in relays until the quarry is overcome by fatigue. Coyotes can prove fairly territorial, creating scent posts marked with urine and bodily secretions, though they've also been known to range great distance.

Although wolves quickly caved under man's persecution, coyotes learned to thrive alongside humans. Coyote size is commonly exaggerated. They measure 23 to 26 inches at the shoulder, and are 41 to 52 inches long and weigh 20 to 40 pounds. Thick fur can make them appear much larger. Even the latter weights are exceptional. In my experience, average Western coyotes weigh about 25 pounds. They can maintain 25 to 30 mph in sustained runs and up to 40 mph in short bursts. Coyotes run with their tails down, wolves with their tails horizontal.

Sign consists of dog-like scat at road or pond edges and along sandy washes.

Tracks are characteristic dog-like prints, though generally narrower. Another sure sign of their presence is distinctive cowboy-western chittering and broken yips, yaps and howls, most common at daybreak and during dark.

This calling helps keep bands cohesive. Lone barking often indicates a warning while guarding dens, kills or carrion. Eastern coyotes are less inclined to calling.

RIGHT: *Gary Sefton, a world-champion game caller, lured this Tennessee coyote into range with a mouth call and eneded its fawn-killing ways. Coyote calling isn't just for Western sports these days. Gary Sefton photo.*

Gray foxes inhabit almost all of the United States, with the exception of the far-northern Rocky Mountains and inland Northwest. They readily respond to predator calling, especially during darkness.

Red Fox Range

Coyotes aren't picky eaters, subsisting on fruits, nuts, carrion, amphibians, reptiles, small mammals, and deer and pronghorn fawns. In mountain and northern habitats — where coyotes attain their largest sizes — they regularly drag down adult deer, working together like wolves.

Hotspots are difficult to supply, as calling can prove productive coast to coast. Yet it's really difficult to beat desolate Western prairies and mountain foothills dominated by public Bureau of Land Management and Forest Service lands — places often offering more action in a week than an entire season in Midwestern or Eastern habitats. If nothing else, there's simply more room to roam without the difficulties of private-land access.

Of the North American foxes, the red and gray species are most commonly pursued by hunters. The 8- to 15-pound red fox is most commonly known to Eastern hunters. It's found in mixed cultivated and wooded areas and brush-lands across much of Canada and the United States, except for much of the West Coast, though I've observed very few west of the Mississippi. Reds are cunning predators capable of learning from experience and are seldom observed in daylight.

Gray Fox Range

The 7- to 13- pound gray fox is generally more prone to foolishness than the red. Grays are common in the eastern

United States west to the Dakotas, Nebraska, Kansas, Oklahoma and south through most of Texas, New Mexico, Arizona and California, and then north through Colorado, southern Utah, Nevada and western Oregon. They're highly nocturnal and readily climb trees — the only true canid to do so.

American bobcats weigh 15 to 25 pounds in most habitats, though they have been recorded to more than 65 pounds. They live in scrubby and broken forests and rocky or brushy arid deserts, and occasionally swamps and farmlands.

They're spottily distributed coast to coast, and are most plentiful in the West from Idaho, Utah and Nevada to the Pacific, and from Washington to Baja. Bobcats are largely absent in the central and lower Midwest. Bobcats aren't so much smart as secretive and cautious. They're usually slow to respond to predator calls, stalking prey instead of arriving on greedy runs like coyotes.

The best calling sites are typically situated around cliffy or rocky areas in the West, or heavy forest or riparian habitats in the East. The Southwest and northern Rockies are tops for regular success, though rugged Eastern locales can produce bobcats periodically.

Bobcat Range

Timber wolves can again be legally hunted in northern and eastern Idaho and northwestern Wyoming, but success remains a matter of luck even in the best habitats. A few hunters develop calling ploys resulting in semi-annual success after persistent efforts, though tracking in snow and glassing open areas where a pack is known to reside are sporadically productive.

Birds of a Feather

Varmints might also wear feathers, as in destructive crows, and invasive starlings, rock and ring-necked doves, and even non-native English sparrows.

The American crow should not be confused with the northern raven, which is generally protected as an important part of the sanitation corps. The easiest distinction is made on overhead flying birds. Crows have squared tails, ravens rounded. The raven is also noticeably larger and often has a goiter-like throat patch and pronounced Roman nose. Crows caw, but ravens generally croak. Crows

American Crow Range

inhabit woodlands, farmlands, agricultural fields and river groves and generally receive scorn for their habit of raiding other birds' nest and destroying eggs. Though most numerous in the East and Midwest, crows range across the West, notably in northern states, and the Four Corners region and major California valleys and its coastline. Its biggest foe is the great horned owl. An owl decoy and crow calls can be used to bring crows into range, sometimes in large numbers.

Starlings were introduced to New York's Central Park by Eugene Schieffelin in 1890 (50) and 1891 (another 40) in a misguided effort to introduce all birds mentioned in William Shakespeare plays to the United States. Today, their

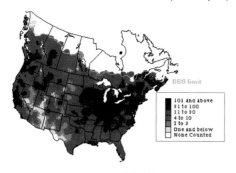

The Range of Starlings

numbers have reached 200 million, and they're found coast to coast, to the detriment of native bird species, as starlings destroy competing nests to take over limited tree cavities. They're spotted, short-tailed blackbirds with a meadowlark shape, but they have distinctively yellow bills. They're fond of cities and parks, but also farms, fields and open groves. They're most

Common feathered "varmint" species include the common crow, top left; common pigeon, top right; ring-necked or Eurasian doves, bottom left; and startlings. The crow eats the eggs and young of other birds, and the others are invasive species that compete with native species.

often shot from backyard bird feeders with scoped air rifles.

Rock doves, or the common pigeon (not to be confused with the band-tailed pigeon, a game bird) and ring-neck doves (not to be confused with native mourning and white-winged doves) are other European imports that constitute nongame where they are found. Ring-neck doves are detrimental to native species, taking over established nesting sites.

Year-round
Year-round (scarce)

Eurasion-Collared Dove Range

Pigeons defecate profusely. The big plus is this is varmint shooting that nets tasty meals. Again, air rifles and bird feeders are common denominators, though pigeons are often sniped near farm buildings or feeding on agricultural fields.

⊕ Chapter 3
Varmint Approaches

I won't tell you how to conduct your varmint hunting business. Traipse through a vast prairie dog town with a Bryco .22 LR pocket pistol, if that's what floats your boat. Use your favorite deer rifle to shoot full-out-running jackrabbits flushed from midday summer cover, just for grins. Sit in the middle of a major ground squirrel colony and burn up a box of .45 Auto rounds from your favorite 1911. Cruise agricultural field edges at night, one person driving, another occupying a pickup bed with a spotlight and shotgun, seeking targets of opportunity — where legal, obviously. Post on a rimrock ledge overlooking alfalfa 200 yards away, taking potshots at feeding

It's safe to say varmint shooting doesn't carry the same fair-chase rules as big-game hunting. Shooting ground squirrels from a truck window (on private lands or from unimproved roads on public ground), for example, is par in varmint country.

jackrabbits with a .50-caliber muzzle-loading rifle and patched roundballs. All are approaches I've enjoyed, having a hoot of a good time while at it.

Were these approaches ideal? Hardly, at least from a standpoint of body count, but this is about enjoying shooting fun, right? There are no etched-in-stone rules. Varmints aren't about the success-at-all-costs mindset permeating big-game hunting today. Outdoor writing is filled with hardnosed dogma, from cartridges

LEFT: *There are many ways to approach varmint shooting, from setting up on a vantage to bang away at concentrations of targets, as shown here, to wandering lonely deserts kicking up game.*

and firearms deemed "acceptable" for specific game and conditions faced, to how much recoil you're required to tolerate, to what degree of skill you're required to attain to avoid shame from peers, to exactly how to approach any situation. This often reveals as much about writers and their world views as any practical information. Again, varmint shooting is about fun and respite from the stresses of everyday life and tedious, mind-numbing toil. As long as you're breaking no laws, do what makes you happy, not what someone else deems acceptable.

With that said, it's also true varmint shooting and/or predator hunting welcomes a variety of tactics, according to current goals, expectations and state of mind — seeking an uncomplicated stroll versus precision shooting skills, or high body count versus long-range bragging rights, for example. So consider this advice not so much as rules of engagement but suggestions in the pursuit of happiness.

■ High-Volume Shooting

Sometimes, varminteers just want to shoot versus hunting in the classical sense. Directing precious ammunition at assorted cans remains wildly popular for this reason. Some varmint shooting lends itself to this mode better than others. You obviously need concentrated varmints — a ground squirrel colony or prairie dog town, or a prime alfalfa field in jackrabbit country, instead of, say, a day of predator calling for wary coyotes or red foxes or goal-oriented quests for bobcats or a bucket-list wolf.

For most of us, rimfires represent the high-volume ideal, being cheap and mostly readily available. I say mostly, recalling recent shortages of rimfire ammo created by highly advertised political ambitions that then encouraged greedy hoarding based on insane conspiracy theories and the idea that rimfire ammo production would suddenly cease or the government was buying it all to deny public access.

. . . .

RIGHT: *Sometimes, the varmint shooter chooses volume, other times challenge. When on a volume bloodlust bent, the author enjoys shooting his autoloading .22 Long Rifle or .223 Rem. AR.*

The AR platform has become hugely popular with varmint shooters because the guns are accurate and just plain fun to shoot, especially in high-volume arenas. Steven Tisdale used an AR in .223 Rem. to shoot Texas jackrabbits.

I worked sporting-goods retail for a couple of years during Obama's anti-gun tenure and learned to loathe the hoarders — especially those cleaning off rimfire shelves while also bragging of the 100,000-plus rounds already squirreled away in bedroom closets. We were forced to institute per-customer limits, but these greedy souls would send in relatives and friends, so major shipments of ammo dwindled in only hours, with most going to the same few folks each week. I was then forced to endure the scorn of regular customers who only wanted some damn .22 shells so they could take the grandkids plinking during the weekend. Those days, fortunately, appear to be behind us. In fact, I anticipate a glut of .22 LR shells after these mostly retired hoarders begin to pass.

The author's father uses a camping pad, bipod and tack-driving Mossbery MVP Varmint in .204 Ruger to snipe long-range rockchunks in Southern Idaho. Setting up like this provides challenging shooting fun.

When I think of high-volume shooting, I also generally think of auto-loading firearms. For some reason, auto-loaders denote a lack of accuracy in my subconscious mind, but that isn't true, as I own auto-loading .22 LRs that assemble tight groups at 50-plus yards, provided I do my part. Maybe knowing an automatic backup shot is available discourages our most precise efforts. Even sitting on a bench, shooting auto-loading .22 LRs for test groups, I must will myself to slow down and concentrate on each shot individually. The various and most popular .22-caliber rimfires are also relatively limited in energy and range, so limitations occur there, too.

But plopping down in the middle of a mob of ground squirrels and plinking away with an auto-loading .22 LR is one of varmint shooting's great joys.

Walking out a desert wash or alfalfa field edge with an auto-loader just seems natural, as an auto-loader is hard to beat on running targets at reasonable ranges, "walking" shots in while swinging, and pulling the trigger and concentrating only on aiming. Of course, rimfire pumps and lever guns can be nearly as fast handling and quick to follow up, so they also have adoring fans. Handguns have a place in this, too. Even my scoped Taurus .22 Hornet or .17 HMR revolvers making burning powder in volume easy and fun.

More recently, ARs (AR stands for Armalite rifle, by the way, not assault rifle or automatic rifle) have become the big thing. Honestly, the AR phenomenon once annoyed me a bit. I began to feel the entire outdoor media and gun-lobby machine was intent on collectively shoving them down our throats to make some political point. Gun-grabbing liberals want to outlaw or at least curtail military-type guns because they appear scary to them, so suddenly we were forced to prove they're viable hunting tools, as if that would make any difference to those who would like nothing more than to eliminate all firearms and further cement their power.

But then I finally borrowed an AR-15 — a Rock River Arms in .223 Rem. with a heavy varmint barrel — and became addicted. After the consignment period was finished, I immediately had my own built and shoot it regularly, often ignoring my custom long-range bolts because it's so damned fun to shoot. When you pop a 30-round clip home, despite ½-inch, 100-yard group capabilities, it's difficult to avoid a high-volume outlook. With a bolt rifle, there's much deliberation between

In certain varmint settings, erecting a portable shooting bench and adding a rifle cradle and staying a while is indicated. This is especially true at concentrated ground squirrel and prairie dog colonies.

In some habitats, it pays to walk away from the vehicle or ATV and set up overlooking target-rich ground. Here, the author found a vantage overlooking a defunct farm taken over by Columbian ground squirrels.

Even when varmints are concentrated, a shooter sometimes simply wants to stretch his legs. Classid walk-about shooting normally includes shooting offhand, but shooting sticks are also welcomed.

shots. With my AR, I greedily engaging targets in shooting-gallery fashion, laying down fire on running targets, burning through ammo at an alarming rate. Luckily, .223 Rem. ammo is affordable and especially cheap to handload.

■ Long-Range Sniping

Other days and in other habitats, I'll slow my pace considerably, settling in and taking my time selecting targets and setting up for the shot. The ultimate goal is precision — doping all factors thoroughly before settling in to squeeze the trigger gingerly. Even in the high-volume ground squirrel fields of eastern Oregon or prairie dog towns of Wyoming or Montana, after an initial day of high-volume bloodlust, I'll find myself in a calm place where I began seeking challenge instead of body count. This normally means gaining a vantage, assembling rock-solid rests and using quality optics to locate targets.

My truck or ATV is often the base of these operations, parked on rises, hillside benches or ranch-road bends overlooking productive fields of target species. A portable bench set up in the truck bed, a rifle cradle tossed across the truck hood or

ATV rack, or a sandbag nestled on a pickup bed edge or ATV seat provide steady shooting. And all my stuff — ammo boxes, cleaning gear, spotting scope and ice-filled coolers holding lunch and cold drinks — remains readily accessible. These are the days I seem to stretch my abilities, seeking ever-farther targets, doping wind, spinning scope turrets and concentrating on consciously controlling my breathing.

I also use pickup beds, which raises me above screening vegetation, as a platform for a swiveling shooting bench that holds a rock-steady rifle cradle. This is particularly useful during late spring or early summer, when vegetation matures to obscure targets. Forcing yourself to slow down and really look is the only way you'll get any shooting during these conditions.

I use height-adjustable cradles to lift my rifle to a particular sight plane, crank scopes to maximum magnification, twist side parallax into gin-clear focus and slowly pivot on the bench, watching carefully for targets to slide into view. With quality high-power optics and a razor-sharp focus, I find ground squirrels I never would have discovered with binoculars alone.

Sometimes, it's just a wet eye shining through grass or the slightest hint of fur or a flicking tail that catches my eye. When I finish reading a line of terrain, I lift or drop the rifle slightly through a precise adjustment of the shooting cradle, starting back on a new line of habitat.

Overall, these are also days when I uncase the big guns, such as my custom .22-250 Rem. with its chunky benchrest stock, 26.5-inch custom barrel, crisp Timney trigger, and ear-splitting, dust-raising Xtreme Hardcore Gear muzzle break. Or, I might choose a 6mm Creedmoor or .243 Win. loaded

Fred Eichler and song Trent stalk a Western jackrabbit while shooting a .22 LR revolver. Such varmint shooting is great fun and a solid foundation for honing overall shooting and hunting skills.

with high-ballistic-coefficient pills pushed to maximum velocity for more retained energy at longer ranges. Or, if breezes begin to stir, my tack-driving, overkill Brown Precision .25-06 Rem., spitting 117-grain payloads to a modest 3,000 fps, might strike my fancy. I could choose lighter 70- and 75-grain .257-caliber pills from Sierra and Hornady, respectively, pushed to 3,600 fps — and believe me, it's tempting at times — but I fear throat erosion, and this rifle still serves as a one-hole-group big-game killer.

In rougher Idaho rockchuck ground, Colorado's marmot high country, a road-less patch of Columbian ground squirrel meadow or isolated New Mexico rock squirrel grotto, hiking a short distance with a shoulder-slung rifle and daypack of gear to set up on a commanding ledge, solitary hilltop or boulder pile can prove quite rewarding. Shooting prone across a sandbag, bipod or portable shooting mat (or standard-issue backpacking sleeping pad), or simply a daypack of gear tossed atop a boulder or stump, is often the way to operate in these situations. There is no better way to tag a hunter-savvy Eastern woodchuck than to find a vantage overlooking his burrow opening and lie prone beneath a swatch of camouflage netting or behind a screen of bushes like a military sniper, patiently glassing and awaiting his emergence.

Of course, there are no rules that say you must use a centerfire rifle in this sniper business. I regularly apply my .17 HMR rifle to this patient approach, sitting on our elevated deck during evenings with a cool drink, a shooting bag set on the railing, popping the Columbian ground squirrels intent on pioneering our pond dike 250 yards below. Now, 250 yards is pushing the effective limits of that hot little rimfire, making for challenging and engaging shooting. When we visit eastern Oregon in spring, my father's goal is often to best his personal record for the farthest .22 LR ground squirrel, using turret scopes to snipe the little rodents at more than 200 yards — proving again that "long" is a relative term in shooting.

■ Walk-About

The varmint shooting of my eastern New Mexico childhood involved mostly aimless walks through likely habitats to see what I might kick up, or sometimes just long hikes across the countryside with no destination in mind, a .22 LR or my love-worn .243 Win. bolt rifle in tow. This was an obvious product of youth, in which some momentum had to be

Relatively new on the shooting scene, ATVs offer a great avenue into productive varmint shooting while saving fuel and wear and tear on your vehicle. The author often uses his ATV to reach remote clearcuts while shooting Idaho ground squirrels.

On private lands, your truck or SUV makes a great stalking horse for varmints such as ground squirrels and prarie dogs. On hotter days, it's nice to have air conditioning and quick access to cold drinks.

maintained to sooth a short attention span. But I shot a lot of varmints and kept my wanderlust thoroughly sated.

This also let me drop by various habitats, acquired after extensive exploring, and enjoy a variety of shooting. I'd grab a rifle and leave suburbia behind by crossing a dry creek bed. Within a half-mile, I'd be kicking across an alfalfa field, sure to produce shots at fat black-tailed jackrabbits. From there, I'd cross a county road, walk down a windrow that sometimes harbored farmland pigeons and visit an excavated pit filled with old cars, piles of tires, home appliances, nail-riddled lumber and household trash — the alluvia of a working farm. There I was sure to receive a shot or three at rock squirrels inhabiting the rubbish. Another couple of

miles of grass pasture, where I might pick up a few more jacks, brought me to the Santa Fe Railroad line, where more rock squirrels were certain to appear beneath two trestle bridges, the camouflaged rodents attracted to extensive riprap deposited to discourage erosion. Near the larger trestle, aside the running creek, was an abandoned house I always stalked, because I once shot a raccoon there (their sign always in evidence) and collected a $20 hide. From there, I'd swing north 2 miles and enter short-grass prairie, where I shot prairie dogs to my heart's content and occasionally got thirteen-lined ground squirrels sharing that open habitat. But I couldn't stay too long, as I had a 6- or 7-mile trek to get home for dinner on time.

While attending college years later in drearily featureless Lubbock, Texas, far from mountains and too destitute to do anything about it, a vast CRP field and adjoining patch of low-lying mesquite behind the house, and a break-action, single-shot .22 LR kept me sane and let me eventually graduate. That field was home to a seemingly endless stock of jackrabbits, which I belabored unmercifully. Once, while decompressing after an especially odious week of full-time work and night school, I shot a coyote — a $35 fur-market gift at a time when a six-pack of staple Milwaukee's Best or Meister Brau cost $2.

Gun-writing legend Jack O'Connor once wrote, "The finest practice in the world for learning to hit running game is shooting running jackrabbits, and if I have some small degree of skill in the department, I owe it all to the long-eared desert speedster. The jackrabbit hunter will get more practice on running game in a week in good country than the deer hunter will on deer in half a lifetime. On many occasions, when I lived in southern Arizona, I have headed out across the desert with 60 rounds of ammunition with me and returned to the car with none." These are forays to which I can readily relate.

Almost all this shooting, from the eastern New Mexico forays of my youth and those western Texas jacks, to the Columbian ground squirrels I stalk in my Idaho backyard today, involve offhand shooting with rimfire rifles and handguns — mostly .22 LR, and only occasionally .22 Mag. or .17 HMR. I might occasionally receive the luxury of sitting to rest off a folded knee or leaning over a fence post, but for the most part, it's all unsupported shooting. Often, obscuring vegetation means I must take the shot presented — and often quickly, as my targets don't hold tight long. So offhand it is.

This is valuable hunting practice. As although much is made of long-range big-game shooting of late, the truth is the careful hunter — especially those still-hunting wooded areas — is more likely to receive more quick offhand opportunities at deer or elk at less than 100 yards than anything else. And what if you run into a rutting whitetail buck unexpectedly while accessing a woodlot tree stand? Will you be prepared?

This is the epitome of basic varmint shooting, really — uncomplicated and free of major preparations. Just a grab-a-rifle-and-go enterprise that's relaxing and allows some welcome exercise and time for quiet contemplation. It can also prove quite rewarding.

■ Drive and Shoot

Many of the fair-chase rules of big-game hunting do not apply to varmint shooting. Take road hunting, for example. To the ethical big-game hunter, riding backroads looking for a potshot at a deer, elk or black bear is considered the lazy man's option, and it's considered downright slovenly in many circles. It might even be illegal. In varmint shooting, especially on private lands with controlled access or remote areas with only unimproved two-rut roads, it's generally par. The ranch rifle is a common theme in firearms manufacturing. This is a compact, easy-handling rifle that

RIGHT: *When pursuing varmints in the boondocks (especially in the West) where human traffic is rare, hunting and shooting from the vehicle is a common approach and completely legal in many cases.*

Getting away from it all is what varmint shooting and predator hunting is about for many riflemen. Taking a tent or camp trailer and staying a while is easy during pleasant spring and summer weather.

lives in a vehicle — even if you don't own a ranch or farm — on the chance you'll need something to shoot an incidental coyote sighted from the truck, a fox caught stealing chickens, a packrat in the hay stack or ground squirrels burrowing into a stock-tank dike or chronically undermining a stretch of ranch road. The compact Ruger Mini-14 in .223 Rem. or 7.62x39 is a classic in this area. Ruger's 10/22 is another common ranch rifle — easy to stash, holding lots of shells and capable of acceptable accuracy. The ranch gun is essentially a road hunting weapon.

I've already detailed the ranch shooting I enjoyed in as a child. It was serious shooting, no doubt, but it was conducted while engaged in serious business — feeding cattle and assuring windmills and steel-tank floats were functioning properly during scorching-hot, lip-cracking-dry summer months when an interruption to water flow could prove fatal to livestock. Frequent stops for shooting no doubt slowed our progress, but failing to accomplish our tasks was not an option, and work always came first. Still, we shot a lot of varmints, that fun taking the edge off of what might have otherwise proven boringly hard work. Seriously, though, I actually enjoyed the hell out of it, simply because of the anticipation of all that shooting.

But that's not what I have in mind here. I'm hinting at simply using your vehicle as a form of blind or stalking horse, shooting from its windows at varmints you pass while going between concentrations, or parking among a colony of prairie dogs or ground squirrels and banging away. We do a lot of this in eastern Oregon while driving between prime sniping sites. Although the big concentrations are generally on specific fields or creek bends, there are enough rats in roadside ditches, at creek crossings and around abandoned buildings and rock outcrops to warrant stopping and wanging away. This is shooting in which the vehicle is only occasionally turned off; stop-and-go action resulting in plenty of shooting — the big .22 LR value pack sitting on the dash, exhausted during an average day, and one of those ammo-bucket deals often consumed in a weekend by a couple of shooters.

Admittedly, that kind of shooting is most appealing during the hottest summer days or at the end of our ground squirrel shooting season in late spring, simply because it's much more pleasant to remain in an air-conditioned vehicle. Though in most cases, you aren't necessarily sacrificing the shooting end for that comfortable, relaxing approach. On farms and ranches, and other places with steady traffic such as oil-field patches or around electricity-generating windmill

Shooting from a vehicular base is usually the way to go on concentrated varmints. It keeps other firearms and gear handy, as well as hydration and lunch.

farms, varmints have become accustomed to vehicles. A passing truck means nothing to them, as they see dozens a day. For this reason, it's often easier to approach within range of varmints if you stay in your vehicle. If you step out and go for a walk, you'll often find varmints are extremely spooky and difficult to approach. In Oregon, for example, it's fairly common to shoot for an hour from a spot while remaining inside or beside the vehicle. But if you walk away from the vehicle to confirm a kill, the field clears completely, sometimes for the rest of the day. You must find another spot.

I wouldn't think of hunting deer from my truck. In varmint shooting, I do it without apology.

■ Public Versus Private Lands

If you're lucky enough to live in, or are willing to travel to, the West or western Great Plains, you can often find top-quality varmint shooting on public lands. I'm certain some small amount of public-lands shooting is available in the East — likely predator calling opportunities — but higher human populations, especially east of the Mississippi, generally makes success on those lands spotty.

Public lands offer the obvious advantage of being open to all, a situation unique to North America and especially the United States. As I have hinted, the more remote public lands are from major metropolitan areas, the more reliable the shooting generally proves — western Colorado wastes versus the Front Range surrounding Denver and Colorado Springs, for example.

Private lands have distinct advantages, such as fewer competing shooters and the ability to do things you might not be allowed to do legally on public lands. The most obvious, for example, includes the ability to shoot from or across private ranch or farm roads not maintained by state or county entities — though in Montana, at least one foot must touch the ground while shooting even varmints, even while on private lands. That means shooting from the elevated position of a pickup truck bed is illegal. Go figure. I know of no situation where shooting from and especially across a public road is permitted by law in any state, for obvious safety reasons. In many locations, night shooting and spotlighting for varmints or predators is allowed on private lands with landowner permission, but the same is forbidden when public lands are involved. Check and re-check game regulations in your state before spotlighting anywhere, or even shooting at night with night-vision or thermal-imaging optics. Many states have laws that are quite vague, as new technology has not yet been addressed specifically. Contacting a conservation department official far up the command chain might be the only safe way to know for certain, or at least provide backup should an overzealous conservation officer interpret the law.

Federal Forest Service, Bureau of Land Management and some state lands — subject to various regulations — also allow camping for long periods without fees outside of maintained camping areas with facilities. There's something to be said for the simplicity of erecting a tent or parking a trailer where you won't have to deal with human noise or intrusions and can sit around a campfire during evenings enjoying a cold one. This can sometimes be done on private lands, of course, but will require special arrangements.

The biggest hurdle to productive public-lands shooting is researching and pinpointing specific hotspots. Contacting state conservation department biologists or forest service and state-land employees sometimes puts you on the right track, but eventually, you'll have to burn some fuel and have a closer look. The range maps and habitat descriptions in Chapter 2 give you good starting points, but you should also purchase BLM or Forest Service land-status maps to learn the basic lay of the land and where you'll be allowed to hunt. After narrowing your prospects, more detailed U.S. Geographical Survey topographical maps provide added terrain detail.

Gaining permission to private lands isn't for the shy. Every time you approach a ranch or farmhouse, you're selling yourself. Permission is often denied or granted because of quick first impressions. Basic manners, as I pointed out, are highly important, but so are appearances. It might sound silly, but comb your hair, wear clean clothes, tuck in your shirt, and smile and talk enthusiastically. How would you dress and address people if forced to sell magazine subscriptions door to door?

Being a local is a definite plus, as landowners feel more secure knowing where they can find you if you do something stupid (offering a legitimate business card sometimes helps in this regard), though I've also played the sportsman who has traveled a great distance to enjoy local bounty, which can illicit sympathy and/or a good-host mentality. Don't get in a hurry. Be willing to chat a while. I gained access to one of my best local white-tailed deer spots only after spending three hours during a prime evening in the middle of hunting season chatting about weather, farming and cattle prices. Make it clear, if the opportunity arises (and you're actually willing), that you'll be willing to help with basic farm or ranch choirs — such as mending fences, stacking hay or rounding up cattle — for the privilege of accessing their land. Varmints make gaining trespass access easier, but a landowner must still trust that you won't burn him out, let his cattle escape through gates left open, cut ruts driving across his fields or leave trash behind.

⊕ Chapter 4
Calling
All Predators

Nothing in hunting is quite as exciting as luring wary quarry into range through calling. In basic terms, predator calling is usually nothing more than the promise of an easy meal. For this reason, 95 percent of predator calling involves distress calls of common prey species; rodent squeaks, the blood-curdling squalls of rabbits being torn limb from limb, or bawling deer or pronghorn fawns separated from mama or caught in fence wire. Others, such as coyote-howl locator calls, are designed to illicit responses and get you on track faster, act as confidence builders in hard-hunted areas or attract attention during late-winter breeding seasons.

But there is more to successful predator calling than just calling. This is a multifaceted program in which the smallest parts are important to the bigger picture. You can produce the best calls and still manage to kill only time. You must first know your prey and understand why they respond to calls according to time and place. Predators are true survivors, especially in environments where they're hunted steadily. Only schooled predator callers score with regular frequency in such environments.

So first, let's meet our cast of characters.

Coyotes are predator calling's most popular target because they are most widely available, harmful to local big-game populations and generally come most greedily to the distress calls of rabbits and fawns.

LEFT: Calling coyotes is normally considered a late-fall and winter game, as pelts are prime during these periods. But you can hunt coyotes year-round to help control numbers and save more big-game fawns from destruction.

■ Coyotes, a Calling Favorite

Since the elimination of wolf competition, coyotes have thrived across North America. Their abundance and widespread availability would seem to indicate easy pickings — and that can prove true in regions riding a peak population wave. In most cases, the opposite is true. You can live in areas where their nightly chittering calls are commonplace and still struggle to earn regular success.

The coyote has it all: excellent eyesight that picks up the slightest movement at distances taxing even the flattest-shooting varmint rifles; sharp hearing allowing it to pinpoint, say, small mice scurrying beneath matted grass; and some of the most astute olfactory senses in the wild kingdom — all tied to hair-trigger survival instincts.

The prolific coyote also thrives in innumerable habitats, including hot, dry deserts; cold, snowy mountains; thronged woodlands and brush country; and wide-open prairies and farmland. Each of these environments presents different challenges. Failing to adjust to terrain can result in hit-and-miss results. No matter the cover type, coyotes must feel secure moving toward calls or will not expose themselves for clean shots. Part of that hinges on realism — as habitats change, so does available prey. So, it does little

The author has been calling predators since his early teens, initially lured into the sport because of high fur prices. Today, he seriously pursues calling success for fun and relaxation, though during the right years, calling can pay for itself via the raw-fur trade.

good to blast away on a coarse jackrabbit call when cottontails dominate. The reverse might be true on open prairies, where cover-loving cottontails are absent and jacks common. In other areas, say Eastern woodlands or mountain terrain, a fawn's distress calls might prove the ticket to success. Sometimes, in harder-hunted areas, off-the-wall stuff does the trick; fighting woodpeckers, squalling raccoons, the cries of domestic puppies or cats, or during the late-winter mating season, vocalizations of other coyotes appealing to sexual urges.

Calling approaches also revolve around seasons, as coyotes are often pursued year-round because of their proclivity for molesting livestock and the young of desirable game. They're seldom afforded the same protection of other furbearers, largely because of lobbying efforts by stockmen associations. An Arizona Fish and Game Department study, for example, attributed 65 percent of Coues whitetail mortality directly to coyotes. Coyotes are especially hard on delicate pronghorn fawns. This makes summertime hunting a matter of imitating young deer or pronghorns, but their winter prey commonly consists of rabbits and rodents.

Other predator species often demand calling in the places they hunt and sleep, but successful coyote calling normally involves luring them onto ground advantageous to the shooter. In mountain habitat, for example, you strive to lure them into open meadows, clear-cuts or pastures for clean shots with scoped varmint rifles. Seemingly endless options and too much cover that limits your calling range means you must cover a lot of ground, listening for calls or looking for tracks in snow to discover concentrations. In Eastern woodlands or farmlands, coyotes are normally pressured more, and stand options are limited because of land access. The smart hunter seeks corners of agricultural fields not easily observed from afar and calls only when wind is ideal, otherwise holding off until another day for fear of educating yodel-dogs. Often, in the thronged swamps of the Southeast, for example, or thorn and cactus flats of southern Texas or southern Arizona, you'll wade right in and call them into your lap, a flat-shooting varmint rifle exchanged for your favorite turkey shotgun.

Generally, coyotes respond to calls fairly quickly, often on greedy runs, usually within 10 to 15 minutes. In more expansive or rugged terrain, and on still days when sound carries farther, I'll give coyotes 20 to 30 minutes to arrive before moving. When faced with more educated Eastern 'yotes, give them plenty of time to slink in — up to an hour. I've had coyotes arrive in full-out gallops and run me over, though they occasionally hang up at 300 to 400 yards, surveying the situation shrewdly, requiring more coaxing or simply fading away. In those situations, a motion decoy is a boon, stopping runners for standing shots or luring the undecided another 100 yards for surer shot placement. I've had worthwhile results with stationary spotted fawn and coyote decoys, too.

ABOVE: *Predator calling has always fascinated hunters, but its popularity is on the upswing, thanks to television shows such as* Predator Nation, *hosted by Fred Eichler, shown here after a successful morning's hunt.*

The decision to take a long stab or gamble on coyotes moving closer is left to experience, with cartridge and rifle capabilities and shooting abilities plugged into the equation. When coyotes arrive in groups, which is not uncommon during Western winters, allow the leading dog to get on top of you before targeting the longest high-odds target first and working on the others before they move out of range. My record is seven western New Mexico song dogs in one sit. Also, even after shooting a coyote, continue calling, as more targets often appear given time.

■ Sly and Not-So-Shy Foxes

Two fox species are commonly pursued in North America: the red and gray. Smaller kit and swift foxes are hunted in isolated plains habitats, though they're often protected because of relative regional scarcity. The red fox has garnered a well-deserved reputation as a sly operator. The reason is twofold: its predominantly Eastern digs and increased exposure to man in those more densely populated regions, but also its general inclination for nocturnal tendencies. Like the woodchuck, the sporting literature of my youth was filled with red fox calling tales, sparking early predator calling ambitions.

Red foxes, like coyotes, are omnivorous but relish meat. It's important to remember red foxes are relatively small, and a 15-pounder is a brute. Consequently, red foxes generally disregard the coarse calls of jackrabbits or deer fawns, though those animals are abundant in some of their range. Shrill cottontail and rodent calls are best, more closely imitating their preferred diet. In general, a caller hoping to lure red foxes begins with squeaky rodent calls, in case a fox is close by, and continues with high-pitched cottontail distress sequences delivered with ascending volume to reach farther or penetrate thick brush. Should a red respond but hang up out of range or refuse to emerge from deflecting brush, use the rodent squeaker as a finisher. Red foxes, especially in hard-hunted areas or places where coyotes or stray dogs roam, seldom gallop into calls, generally emerging at cover edges to survey the situation carefully before slipping forward. Give them time. The most wary reds generally attempt to swing downwind while responding to calls, so choose battlegrounds accordingly.

The best bets for red fox setups typically involve old clear-cuts, open glades in river bends, fallow grass- and brush-choked farm fields, or secret corners of agricultural fields not easily observed by a passerby. An abundance of brush piles, and areas around thick creek bottoms or hedgerows are places reds normally hunt, and they're welcome elements to successful setups. Reds can show up quickly, but as often, they'll take up to an hour steeling their nerve to show themselves, so be patient. A motion decoy can help speed the process.

Gray foxes aren't the sharpest tools in the woodshed. In reality, their proclivity for climbing trees aside, they behave more like cats then canines; curious animals sometimes prone to silly behavior. The only thing that

RIGHT: *Predator calling is not just an American institution. Swedish hunter Olof Reinhammar takes predator hunting seriously, protecting his family's sheep farm from red fox predation. Olof Reinhammar photo.*

The author enjoyed a highly successful nighttime spotlight hunt on private property with landowner permission, collecting six gray foxes and a prime bobcat in a single night. He used a scoped .223 Rem., but a shotgun would have been better.

saves them is nocturnal tendencies. After spending much of my life in prime gray fox habitat and calling obsessively, I've only lured three out of hiding during daylight. This, I believe, is a feature of living alongside coyotes and bobcats that happily devour them given an opportunity, but that's only theory. This makes them largely a spotlighter's concern, which limits options because of obvious conservation department laws. In West Texas and New Mexico, where I hunted grays when young, spotlighting was permitted on private lands (don't take my word for it; laws occasionally change) and only with permission from landowners. Having a signed note was a precaution against citations. Night-vision and thermal-imaging technology have a place here.

At night in prime habitats and aided by artificial light, grays are almost too easy. This is where my perceptions of grays as the dunce of the fox family really developed. I've witnessed grays jumping into pickup beds full of hunters more than once looking for the source of our calls, attacking dirt clods when hit with a light (a turn of shadows creating a ball-before-a-housecat scenario, maybe) and sticking around to be shot at multiple times before meeting their fate. Grays will often approach vehicles parked beneath full moons. They don't seem to heed their noses, though from my trapping experiences, I know their sense of smell is sufficiently honed. For those reasons, I generally prefer a magnum shotgun for nighttime gray foxes, as ranges are typically intimate and targets seldom stationary — unless you're in

it strictly for sport. They wise up when hunted but never possess the native street smarts of the average red fox.

You can find productive calling sites in riparian or brushy areas, or along vegetation-choked draws in more open desert. The typical approach is to call continually, tipping a spotlight 45 degrees skyward occasionally and scanning surroundings, seeking telltale orange-or green-glowing eyes. A red-, green- or blue-lens filter is also a boon (though this also reduces light intensity and reach), as canines are colorblind. However, they discern shadows, which can cause strange behavior — such as attacking dirt clods — or spook predators that have seen the show before. As the hunt reaches a climax, the shooter is cued, and the fox is coaxed closer — if the shooter is using a shotgun, which is only fatal to 50 or 60 yards — and hit full on with the light. You can often take your time aiming a rifle, but not all grays are fools, so don't count on it. Be on them and ready to shoot, first confirming beyond a doubt you're not mistaking deer or livestock eyes for a fox.

Grays usually arrive quickly — sometimes within five to 10 minutes — though I always call much longer, anticipating laggards or a bobcat sharing their habitat. Foxes usually have established seasons, typically when fur is prime during fall and winter, so check regulations carefully.

■ Bobcats: the Secretive One

Bobcats are North America's most aesthetically attractive predators and also the hardest won. They are strict carnivores, shunning carrion and preferring only fresh-killed meat. This makes them an apex predator, with population densities never matching those of more common coyotes or foxes. Calling in and tagging a bobcat is one of predator calling's real highlights, setting aside the fact a prime pelt can also prove valuable in certain regions. I've received $350 to $450 from fur buyers for prime Western bobcat pelts.

A prime bobcat can mean a big payday while predator calling. Sportsman's Channel Predator Nation television host Fred Eichler tagged this gorgeous winter bobcat while calling in southeastern Colorado. Fred Eichler photo.

Another "yuge" part of the equation, besides relative scarcity in most habitats, is that bobcats are highly secretive and deliberately cautious. I've had a handful of bobs sprint into calling setups, but more often, they'll stalk your calls, appearing suddenly or observed stalking between patches of cover after 30 to 45 minutes. They'll often mount a distant vantage and stare endlessly at a calling site before committing. This makes decoys (namely quivering or wagging arrangements) welcome additions to any calling arsenal, giving Mr. Bob something to fixate on other than the caller. Interestingly, though, even after spotting a caller, bobcats often sit at a safe distance or peer from behind cover and watch — part of a cat's advertised curiosity, I suppose.

I remember calling a huge tom bobcat in while bowhunting. I was using an Expedite cottontail-rabbit decoy that quivered and emitted a squeak at timed intervals. I was so rattled by the sudden and unexpected appearance of a prime tom I muffed the first shot, shooting over his back. The cat jumped and stared at the spot my arrow rattled into below, letting me stealthily nock another arrow. Just then, the quiver decoy did its thing, letting me slowly draw and take my time on the second shot. I didn't miss that time.

I've seen no evidence that bobcats are smart. They're just deliberate in every motion, likely a result of the hungry coyotes typically sharing their habitat.

When targeting bobcats, calling sites normally revolve around cliffy, rocky terrains — places bobcats regularly hunt rodents and rabbits and lay up during midday. If a rocky place supports copious cottontails, packrat nests and rock squirrels, it constitutes potential bobcat habitat, though sure cat sign such as tracks and "toilets" (loose or sandy patches of ground where cats deposit scat like a housecat's litter box) provide more confidence a cat is present. Scouting after fresh skiffs of snow is another sure indicator.

Though you never really know. That's why that big tom caught me so flat-footed, called in on a barren flat of scattered mesquite well removed from rocky or brushy cover. In South Texas and western Mississippi, I've called bobcats in brushy bottomland habitats. Remember, too, bobcats wander widely, covering vast circuits of established territory (males range most widely, especially in the West), often arriving at a spot only periodically. Bobcat hunting is normally permitted only during winter, as it would be a shame to waste so valuable a predator for mere sport, even if they're especially hard on game birds such as turkeys.

■ Crying Wolf

Bringing wolves to the call is a highly specialized and regional segment of predator calling. Wolf hunting is legal in Idaho, Canada and Alaska, and has been off and on in Montana, Wyoming, Minnesota and Wisconsin, according to current anti-hunting lawsuits and court injunctions. Admittedly, it's outside my expertise. I cannot imagine wolves not being interested in the distress calls of deer fawns or elk calves that share their habitat, but from my understanding, the most successful wolf callers use wolf howls to their advantage. Wolves are strong pack animals that run in tightly knit social units, or packs. They compete viciously for prime hunting grounds, defending territories like warring tribes. Young males kicked from an established pack or competing packs that wander into another pack's territory in search of better hunting during lean times are attacked and killed without mercy. Successful hunters approach wolf hunting much the same way as coyote calling, scouting until a wolf pack is located, and carefully minding topography and wind. But instead of issuing distress calls, they offer realistic wolf howls in hopes of sparking territorial disputes. Of course, with a 175- to 250-pound timber wolf, you might want to leave the varmint shooter at home, opting for your favorite deer rifle. I can only imagine the thrill of tagging one of these once-in-a-lifetime trophies.

RIGHT: *Bringing wolves to a call is only a dream for most predator callers, because there are so few places where it's possible.* Predator Nation TV host Fred Eichler traveled to Canada to fulfill that dream, luring this wolf into range with territorial wolf calls. *Fred Eichler photo.*

Electronic calls are all the range today, but predator callers have been getting the job done with mouth calls for decades. The biggest disadvantage is that predators can more easily pinpoint the source of the calls. A quivering decoy helps shift attention elsewhere.

■ Mouth Calls, Pros and Cons

It started with mouth-blown calls, of course, as pioneers such as the Burnham Brothers opened a new world of sport in the 1950s and '60s. I've won numerous predator calling contests with mouth calls and collected thousands of dollars of fur by producing calls with my lungs. Mouth-blown calls, despite the proliferation of electronic options today, still sell briskly. They're extremely affordable, costing about $10 to $15 opposed to the cost of a quality $150 to $500 electronic unit (sub-$100 units seldom produce realistic sounds, offer limited calling options and have little way of manipulating them when switched on). Mouth calls give you more control, as you can call when you wish and as loud or quiet as you need, putting more heart into a call when a predator hangs up, without taking your eyes off the game to operate a remote control.

The problem with mouth calls is they require lung power. Predator calling done right, with heart (recall, you're imitating an animal fighting for its life), can take your breath away, which then affects shooting proficiency. You need to be in decent cardiovascular conditioning to call at your best, especially through an entire day of hunting. Mouth calls also have a tendency to freeze up or wear out at the worst possible moments, rendering them inoperable. Without a backup, you're finished for the day.

■ Electronic Calls: The Modern Edge

A mouth-call aficionado from way back, I caved to the electronic rage late in the game. Part of that is because I'm a cheapskate and also because I've always gotten along fine without one. Still, there are definite advantages to electronic calls. Their biggest selling point is the vast variety of call options afforded by better units. You get all the usual calls — rodent squeaks, and cottontail, jack and fawn distress — but also some unique stuff that can really turn the tables on hunter-wise predators. FOXPRO's Banshee Pro, Western River's Mantis and Primos' Turbo Dog include woodpecker distress calls and cottontail and jackrabbit distress cries mixed with coyote talk, straight coyote calls, bobcat distress mews and many other options, in addition to standard predator fodder, controlled from a distance with menu-equipped remote controls.

Remote control is another feature I like about electronic callers; the ability to move units away from your immediate position. This might seem like a small thing, but it presents distinct advantages. It allows you to better play wind in marginal situations. It's common for savvy predators to swing downwind of the call source, scent-checking for danger. Electronic calls put attracting calls and human scent on different slipstreams. Also, predators, with their sharp hearing, easily pinpoint the source of sounds. Moving calls away from the caller means a predator's attention is directed elsewhere, allowing careful shot execution, instead of the sometimes hurried or twisted shots that result after luring predators with mouth calls. Finally, electronic calls save your wind, leaving pulse rates steady and lungs at rest for precision shooting.

■ Time and Place

I know I'm repeating myself, but it bears reiteration: The best predator calling is typically found farthest from civilization, where they're less apt to have been subjected

....

Electronic predator calls have several huge advantages, the largest of which is the ability to set a caller away from the shooter and operate it remotely. This makes playing the wind easier and shifts attention away from the shooter.

005848   2013.02.10 06:57:55   KANH-0573

Nighttime hunting is a mainstay of serious predator calling, as hunting predators are most active during darkness. Spotlights have long been the key to success. More recently, thermal-imaging technology is the new normal.

to educating hunting pressure. For quality coyote calling, two to three hours of driving from cities seems about right for finding productive ground. For the Eastern red fox hunter, begging permission to access exclusive private property is the best advice I can offer. Beginning predator callers and simple mistakes (or lucky predators) culminate in smarter critters reluctant to investigate calls. I've called in areas where all you get for your efforts are repeated, mocking howls — a sure sign they've been called before. My best predator calling forays involve overnight stays, sometimes sleeping in my truck to get an early start the next morning. If the thought of a breakdown or two flat tires causes uneasiness, you're probably at an excellent predator calling destination.

Like fishing, the best time to go predator calling is whenever you can get away, but certain conditions prove better than others. Calm days are obviously better than windy conditions, though don't let moderate winds discourage you. I've shot plenty of coyotes in modestly windy days at the front end of winter storms, snow swirling from the sky. I prefer still, overcast days immediately preceding major storm fronts, as predators feel barometric pressure drop and know they're likely to be holed up a while, so getting a bite to eat becomes more urgent. Likewise, immediately after major storms can be excellent for similar reasons, as predators have been laid up, and their

Decoys, especially battery-operated motion decoys, can give a predator caller an edge, directing responding predators to places more favorable to wind or shooting lanes, or coaxing a reluctant critter into the open.

bellies are empty. Cold mornings and evenings or bitterly cold days are also generally best, as predators' heavy winter coats can discourage daytime activities.

One of my secret weapons is calling coyotes during bright full-moon nights, with only lunar reflection by which to shoot. This is best conducted during snowy months when moonlight is amplified and predators highlighted in greater detail, but I've had good luck hunting in prairies, open desert and harvested or plowed fields. This approach also allows effectively plying those wide-open, featureless areas where predators are present but out of reach during daylight. I've hunted pan-flat areas by laying flat, sitting to shoot only after hearing 'yotes pattering across crunchy snow or dry ground. Your biggest problem in open habitats is effectively stashing your vehicle. A turkey shotgun fed appropriate shells (see Chapter 6, "Pelt Shooting") is generally best, allowing point-and-shoot reaction to approaching coyotes, though I've done well with large-objective scopes and rifles on the brightest nights — namely sitting atop blanketing snow.

Of course, nighttime spotlighting is a productive and time-honored approach to predator calling, as coyotes, foxes and bobcats tend to be naturally nocturnal, and you're only operating when they are most active.

Game laws, obviously, play into this, as no one needs a game violation. Pore over regulations carefully. Spotlighting has traditionally been conducted from open pickup beds, though smaller ATVs and especially portable, handheld spotlight units have opened more options and eliminated the problem of camouflaging large, conspicuous trucks. Truck-based hunts are best conducted during the darkest nights, especially under heavy overcast that blots out even the stars. Portable units allow hunting during any moon phase, with the rules of engagement much the same as during daytime hunts.

■ Winning Setups

A productive predator calling site must include six important components:

- **1) Ply appropriate habitat:** Calling sites should be adjacent to likely cover, even places predators are known to inhabit, to give you the best start and higher odds of reaching a predator's ears. There's no use playing to an empty concert hall.

- **2) Stash your ride:** You must get to predator calling sites somehow, especially when making a day of it and calling from many spots. You need a place to ditch your truck or ATV that's out of sight and well upwind. Park in a wash or behind a shallow canyon lip, and climb atop a mesa or canyon edge. Walk over the crest, inside a finger of trees or behind a small hill or large pond dam — you get the idea. In high-volume calling, you want to walk as little as possible, conserving more time for calling. One trick I used successfully during predator calling contests was parking in low spots along major highways,

RIGHT: *Predators are hunters and possess ultra-sharp eyesight. Donning camouflage that blends well is imperative. Ghillie-type outfits such as this Rancho Safari Shaggie coat are tops in this area, as they more effectively break up the human outline. Vista Outdoor photo.*

Successful predator calling is a multi-pronged program, from watching wind carefully, entering the area without being detected, adopting convinving concealment and choosing the right call for the preys' habitats.

even busy interstates, and walking over a raise to call coyotes no one ever considered plying.

- **3) Slip in undetected:** If you make a lot of noise while parking, gathering gear, slamming doors or crashing through brush while accessing your spot — commotion sharp-eared predators can easily hear — you'll receive few takers. Hiking across skylines or vast open pastures will likely result in more of the same: no sale. And never walk upwind of likely cover, as you'll clear out predators before you begin.

- **4) Play the wind:** Predators, as we have established, have delicate noses. Sending your most tantalizing calls downwind of your position only educates predators and will result in no shooting or only very long shots as predators hang up.

- **5) Get out of sight:** After you arrive at your calling site, you must get out of sight, falling into cover or tucking against rocks or vegetation that disrupts your human outline. Leaning against the trunk of an umbrella-like tree is ideal, lending comfort that encourages you to hold still and disguising shade when viewed from a distance.

- **6) Set up for clean shooting:** Getting slightly above surrounding ground — a hillside, hillock, ridge or cliff edge — gives you a more commanding view of incoming game, and meadow, clear-cut or power-line right-of-way openings offer obvious deflection-free shooting.

■ Camouflage, Sight and Scent

Camouflage deception is also an important feature in predator calling. Even after seeking refuge in disguising vegetation or tucking into rock piles, it's important to blend in convincingly. Predators, especially patient bobcats, are as

sharp-eyed as anything you'll hunt. Choose camouflage patterns that melt into habitats you're hunting. Use woodland or tree stand patterns such as Realtree's Xtra or Mossy Oak's Break-Up Country in wooded or farmland areas. Open-country patterns such as Realtree's Max-1, Mossy Oak's Brush or ASAT work well in deserts or sage country. And even waterfowl patterns such as Realtree's Max-5 or Mossy Oak's Shadowgrass Blades work on open prairies or grassy areas.

Better, invest in a ghillie or 3-D camouflage outfit with leafy tatters and irregular edges that shatter the human outline. My favorite, because it works well in all seasons and habitats, is Rancho Safari's Shaggie System. This is an industrial-grade camouflage netting shell holding hundreds of hanks of hand-sewn burlap, jute rope and lightweight camouflage material in many basic configurations, including woodland, mountain, prairie or desert hues. It allows taking cover with you, including pants, a long jacket and head and face cover. It can be worn over shorts and a T-shirt during warm months or cover insulated duds when it's cold.

Scent-control outfits from ScentLok Technologies or Under Armour represent another modern marvel. They use filtering agents. ScentLok has activated carbon and chemical compounds to absorb a wide spectrum of organic and inorganic compounds. Under Armour uses specially engineered Zeolite lava that attracts and captures scent molecules. I also believe in scent-killing sprays (and laundry detergents), preferably wide-spectrum oxidizers such as Atsko's N-O-Dor (or Sport's Wash). More recently, Ozonics' HR300 ozone generators accompany me to stands, as ozone is an aggressive oxidizer that captures and destroys downwind odors. Short of a plastic bubble, no product eliminates 100 percent of human odors, but they eliminate just enough to make a wise predator believe you're farther away than in reality, maybe giving you a few extra seconds to pull off a clean shot. And seconds are often all you need.

⊕ Chapter 5
Feral Hogs, Stemming The Tide

nly a hunter could love a wild boar. Even after killing something approaching 100 hogs from coast to coast and with everything from primitive bows to ARs, I still can't get enough. They're smart, tough and tasty, and generally involve fewer regulations and more liberal, if any, bag limits. They can generally be hunted year-round, most notably during summer off-seasons when no other hunting options exist.

To others, wild swine aren't welcomed. U.S. Fish and Wildlife biologists tell us 42 of 50 states harbor established populations of hogs, with predictions of further pioneering. These intrusions cost the American taxpayer up to $1.5 billion annually in damage to property and control efforts. In Texas, the annual cost to the livestock industry is an estimated $52 million, a situation that has the Texas Agriculture Commission discussing poisoning hogs with warfarin-based pesticides. The announcement has been met with mixed opinions. Landowners — farmers and ranchers, especially — are more likely to revile hogs, which is more good news for hunters looking for shooting opportunity on private lands.

Hogs are destructive, wrecking fields and pastures like run-amok tillers, ravaging and trampling crops with insatiable appetites, chewing waterlines and sullying livestock tanks with incessant wallowing and defecation, breaching livestock fences and even consuming young livestock and game. They also devour mast native game depends on for survival, reducing a land's carrying capacity. Hogs breed like rabbits, and can reproduce as early as 6 months, with sows dropping two litters annually, averaging four to six piglets or up to 10 or 12 in better habitats. Hogs live four to five years on average. One university study deduced that to remain abreast of hogs' reproductive pace, 66 percent of their population must be eliminated annually, yet hunters only account for annual harvests of 10 to 50 percent of overall populations, depending on the region.

LEFT: *Wild boars offer the average guy an opportunity to hunt big game affordably and outside traditional big-game seasons. The author's father shot this eating-fat boar while spot-and-stalk hunting along a thick creek bottom, taking it with his .260 Remington deer rifle.*

The U.S. Fish and Wildlife Service estimates that established populations of wild hogs inhabit 42 of 50 states in the United States. This is bad news for farmers and ranchers who must contend with the destruction, but good news for hunters looking for opportunity.

Hog diseases aren't a significant threat to human health, but they can prove problematic to livestock and native wildlife. Even so, wear rubber gloves while gutting and processing wild hogs, and/or wash your hands thoroughly immediately after exposure, just in case. Wild hog meat mirrors free-range pork but should be cooked thoroughly. Young animals obviously provide the most succulent eating, but older animals can be salvaged with proper care.

■ Understanding Wild Boars

Despite the runaway populations and widespread availability of pigs, hunting success can prove hard won. Hogs are quick studies and learn from every human encounter they survive. Their eyesight is relatively poor, though they perceive conspicuous movements. Their hearing is only average.

It's their noses that really shine. In my opinion, hogs have a more highly developed sense of smell than white-tailed deer. You might get away with small amounts of noise and get closer if you move slowly, but you'll never fool their noses, even from hundreds of yards away.

Wild boars remain most active during day from fall through early spring, though they're averse to extreme cold (relative to regional norms). Hogs become increasingly nocturnal during warm months, especially the largest, oldest boars, though they'll venture into daylight when isolated and/or limited food is available and hunting pressure light. For example, in West Texas, the sweet wild plums of late-June and early-July bring even wise old boars into daylight. Also, during hotter portions of summer, hogs venture to water any hour of the day. Hogs have no sweat glands, so they must consume water to survive when temperatures soar.

Florida remains one of the best places in the country to pursure wild hogs, with private lands offering the most liberal regulations. European hogs arrived in America here first, so it's fitting the state remains top for hog hunting.

In areas where feral hogs have just arrived and begun to cause a nuisance, gaining hunting access can be easy. Even in established areas, hog hunts can be arranged for much less money than most game birds or big game.

88 : Chapter 5

Texas is considered by most as the country's top hog destination, and one with the most open rules. The author took these behemoth boars while hunting at night with ARs and thermal-imaging scopes at the landowners behest.

■ Rules of Engagement

Though hogs are found across the nation, the most popular strongholds remain Florida, Texas and California. Not incidentally, that's where hogs first arrived in the New World. Initial feral hogs arrived during Florida explorations by Hernando de Soto in 1539. More interesting, these hogs came from Cuba, descendants of hogs introduced during Christopher Columbus' second voyage in 1493. Texas hogs arrived later, about 300 years ago, brought as a reliable food supply by Spanish explorers. Limited stocks of European Russian boars arrived in the 1930s and soon escaped, mixing with feral populations. In California, Juan Rodriguez Cabrillo ventured north as far as modern Santa Barbara in 1542. It's conceivable hogs escaped during those explorations, though it wasn't until 1769 that Spanish and Russian outposts were permanently established, likely leading to most of today's stock. Limited European boars were introduced to California as early as the 1920s.

These traditional wild boar strongholds serve as a cross section of the wide variety of conservation department rules you can expect to encounter while hunting hogs. Of course, always check regulations thoroughly before hunting.

Like Florida and Texas, California received early influxes of wild hogs via Spanish exploration and settlement. Despite more convoluted regulations, the Golden State remains a top draw for quality hog hunting -- mostly on managed private lands. Fred Eichler photo.

■ Florida

Wild boars inhabit all 67 counties of the Sunshine State, with best estimates putting their numbers at more than 500,000. Florida hogs generally run a bit smaller than those in other regions. Hogs are defined as wildlife in Florida and thus garner various degrees of protection. Wild boars can be hunted year-round on private lands with any legal weapon with landowner permission. No size or bag limits are included, and no license is required. Night hunting (with spotlight or thermal imaging) is allowed with gun and light permits,

though suppressors aren't directly addressed. Limited-entry quota hunts, with application deadlines, are offered at many public lands and managed to prevent overcrowding and provide top-notch experiences. Florida's many wildlife management areas are also open to public hunting. Public lands include highly defined seasons and permits, with hunting licenses required. Daily limits apply, and minimum size requirements are instituted in some areas. No lights or night hunting are allowed. Residents pay $48 for a yearly hunting/fishing license and nonresidents $46.50 for a 10-day temporary licenses or $151.50 annually. Additional permit fees apply to public-land hunts. See the Florida Fish and Wildlife Conservation Commission website for current information: myfwc.com.

■ Texas

Lone Star State hogs number 1.5-plus million and counting. In Texas, hogs are designated as exotic livestock and essentially belong to landowners. So, technically, landowners or their agents are allowed to kill feral hogs causing damage to livestock, farming operations or private property without a hunting license. To add confusion, Texas Parks and Wildlife requires hunters to purchase a hunting license if hunting for "trophies or food." Though landowners want hogs killed, I donate $48 for a nonresident five-day special permit when hunting Texas' summer hogs and a $300-plus hunting license if also hunting turkeys or deer. Texas allows hunting hogs at night with artificial light, silenced firearms, night vision and thermal imaging. Even so, it's a good idea to drop a courtesy call to the local game warden to avoid wasting his and your time explaining yourself in the field. Baiting is legal. Even aerial gunning is allowed (more later), though this requires a permit from TPWD. Learn more by visiting Texas Parks and Wildlife Department's website: tpwd.texas.gov.

■ California

There are no solid numbers for Golden State wild boars, but to provide an indication, hunters killed 5,453 hogs from 44 of 58 counties during the 2005-'06 seasons. Hog populations have since expanded to 56 of California's 58 counties. The People's Republic of California, naturally, includes a plethora of tedious regulations, including those specific to various areas and counties. I'll give you the basic rundown, but I highly encourage you to read hunting regulations carefully, as rules often apply to one set of counties and not others. California also has condor zones, where shooting lead bullets is forbidden. Homogeneous-alloy pills — such as Barnes' TSX, Nosler's E-Tip or Hornady's GMX — solve this problem, and are controlled-expansion designs highly welcomed on tank-like hogs. California not only requires a hunting license ($47.01 [seriously?] resident, $163.65 nonresident) but also tags to attach to each hog taken ($22.42 resident, $75.34 nonresident). You must report each harvest. Seasons are open year-round, and limits are limited only by your tag purchasing power. No baiting is permitted.

Straightforward hunting ploys work as well on wild hogs as commonly hunted deer. Spot-and-stalk ploys – gaining a vantage and glassing for animals before planning a stalk – is highly productive in broken or rolling terrain.

Regulations regarding night hunting and lights change with areas and units. In some areas, lights are legal for furbearing (like coyotes) and nongame (hogs) mammals, but not during open big-game seasons or from vehicles not parked and switched off. In other areas, you can use lights powered by batteries no larger than 9-volt, with exceptions made for larger lights on private land when landowners are suffering damage to livestock or property. In other areas, nongame can be taken any time with landowner permission. To sort it out, visit California Department of Fish and Wildlife's website: wildlife.ca.gov.

In states or areas where baiting is legal, there is no better place to ambush a greedy feral pig than near a corn feeder. This is a common approach in states such as Florida (private land only) and Texas, but it's not legal in California.

■ Basic Approaches

The wonderful thing about hogs is they allow basic or sophisticated approaches, and the choice up to you. Because hogs share habitats where you might hunt deer, the same ploys are easily adopted. Still-hunting, spot-and-stalk and stand-hunting (sometimes in conjunction with baiting) account for most hog-hunting success.

I prefer spot-and-stalk hunting when possible. This is a matter of gaining the high ground during prime hours and putting quality optics to work. Hogs generally blend well, especially calico or spotted specimens common to certain habitats. As often, hogs really stick out, especially jet-black hogs silhouetted against yellowed grass or those traveling in large groups. I've also located hogs after they let loose ear-piercing squeals while tussling for food or fighting for receptive sows. I seldom spend a lot of time poring over ground like I might while seeking deer, as hogs are generally easier to spot than naturally camouflaged deer. On Texas ranches, we often conduct recon from a truck, driving to rims overlooking lower ground, or high spots above field or food-plot edges, even stopping to climb windmill towers or oil-field collection tanks to gain a vantage.

Long-distance glassing is most productive in broken or semi-open habitats. In northern and western Texas, for example, gypsum rimrock, clay hills and the aforementioned oil-field and windmill perches allow glassing over miles of scattered mesquite, blueberry juniper and prickly-pear cactus grasslands. In northern California, glassing tilted topography and open grass swales between manzanita, madrone and live-oak thickets reveals hogs, especially near bottom or hillside springs on warm afternoons. Spot-and-stalk ploys, by contrast, would prove fruitless in flat, thickly vegetated Florida or South Texas.

In thicker habitats, still-hunting is the preferred mode of operation. During hot summer months, I enjoy quietly slipping along thronged creekbeds or washes, pausing regularly to glass shadows or inspect suspicious highlights. It's common to locate sleeping hogs shaded in tight places for point-blank shooting. And keep your ears open, because more than once, I've heard the soft grunts of rooting or traveling hogs. Once, while still-hunting a series of extensive wild-plum thickets, I located a big-old boar through his loud snoring. A sleeping adult hog isn't as on edge as a deer, making approaches easier. It's also common to find piles of sleeping hogs in tight cover during colder periods or while camped out on isolated food sources, like those wild plums I've hunted often. I recall jumping 25 hogs out of a thicket, blazing away with a .44 Mag. revolver — exciting sport for sure.

Stand-hunting proves exceptionally productive in areas where glassing isn't feasible and footing is too clamorous for still-hunting. Sites overlooking runways or trails filled with blunted tracks and dog-like droppings following thick strips of cover or low places are productive. Food is always the primary attraction, especially bounty such as acorns, wild plums, feral apples, small food plots or beaten-down trails leading to agricultural fields. During warm periods, never dismiss water, especially isolated stock ponds or pockets in creekbeds where water remains during dry periods. During summer, I've witnessed hogs on water during every hour of the day, even when it was 98 in the shade. If you're going to sit still during warmer off-seasons, remember to spray down with mosquito, chigger and tick repellent. ThermaCell units are excellent, producing a barrier of insect repellent without game-spooking chemical odors.

Of course, the most productive stand site in hog country is near a corn feeder. I've taken hogs in Florida and Texas hunting in this manner. It's where I hunt when I'm tired of window shopping and ready to make a purchase. It's deadly effective, because wild boars are, as they say, greedy as a pig.

■ Hog Medicine

Much is made of hogs' tenacity for life. This is largely true, though I think part of the problem is that many hunters fail to place shots precisely. The vitals of North American big game are set farther back than animals across the Atlantic. To kill North American deer, elk or bear cleanly, aim a couple of inches behind the shoulder and mid-body, and they'll seldom get out of sight. Hog vitals, like other European and African animals, are situated farther forward and on the lower third of the body, essentially beneath the lower shoulder. On broadside hogs, place your shots tight into the armpit. If slightly quartered away, shoot to send bullets forward low between the shoulders.

Wild hogs are destructive, a trait that makes them despised by most landowners. This damage was caused when hogs chewed through a plastic water line, wasting precious water meant for livestock and making a mess.

There's also much ado regarding boars' protective shield, which is essentially accumulated scar tissue resulting from love's labors lost. I've heard claims this gristle plate will stop a .30-'06 Springfield bullet. This is plain nonsense, obviously, as even modern bulletproof vests won't accomplish that. I once shot a sheep-eating boar that weighed 508 pounds on a certified wool/mohair scale, and its shield slowed the penetration of a heavy arrow shot from 65 pounds considerably, but I obviously didn't hang him on that scale alive. Yes, some old boars wear gristle shields. But no, it won't stop rifle or pistol bullets — especially quality designs. In reality, you won't shoot many of these old warriors (except at night, in which case shots are typically short and shots to the ear welcomed) any more than you regularly shoot record-sized white-tailed bucks.

Hunters also tend to exaggerate the size of many hogs seen or shot. Of the multitudes of hogs I've shot, I can count on my fingers how many weighed more than 300 pounds. Ninety percent of hogs shot weigh less than or no more than the average deer in the same habitat — 90 to 175 pounds. So, the cartridge with which you've been collecting yearly venison will be acceptable for hog hunting. That said, if you hunt hogs long enough, you'll eventually get a chance at one of the big boys. The solution doesn't necessarily lie in bigger artillery but with choosing high-quality, controlled-expansion bullets made to drive deep while retaining most of their starting weight. Prime examples include Barnes' X series, Hornady's GMX, Cutting Edge's Raptor or Nosler's venerable Partition. I'll get into more details in Chapter 10, "Handloading To Needs."

The other aspect of hog hunting played up for maximum sensationalism is the status of wild boars as dangerous game. You can bet your best rifle that 99 percent of the hogs you'll encounter, after detecting your presence, will depart hastily and with fear in their hearts. Wounded hogs might prove a different matter, of course, but a white-tailed buck or coyote might also prove dangerous if wounded and cornered. So although I've no fear of wild boars, I show due respect, taking appropriate precautions while trailing in heavy cover. A magnum handgun is welcomed insurance in tight quarters and a viable alternative at intimate ranges.

The exception to this nonchalant attitude arrives while chasing hogs with hounds, in which case things can turn ugly in a hurry. A pissed-off boar-hog being harried by a pack of screaming, nipping dogs can prove downright and suicidally wicked. I've a ragged scar on the back of my scalp to prove that point. That boar had to be shot off me with hand cannon — and I was only along to take pictures, damn it!

■ Texas Stands Alone

Obvious aspects make Texas the king of hog hunting. The dominance of private land is an obvious factor, as are the large acreages of average Texas ranches. Because hogs are treated as exotic livestock owned by landowners, they're more apt to be viewed as targets than game animals like they are in California and Florida. Now, don't get me wrong, I respect hogs as I do all living creatures, believing they deserve quick and dignified ends. But most farmers and ranchers don't see things that way, and they don't much care how you go about killing them. To the average Texas landowner producing commodities, the only good hog is a dead hog. This makes approaches that might be viewed as unacceptable in other places common modes of operation in Texas. Baiting? A regular institution. Night shooting with spotlights? No problem. Night-vision gear or thermal scopes? Yep. Shooting from helicopters? Yes, that, too.

■ Spotlighting Success

Spotlighting has remained a standard approach to Texas hog control because of the species' nocturnal tendencies. Yet one of the unique aspects

Decked-out ARs ready for nighttime hog action, left to right: Alexander Arms 6.5 Grendel, Trijicon IR-Hunter and Truglo TRU-Point Laser/Light Combo; custom 6.8 SPC, FLIR ThermoSight R-Series and Cyclops VB250 Varmint Light; and Sig Sauer M400 .223 Rem., Sig ECHO1 Thermal Reflex Sight and Streamlight TLR-1 Game Spotter light.

nighttime hunters must understand is that hog eyes lack a *tapetum lucidum*, fancy words describing the reflective layer behind the retinas of cervids such as deer and predators such as coyotes and raccoons. So, although nighttime spotlighting can prove effective for controlling hog populations, you cannot depend on the telltale blink of shining eyes common to other forms of varmint and predator shooting, a feature that generally lets you pick up animals at much greater distances. This makes black or otherwise dark-hued hogs sometimes difficult to see in brushy areas. Still, untold numbers of hogs have been eliminated in this manner.

Recently, feeder lights or motion-activated lights set aside feeders have become common, allowing night hunts over established bait sites. Some

Outdoor writer and TV host Scott Haugen and his boy bagged these wild hogs in Florida at night by old-fashinged spotlighting. Artificial light is still a viable way to find nighttime action. Just recall that hogs' eyes don't shine like those of predators. Scott Haugen photo.

products replace the protective cap beneath feeder motors with motion-activated green or red LEDs to provide shooting illumination. Other motion-activated units are mounted to posts or trees beside feed stations, lighting up the scene when movement is detected. In either case, the best results are obtained after the system has been in place a while so hogs become accustomed to a play of shadows beneath color-filtered light or outright white light.

Even with artificial light, problems remain with sighting devices. Lighted dots or reticles solve the problem of sure aiming during nighttime assaults. Dot scopes are popular with the black-gun community, so they're common and cover the gamut from highly affordable (TRUGLO) to pricey (Trijicon or

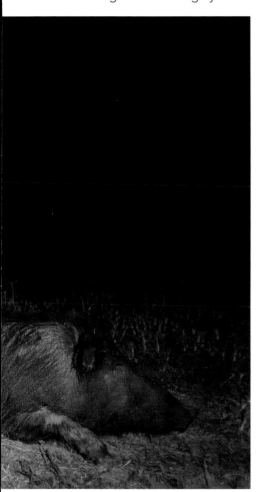

EOTech), though that extra money generally translates into more durable construction. The better stuff is what many U.S. military forces use in combat, if that's any indication, Trijicon's ACOG, for example, is lighted by tritium and requires no batteries — but also retails for more than $1,200. Dot-scope models often allow selecting from various reticle styles, hues and, invariably, brightness intensity. Lighted-reticle optics provide another option, with a rheostat switch allowing intensity adjustment to match available light. Otherwise, these serve as standard-issue rifle/pistol scopes at every price point imaginable. Two of my high-end Vortex Viper PST varmint scopes include lighted reticles. This is like four-wheel drive in a truck or SUV. You won't use it most of the time, but when you need it, you need it desperately.

The spotlight is another matter for contemplation. When I was young and spotlighted for varmints or predators, spotlights plugged into cigarette-lighter receptacles attached to a coiled telephone-type cord. Such systems still exist and are more efficient than ever.

But rechargeable cordless units have become standard issue. The biggest drawback to portable units is they eventually require recharging, which can take hours. A dead unit halfway through the night is unacceptable. When purchasing a rechargeable unit, check to see if it can be operated while plugged into the charger (cigarette lighter, usually). Some can, but others cannot. Another solution is to have two rechargeable lights on hand; one on the charger, another in use, switching occasionally to assure maximum output. Something in the neighborhood of 1 million candlepower seems standard.

I also install a weapon light — something with at least 250 lumens, though more is welcomed, granted it doesn't become burdensome. Handguns so equipped are also welcomed for backup, finishing weapons or close-range work. Weapon lights can be set atop your scope via dual-clamping rings or to Picatinny rails like those common on AR platforms. Aftermarket pic rails can be purchased and easily attached to any rifle with a little ingenuity, lending better balance than piggyback scope systems. Even while using night-vision or thermal-imaging optics — more on this later — I insist on an attached light, even one including an incorporated laser, such as TRUGLO's affordable Tru-Point Laser/Light Combo. Let's say you've knocked over a big boar lit up by spotlight while aiming with a dot or lighted-reticle scope. You bail out of the truck, traipsing through thorn, cactus or simply treacherous footing. You need light to make your way safely. You might as well keep it handy by attaching it to your firearm. You then arrive at the scene to find your hog spine-shot and flopping at 10 yards

— a potentially dangerous situation — with the spotlight blinding you from behind. You can use the laser to administer a quick, humane finish. Most units include convenient pressure switches. Attaching "tacticool" stuff to your weapon for show is one thing. In nighttime hog hunting, these tools actually serve practical applications.

■ Own The Night

Night-vision and thermal-imaging weapon scopes are more recent developments, at least in the sporting industry. Military units have long used such technology to gain the tactical advantage in modern

FLIR thermal imaging has changed the hog hunting game, letting hunters own the night, see through brush to discover more hogs and shoot precisely on the blackest nights. Thermal imaging isn't legal everywhere, so check regulations where you hunt.

warfare. Night vision is the older of these technologies, but it's by no means dead. Thermal imaging is considered the latest and greatest.

Night-vision units amplify available star or moonlight, providing a green-hued view of the world visible to the human eye. During the darkest nights — overcast or foggy conditions, for example — better night-vision units can be switched to project IR light invisible to animals and humans but allowing the unit to provide visible imaging. Night-vision and thermal-imaging optics require battery power, obviously, but night vision has the advantage of offering clear images during even the hottest summer nights across rocky terrain — conditions that can cause confusion with more affordable thermal units (not an issue with the best), which require a marked difference in ambient and target temperatures for maximum efficiency. Night vision tends to be relatively more affordable than thermal, which isn't to say it's cheap.

Human eyes perceive a narrow band of wavelengths known as — big coincidence — visible light. This is but a fraction of the bandwidth of our universe's electromagnetic energy. Beyond the red/orange bandwidths at one extreme of the visible spectrum (blue/purple at the other end), we find infrared, or IR, light, which is not visible to your eyes but felt as heat. Thermal imagers capture this heat and translate it into visible light. Technically, you don't see the object but rather an interpretation on a small LCD screen. Because thermal units project no artificial light, they're often legal where night-vision units projecting IR light aren't, though such new technology is often not addressed, and laws and regulations remain gray in many states. Modern thermal units provide sharp high-definition images, not that blobby stuff you saw in the Arnold Schwarzenegger movie *Predator*.

Quality thermal scopes aren't cheap, starting at $3,000, with the best retailing for as much as $10,000. Thermal-imaging mechanics depend on a silicone-like element called germanium. A germanium lens focuses thermal energy that then hits a focal-plane array using a series of registers that generate electrical impulses. These impulses are translated into video pixels and displayed on a cross-hair-equipped screen for viewing, aiming and capture. Greater resolution and larger lenses translate into more detailed video readout — and higher prices. Germanium is expensive. To further complicate matters, manufacturers don't know if a particular FPA is operational until final assembly. A certain degree of rejection adds to cost. This technology is evolving quickly, so costs will undoubtedly decrease with time.

One final note on Texas hog hunting: aerial shooting. This was once a means of effectively controlling hog numbers at specific properties at

Craig Meier and Terrell Coleman, owners of Heli-Hunter LLC.

Once a means of controlling hog populations, Texas recently approved legislation allowing pilots to host shooters for pay. Here, Predator Nation host Fred Eichler prepares for takeoff and an aerial hog hunt. Fred Eichler photo.

the landowner's behest, but Texas Parks and Wildlife recently approved legislation allowing helicopter pilots to host paying guests, leading to a new world of shooting sport. This isn't hunting by any means, but it's as exciting as shooting gets, hanging from the open door of a chopper shooting full-out running hogs. Shotguns fed 00 buckshot or AR platforms with low-power dot scopes are standard weaponry. The interesting thing about this, as I discovered while shooting from a Piper Cub conducting county-sponsored coyote control, is you'll be leading running targets from behind, or backward, as the aircraft is simply moving faster than even running game. With choppers, the pilot can sometimes cut hogs off to provide standing or at least milling shots, but more often, hogs flee straight away from the chopper, so Obama's foreign policy of "leading from behind" remains most productive. Like night-vision and thermal-imaging technology, chopper hunts don't come cheap ($350 to $475 an hour), but they offer once-in-a-lifetime thrills unlike any other.

Hornady Manufacturing photo.

⊕ Chapter 6

Varmint
& Predator Cartridges,
Rimfire to Centerfire

The term varmint cartridge usually denotes a smaller cartridge spitting light bullets at very high speeds. By this definition, the .22-250 represents the archetype varmint cartridge. But this doesn't complete the picture. A varmint cartridge could also be defined as one generally useful for shooting any of the critters discussed so far (wolves and hogs excluded). I like this definition better, especially for our purposes. But there are gray areas — for example, the one-gun owner pushing his favorite deer rifle, loaded with the lightest bullets practical to the cartridge, into varmint shooting service.

In reality, the perfect varmint cartridge doesn't exist, as the needs of the Northeastern woodchuck shooter differ greatly from, say, a Montana prairie dog sniper. You can press just about any cartridge into service when necessary, but that isn't ideal. For most of us, this means owning a battery of firearms chambered for various cartridges and matching cartridges to conditions at hand or a particular mood. Owning many firearms is also more fun than owning only a few.

This starts with rimfires, such as a requisite .22 Long Rifle or sexy .17 rimfire. The tiny centerfires follow; the Hornets, .218 Bee and .221 Rem. Fireball, with their mild recoil and quiet

A sampling of viable varmint cartridges, left to right: .17 Hornet, .17 Rem. Fireball, .17 Rem., 204 Ruger, .22 Hornet, .22 K-Hornet, .218 Bee, .221 Fireball, .222 Rem., .223 Rem./5.65mm NATO, 22 Nosler, .225 Win., .22-250 Rem., .220 Swift, .243 Win., .224/6mm Rem., Win., .308 Win. and 30-'06 Springfield.

The quintessential varmint cartridge propels a small bullet at high velocity -- 35 to 55 grains in excess of 3,500 fps, for example. These cartridges provide mild recoil, flattened trajectory and often explosive bullet performance on smaller targets.

nature welcomed in populated areas where ricochets and loud rifle cracks aren't appreciated by residents. Standard varmint centerfires, such as the .222 and .223 Remingtons, dominate because they do it all while proving accurate, not too loud, powerful enough to reach 300 or 400 yards, and affordable to shoot and especially handload. Rounding out the true varmint arsenal are the fastest boomers, including the newer .204 Ruger, popular .22-250 and older .220 Swift. Finally, there is what I label the windy-day option; technically light deer cartridges that perform well for varmints when loaded with lighter, faster bullets, including select 6mm and .257 calibers.

A friendly bit of advice: When choosing varmint cartridges, stick with standard rounds easily located on sporting-goods shelves. High-volume shoots like prairie dogs or ground squirrels require keeping large volumes of ammo on hand or owning plenty of brass for handloading. Antique, wildcat or other cartridges that didn't catch on (no matter how wonderful they might be) make it difficult to assemble quantities needed for prolonged outings. While ordering my first custom varmint rifle, for example, I desperately wanted a 22 PPC — a fine cartridge, no doubt. Ultimately, my gunsmith talked me into a boring .223 Rem. I'm darned glad he did. I now own almost 3,000 .223 brass (most loaded) and can easily acquire more. The list that follows reflects that philosophy.

Common rimfire cartridges, left to right: .17 Mach 2, .17 HMR, .17 Win. Super Magnum (WSM), .22 Short (Remington), .22 Sniper Subsonic (Aguila), Subsonic Hollow (ELEY), .22 LR (Remington Golden Bullet), CCI Stinger (hyper velocity), .22 Mag. 35-grain (Hornady), .22 Mag. 45-grain (Aguila) -- with the .223 Rem. for comparison

Rimfire ammunition is an American favorite because it is relatively cheap, produces negligible recoil and noise, and easily dispatches most small varmints. It comes in a wide variety of makes and brands.

Rimfires

■ The Venerable .22 Long Rifle

Americans burn an estimated 3 billion rounds of .22 rimfire ammo annually, mostly .22 LR. Rimfire shooting might not be the most important form of marksmanship we enjoy, but it's the most significant in terms of volume. The 125-plus year-old .22 rimfire cartridge is fun, affordable and deadly on small varmints, from invasive starlings to prairies dogs and ground squirrels to, perhaps, 150 yards. I've likely taken more Western jackrabbits, a not-so-delicate target, with .22 LR than all other cartridges combined. Rimfire offerings in .22 range from diminutive CB caps and shorts (great for potting small targets at close range when silence is paramount) to nearly defunct Long (still offered by Winchester and CCI) to larger .22 Mag., with LR dominating. LR rounds are further broken into standard, high, hyper and subsonic velocities.

Actual numbers are somewhat subjective, but "standard" .22 LR velocity seems to hover at about 1,250 fps, high velocity at 1,350 fps and hyper velocity indicating anything pushing beyond, say, 1,450 fps. Newly popular subsonic rounds typically clock at less than 1,050 fps.

CCI's 32-grain Stinger and Quik-Shok, for example, chronograph at about 1,640 fps. Aguila Supermaximums push a 30-grain bullet to 1,700 fps, the fastest .22 LR shells made. The company accomplishes this by seating a lighter/shorter bullet into a slightly longer case. Other hopped-up .22 LRs include Aguila's 1,470 fps Interceptor (40-grain bullet), CCI's 1,435 fps Velocitor (40-grain), Federal's 1,435 fps Hyper Speed (40-grain) and 1,400 fps Varmint HE (37 grain), or Remington's 1,410 fps Viper (36 grain).

American shooters burn .22 LR ammunition to the tune of about 3 billion rounds annually. The basic .22 was likely the average shooter's first rifle and is suitable for most small varmints at moderate ranges.

In most cases, varmint shooters enjoy greater accuracy by choosing standard- or high-velocity .22 shells. I shoot hollow-points whenever possible because they anchor burrowing varmints more convincingly, preventing prairie and sage rats, for example, from disappearing down holes after vital hits.

Excellent hollow-point options include CCI Mini Mag (36-grain, 1,260 fps); Federal Game-Shok 38-grain High Velocity (1,280 fps) and new Hunter Match (40-grain, 1,200 fps); Remington

Golden Bullet (36-grain, 1,280 fps; and 40-grain, 1,255 fps) and Cyclone (36-grain, 1,280 fps); RWS High Velocity (40-grain, 1,310 fps); Winchester Super-X (37-grain, 1,280 fps) and X-Pert (36-grain, 1,220); and Eley High Velocity Hollow (40-grain, 1,250 fps), just as examples. Some are plated, others waxed lead, providing excellent accuracy and killing impact.

Remington Subsonic (38-grain HP, 1,050 fps); RWS Subsonic (40-grain HP, 1,000 fps); Aguila's Sniper Subsonic (60-grain, 950 fps); and Eley Subsonic Hollow (40-grain HP, 1,040 fps) are excellent options for quiet shooting at

shorter ranges. Though, when I first shot Eley Subsonic Hollows at ground squirrels, I expected a looping trajectory but found they worked well to 90 to 100 yards and hit with authority.

■ .22 Winchester Magnum Rimfire

The .22 WMR appeared in 1959 in response to those wanting more rimfire punch. The originals fired 40-grain hollow-points at a publicized 2,000 fps (advertising fudging), changed to a more realistic 1,910 fps after gaining widespread acceptance.

Modern loads include CCI's 30-grain HP+V Maxi-Mag and 40-grain CCI Troy Landry, Federal's 30-grain TNT HP and 50-grain Game-Shok HP, Aguila's 40-grain Silver Eagle, Hornady's 30-grain V-Max, Remington's 33-grain Accu-Tip, and Winchester's 34-grain JHP and 45-grain Dyna-Point. The lightest pills, such as Hornady's V-Max and Winchester's Speer TNT HP, push 2,200 fps, 40-grain loads at about 1,875 fps. All do a job on small varmints to 175 yards.

The .22 Mag. has generally garnered a reputation for mediocre accuracy. The solution is to audition many brands and loads of ammunition until discovering one your rifle prefers — admittedly problematic considering the current state of affairs. It seems .22 Mag. ammo is manufactured only occasionally today, manufacturers focusing on .22 LR to keep hoarders supplied. Changing political tides should ease this situation — at least we hope.

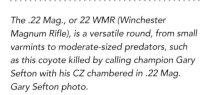

The .22 Mag., or 22 WMR (Winchester Magnum Rifle), is a versatile round, from small varmints to moderate-sized predators, such as this coyote killed by calling champion Gary Sefton with his CZ chambered in .22 Mag. Gary Sefton photo.

The .17-caliber rimfires have become extremely popular, providing flatter trajectory and hitting harder than .22 rimfires. Examples, left to right: .22 LR for comparison; .17 Mach 2, .17 HMR (Hornady Magnum Rimfire), .17 WSM (Winchester Super Magnum) and .17 Hornet for comparison.

■ Rimfires in .17

Small-varmint shooters welcomed the advent of .17-caliber rimfires. They were more successfully marketed than the 1970s ill-fated 5mm Remington Rimfire, which died on the vine despite being an outstanding cartridge.

The .17 Mach 2 uses a .22 LR Stinger case, necked to .172 inch, spitting 17-grain pills to 2,100 fps. Sadly, this excellent and highly accurate .17 rimfire seems to be slowly circling the drain, plagued by ammo shortages and fewer available rifles. The Mach 2 has rabid fans, offering extremely pleasant shooting and deadly impact on smaller varmints to 150 yards. The recent .22 LR rush no doubt factors, so maybe things will turn around. Hornady still offers Mach 2 ammo.

The .17 HMR (Hornady Magnum Rimfire) has proven the most popular of the .17 rimfires. Created by necking down the .22 WMR, the HMR's most efficient with 17-grain bullets, and 15.5-grain NTX Hornady and 20-grain bullets are also loaded. A 17-grain pill clocks 2,550 to 2,600 fps and delivers the goods on smaller varmints to 200 yards. With turreted scopes on calm days, I've shot sage rats to 350 yards with my HMR, resulting in killing impact despite 68 clicks of elevation. The HMR is suitable for foxes and bobcats within 150 yards with careful shot placement. I've killed a coyote with my HMR, but it's not something I'd recommend. Outside 150 yards, it provides marginal energy.

The newer .17 Winchester Super Magnum provides 3,000 fps speeds with 20-grain pills and about 2,600 fps with 25-grain (Winchester offers a 15-grain lead-free pill at 3,300 fps). Created from a nail-gun brass, the WSM didn't live up to accuracy expectations upon release. The real problem wasn't the cartridge but the budget-priced rifles in which it was introduced. Gun manufacturers began offering higher-quality rifles, and reports of improved accuracy followed. That's good news for those who want a hotter rimfire. The .17 WSM can dispatch foxes and bobcats to 200 yards, coyotes with carefully placed shots to 150 and any manner of small varmints with a tad more reach and splat factor on impact.

Centerfires

■ .17 Hornet

Of all of my true varmint rifles, my Savage 25 Walking Varmint in .17 Hornet is far and away my favorite. It's incredibly pleasant to shoot, with the report and recoil of a .22 WMR but the trajectory of a 55-grain .223 Rem. It also assembles one-hole groups. Handloading the .17 Hornet is cheaper than shooting .17 rimfire, a pound of powder charging up to 450 to 500 rounds. Its maximum practical range is 330 yards, after which it drops off exponentially. Inside that, it spatters or rolls up ground squirrels and prairie dogs with authority. The round is similar to P.O. Ackley's 1950s 17 Ackley Hornet, with Hornady making slight changes and standardizing it in 2012. Several reputable firearms manufacturers, such as Savage and CZ, have chambered rifles for the .17 Hornet.

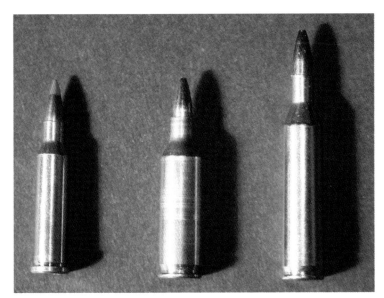

Although many .17-caliber wildcat cartridges have come and gone, only a few have survived as commercially successful rounds, left to right: Hornady's .17 Hornet, .17 Rem. Fireball (necked-down .221 Fireball) and .17 Rem. (which has become less popular today).

The .17 Hornet does its best work with 20-grain pills, with velocities of 3,750 fps possible but 3,650 fps the apparent sweet spot. Adding just 5 grains of bullet weight slows the cartridge 300 to 550 fps, sacrificing everything that is good about the .17 Hornet. Common 25-grain pills and Berger's 30-grain offering make exceptional predator calling options in populated areas where ranges seldom exceed 150 yards and quiet reports ingratiate you to residents.

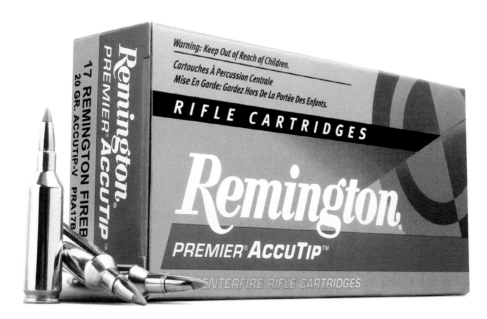

■ .17 Fireball

The .17 Fireball, like its parent .221 Fireball, is extremely efficient, easily pushing 20-grain bullets to 4,000 fps with only 16 to 19 grains of powder and 25-grain pills to 3,700 fps with the same measure of propellant. Back away from maximum loads slightly and the .17 Fireball provides impressive accuracy, though even at "only" 3,900 fps, results are dramatic when bullet meets varmint. Its flat-shooting demeanor requires little adjustment from 100 to 350 yards, though light bullets bleed velocity quickly beyond that point. The older (1960s) .17 Mach IV almost mirrors it in velocity and performance.

■ .17 Remington

The .17 Rem. was the first commercial .17. Standardized in 1971, it was hamstrung early by rumors of short barrel life and, unbelievably, lack of commercial .17-caliber cleaning rods. All .17-caliber barrels require frequent cleaning (say, every 100 rounds) to eliminate chronic barrel fouling, with the .17 Rem. most notorious because it burns larger volumes of powder. Newer propellants minimize this effect. Modern powders and better designed bullets give the .17 Rem. new life. I purchased an early .17 Rem. because I wanted flatter trajectories while hunting coyotes in the days when they averaged $55 apiece. My first experiences were disastrous, with the fragile bullets of the day splattering on hides and inflicting superficial wounds. Handloading and sacrificing some speed solved the problem, but I still don't consider the .17 Rem. ideal for long-range coyote hunting, as unpredictable bullet performance often results in hide damage or dogs escaping after marginal hits. The .17 Rem. is tops in ground squirrel, prairie dog and chuck settings. Twenty-grain bullets can be pushed to 4,200 or 4,300 fps, with ballistically superior 25-grainers attaining 4,000 fps maximum, making it one of the flattest cartridges around.

■ The .204

There have been other 20-caliber centerfire cartridges developed, but only Hornady's .204 Ruger has stuck. In the world of do-it-all long-range varmint cartridges shot on less-than-windy days, the .204 Ruger is pretty darn hard to beat. Based on the old .224 Rem. Mag., the .204 gives you 4,100 fps (maximum loads) with 32-grain bullets, the weight at which the .204 seems to shine. Hornady offers a 24-grain NTX that can be pushed to 4,300 to 4,500 fps. Other 40-grain fodder allows velocities to 3,800 or 45 to 3,500 fps. The heavier bullets make better options for larger predators and superior ballistic coefficients on windy days (better than .224 40-grain bullets, in fact). A 32-grain loaded at 4,100 fps drops only 15 inches at 400 yards, making this a long-range juggernaut.

The Hornady-designed .204 Ruger remains the sole successful commercial .204-caliber cartridge. Created from a necked down .224 Mag. casing, it pushes 32-grain bullets to more than 4,000 fps, with 40-grain bullets offering superior BC to 40-grain .224 pills.

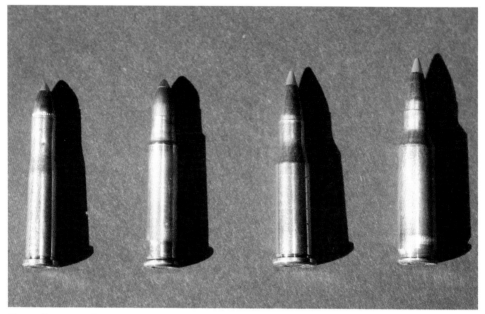

The smallest .224-caliber varmint rounds are extremely pleasant to shoot and best in populated areas where loud reports aren't welcomed. Left to right: .22 Hornet, .22 K-Hornet, .218 Bee and .221 Rem. Fireball.

POPULAR .224S

■ .22 Hornet

Apparently, I'm not alone in my unreasonable affection for the .22 Hornet, as the antiquated cartridge should have passed away peacefully many years ago. But the pioneer 1930s varmint round, with its troublesome bottleneck profile and prominent rim, persists. The .22 Hornet can be coaxed into acceptable accuracy through careful handloading (see Chapter 10, "Handloading to Needs"), but you'll never hear someone bragging of their "one-holer" .22 Hornet. But the original Hornet is quiet and recoil free, with modern powders and bullets extending its usefulness to 250-plus yards. It also helps that many respected gun manufacturers continue chambering quality weapons in .22 Hornet.

Modern factory ammo is commonly loaded with 35-grain poly-tipped bullets, helping the Hornet break 3,000 fps, if not always delivering exceptional accuracy. The .22 Hornet does best as a small-varmint cartridge shooting modern 40-grain pills, with 45-grain bullets better for predators inside 150 yards. I killed hundreds of coyotes with my .22 Hornet and Nosler's now discontinued 45-grain Solid Base bullet. It's ideal for Eastern foxes and woodland bobcats. The newer K Hornet — with blown-out shoulders, 10 percent more powder capacity and 200 to 300 fps greater bullet velocities — offers generally superior accuracy and less tedious loading, but it somehow didn't gain traction.

■ .222 Remington

Remington brought us the .222 in 1950, an original design not based on any other cartridge. Its inherent accuracy accounted for many bench-rest records, and it remains popular with serious varmint shooters today, with an effective range of 250 to 300 yards. The .222 Rem. does best on small varmints when loaded with thinly jacketed bullets, ensuring ample expansion at its moderate 3,100 to 3,200 fps pace. Loaded with 36- to 40-grain pills, it's a small-varmint bomb, with bullets from 50 to 55 grains ideal for close-range work (within 200 yards) on predators without fear of undue pelt damage.

■ .233 Rem./5.56mm NATO

It's no mystery why the .223 Rem. emerged as a varmint/predator-shooting favorite. Adopted by the military in 1957 (later labeled 5.56mm NATO), later standardized as a sporting round by Remington (as the .223), the round is chambered in an endless array of firearm choices, including newly popular AR platforms. Note: .223 ammo can be shot in 5.56mm chambers, but the opposite should be avoided, as the latter includes higher SAAMI pressures

In varmint shooting, mid-sized to larger .224-caliber rounds prove most popular, including, left to right: .222 Rem., .223 Rem., newer 22 Nosler, nearly defunct .225 Win., .22-250 Rem. and venerable .220 Swift.

and can prove unsafe. A ready abundance of military brass and the popularity of ARs (resulting in .223 brass strewn about every popular shooting site) make handloading cases easy to collect in volume. The .223 is highly versatile, handling everything from light 35- to 45-grain varmint bullets, mid-range 50- to 55-grain predator medicine, and pills up to 80 to 90 grains, suitable for cleanly harvesting wild hogs (granted your rifle has rifling fast enough to stabilize longer bullets — that is, 1:8 to 1:6). The average .223 isn't picky about loads or ammo. With streamlined, polymer-tipped 40-grainers, my custom .223 bolt makes easy work of sage rats and prairie dogs to 400 yards, and 55 FMJ bullets from my AR-15 are now my standard coyote medicine.

■ .22 Nosler

The new-for-2017 .22 Nosler neatly fills the gap between the .223 and .22-250 Remingtons, shooting a 55-grain bullet about 300 fps faster than the .223, or about 3,500 fps. Even more velocity gain (about 500 fps) is realized with heavier bullets, such as Nosler's 77-grain Custom Competition. The .22 Nosler was designed for the AR platform, providing one of the most powerful .224-caliber cartridges that will reliably function in that format after a quick switch of the upper and using a 6.8 Remington SPC magazine. I expect this cartridge to gain quick traction among serious predator callers.

■ .22-250 Remington

The popular .22-250 Rem. started life in the late 1930s as a wildcat cartridge based on a necked-down .250-3000, or .250 Savage, case. It has evolved into one of the most powerful and flat-shooting varmint/predator cartridges. The .22-250 is versatile, providing explosive, grenade-like impact via 4,000-plus fps loaded with the lightest bullets (40 to 45-grains), making an excellent long-range small-varmint or predator cartridge when matched with 50- to 55-grain bullets at 3,750 to 3,500 fps, respectively. As most .22-250s

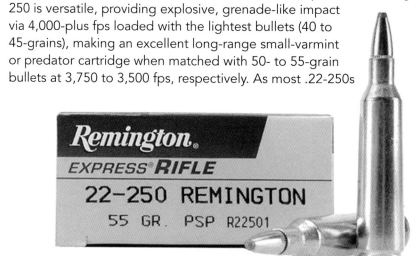

include traditional 1:14 to 1:12 twist rates designed to stabilize lighter bullets for maximum velocity, they don't stabilize longer, heavier bullets reliably. My .22-250, a custom job built on a '98 Mauser action and holding a powerful turret scope, serves as a 400- to 450-yard ground squirrel rifle when loaded with 50-grain Sierra BlitzKings or Hornady V-Max.

■ .220 Swift

Introduced by Winchester in 1935, and based on a necked-down, semi-rimmed 6mm Lee Navy case, the .220 Swift is still revered by many serious varmint/predator shooters. I killed scads of coyotes with my Swift in the day. Early on, the Swift developed a reputation as a barrel burner (something I didn't experience), but stronger steels, newer powders allowing lower operating pressures and improved cleaning techniques reduced this tendency. Still, as with any of the hottest varmint rounds, if you want to save your barrel, load them down a bit, and when barrels began to heat up, lay off. The Swift is appropriately named, as it's fast enough to minimize pelt damage by peeling away bullet noses before exiting, and it's death on running 'yotes because of minimal lead margins. It spits 40-grain bullets to 4,200 fps (which can be hard on barrels) and 50- to 55-grain bullets at 3,800 to 3,700 fps.

■ Federal .224 Valkyrie

Federal Premium's .224 Valkyrie dominated the shooting press early in 2018, creating buzz by delivering 90-grain .224-caliber bullets at 2,700 fps from an AR-15 platform (Savage MSR15 Valkyrie, 18-inch barrel). Created by necking down the 6.8 Remington SPC, the Valkyrie also pushes 60-grain pills to 3,300 fps and 75-grainers to 3,000. The cartridge alone would have proven worthwhile, but Savage released new Valkyrie rifles with generous free bore and fast rifling twist, allowing them to stabilize long-for-caliber bullets. This lets it shoot 90-grain bullets with ballistic coefficients of .450 to .563, so bullets remain supersonic to 1,300 yards. In other words, the .224 Valkyrie is a long-range shoe-in. The cartridge is also compatible with bolt guns, and I predict it will soon become a varmint-shooting mainstay.

LIGHT 6MMS

■ .243 Winchester

For many shooters, deer rifles must double as varmint guns, and the light 6mms are up for the task, especially via handloading. As a teen, I chose a .243 Win. for this reason. I had developed big-game ambitions, but it was fur trapping and calling that earned me the money to buy that rifle, so I also wanted a coyote gun. The .243

filled the gap acceptably, accounting for my first deer and elk, as well as too many coyotes to accurately recollect. Loaded with Sierra 60-grain hollow-points, my .243 served well as a small-varmint killer on anything from prairie dogs to jackrabbits (bullets from 55 to 65 grains now available, providing velocities pushing 3,800 to 3,550 fps). Loaded with payloads up to 85 to 100 grains, the .243 serves as a windy-day solution, with Hornady's 80-grain GMX making an ideal coyote bullet that won't spoil hides, and high-ballistic-coefficient 105-grainers making an excellent extreme-range option.

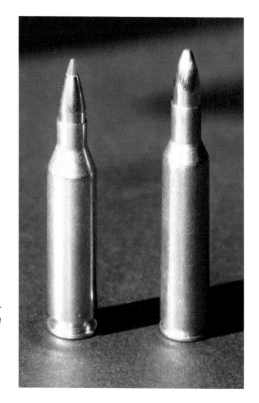

The .243/6mm, calibers can make excellent varmint and predator rounds, especially when ranges stretch and wind becomes a factor, as heavier 6mm bullets include superior ballistic coefficients. The two most popular remain the .243 Win. and 6mm Rem.

■ 6mm Remington

The 1955 .244 Rem., eventually renamed 6mm Rem., is based on a necked-down 7x57mm case, improving on .243 Win. ballistics by a couple of hundred fps. For example, a Hornady 58-grain V-Max can be pushed to almost 3,700 fps, and the 65-grain version nips 3,500 fps, for explosive small-varmint impact. Heavier bullets to 85 to 100 grains provide excellent windy-day options. The 6mm Rem. has long lived in the shadow of the more popular .243 Win.

There are no rules about what serves as a varmint round, as some shooters happily use their deer rifles for varmint work. Left to right; .250 Ackley Improved, .257 Roberts with 60-grain HP, .257 Roberts with 87-grain HP, .25-'06 with 75-grain Hornady V-Max, .308 Win. with 110-grain HP and .30-'06 Springfield with a controlled-expansion bullet excellent for collecting fur.

STRETCHING THE .25S AND .30S

Even as a big-game hunter, I generally preferred light cartridges, so I find .257 calibers a bit much for varmint and predator shooting. Still, a case can be made in their defense, especially for those who can't afford to own many specialized rifles. Of the .25s, I see potential in the .250 Savage, .257 Roberts and .25-'06. Load the .250 Savage with a 60-grain flat-point (Hornady) pushed to 3,450 fps, and I see a lot of fun on running jacks or stalked woodchucks. Hornady's 75-grain V-Max, or the industry's standard 87-grain .257 pills, make worthwhile varmint rounds, departing at around 3,000 fps. The same bullets can be loaded to 3,700 fps (60-grain FP), 3,450 fps (75-grain) or 3,250 (87-grain) from the Roberts; 75- and 87-grain pills easily reaching 3,550 to 3,300 fps launched from a .25-'06. For a long-range round, a heavier, higher-ballistic-coefficient bullet would make lethal .25-'06 medicine.

In a pinch, common 110-grain pills from .308-caliber rounds such as the .300 Savage, .308 Win. or .30-'06 Springfield can open a can of fun, but they require handloading.

⊕ Chapter 7
Varmint Rifles

The term varmint rifle can prove as confusing as the varmint cartridge moniker. Technically, we might use any type of rifle/cartridge combination to shoot varmints. I happily shot prairie dogs with a 7mm Rem. Mag. when young, and varmint cartridges are chambered in many firearm classes. Which you choose really depends on where and how you plan to use it, or a particular mood. Still, to most, the quintessential varmint rifle includes a heavy barrel to retard heating during high-volume shooting, also lending accuracy when shooting small targets way over yonder. It sits in a blocky stock for added steadiness off a rest, might weigh as much as 10-plus pounds and is chambered in one of the smaller rounds discussed previously. Is this classic representation then suited to every varmint/predator setting and need? Is then, say, a .22-250 chambered in a trim, thin-barreled rifle not a true varmint rifle? No and no.

The classic varmint rifle — the bull-barreled, tactical-stocked firearm—is most at home in settings where it won't be carried far; set atop a portable bench, shooting from a cradle off the hood of a vehicle, or lying prone and resting over sandbags or bipod. Such rifles allow precise sniping at small or distant targets — such as ground squirrels, prairie dogs, chucks peeking from burrows or crows perched on a fence post — and minimal bullet stringing as barrels warm after extended shooting. Because heavy varmint rifles typically wear high-powered scopes, the extra weight minimizes muzzle jump, letting you witness hits or perform corrections after misses.

Conversely, fast-handling, relatively lightweight rimfires also constitute varmint medicine, plinking at smaller vermin within reasonable ranges or being used for walk-about pursuits. No one wants to tote 10-pound bench-rest rifles around while walking a desert wash kicking up jackrabbits or clambering across treacherous terrain seeking scattered rock squirrels. This isn't the same high-volume shooting enjoyed by snipers parked over condensed prairie dog or ground squirrel colonies. Lightweight rimfires are affordable and just plain fun to shoot. Every earnest varmint shooter owns one.

LEFT: *There are no hard-and-fast rules about what makes a varmint rifle. The author's father enjoyed shooting Savage's A17 autoloader in .17 HMR, and the author used his custom .22-250 bolt while sniping Idaho rockchucks.*

Customized Ruger 10/22s

No rifle besides the AR platform offers so many aftermarket options as Ruger's revered 10/22. Basic 10/22s ring up at about $225, but serious varmint shooters often invest $1,000, all in, creating their vision of the perfect auto-loading .22 rifle.

This usually starts with an aftermarket stock, eliminating the standard constricting barrel band and creating a more accurate free-floating barrel. Hogue offers an overmolded-rubber Tactical Thumbhole, which turned my 10/22 into a different beast. It includes a cozy ambidextrous thumbhole pistol grip and palm forend swells for improved off-hand

shooting and an integrated cheek piece optimizing scope alignment, among other features. It just looks cool, and aluminum pillar bedding boosts accuracy. ProMag's Deluxe Target (thumbhole), Archangel Precision (target) or Tactical (folding) are also interestingly novel. Tactical Solution's (TacSol) X-Ring Ambidextrous is a pistol-grip stock milled from laminated-wood, and the AdTac synthetic M4 Adaptive Tactical Stock includes two magazine-storage ports, a pistol grip with an extendable monopod and a front Picatinny rail to attach bipods.

Your second step is installing an aftermarket trigger assembly, an investment of $90 to $200 that makes a world of difference to accuracy. Ruger sells the BX 10/22 Trigger, the most affordable available, with set breaking points of 2.5 to 3 pounds. Other sources include the fully adjustable JARD 10/22 Trigger by Slide Fire and Timney Triggers' complete assembly with extended magazine release.

From there, everything becomes optional, though no less appealing. An extended magazine release from TacSol facilitates easier magazine exchange. High-volume aftermarket magazines are also awesome, including banana clips such as Butler Creek's 25-round Hot Lips and Steel Lips, Ruger's 25-round BX-25 and 50-round BX-25X2 (two 25-round mags fused together), and ProMag 25- and 32-round magazines, all in clear or black. ProMag also offers 50-round drum magazines. My preference is magazine clamps such as TacSol's Tri-Mag, joining three standard 10-round Ruger magazines in a tri-star configuration to create less protrusion while shooting atop flat surfaces.

Tactical Solutions also offers 16.5-inch X-Ring SB-X and X-Ring aftermarket barrels, the former allowing installing suppressors without adding length, and the latter anodized, fluted aluminum (six colors) with stainless-steel liners and suppressor/compensator threads. Both provide excellent accuracy and better balance while reducing overall mass. Heavy .920-inch fluted stainless and blued barrels can also be had from Green Mountain Barrels and Ruger in 16-, 18- and 20-inch lengths — all easily installed without gunsmith assistance.

Finally, for devoted predator hunters luring foxes, bobcats and coyotes into sure rifle range with calls, rarely firing more than two or three shots in a row and sometimes walking considerable distances to set up, a heavy varmint rifle isn't needed. A standard off-the-rack sporter mirroring the average deer rifle — chambered in a varmint round that won't shred hides and shoots flat should a long poke be required — offers faster handling in unpredictable settings. Predators are larger than ground squirrels or prairie dogs, meaning pinpoint accuracy is appreciated but not vitally important. It might also be argued that not all rodent hunts require more rifle than this; shots in broken country or while stalking resulting in shorter ranges, often less than 150 yards. Such rifles are capable of long-range accuracy (I own pencil-tubed rifles capable of sub-MOA groups) and are welcomed where shots don't come one after another. Another important aspect is cost. Heavy-barreled, tactical-stocked varmint rifles are sometimes double the price of a decent sporter — upward of $2,000 in custom wares.

THE EVER-POPULAR .22 LR

I can't imagine varmint outings without a .22 LR or one of the newer .17 rimfires along. After a few hours of centerfire bluster and muzzle-break concussion, a quiet rimfire offers a welcomed break, and there are normally plenty of short-range volunteers on hand. A .22 LR was most shooters' starter gun; a simple single-shot that provided years of joy while establishing solid shooting fundamentals. For others, pumps and lever guns are preferred, some of those handed down through generations, and varmint shooting classics. Still, serious varmint shooters likely fall into two groups in this area: tack-driving bolts or reliable semi-autos.

■ Tack-Driving Bolt Guns

A scoped bolt-action promotes deliberate shooting and an accuracy edge, especially when pushing .22 LR capabilities. Such rifles hit every price point, from basic models with classic wood stocks to tactical versions bedded in heavier synthetic or laminated-wood stocks and offering accuracy potential matching centerfires within their respective capabilities. Savage serves well as a cross-section of possibilities. The Mark II series comes in four budget models, including camouflage, wood and black synthetic stocks, and a complete package including a 3-9x40mm Bushnell scope. Stepping up a bit, the new-for-2017 B-Series guns, with adjustable fit and groundbreaking AccuTriggers, are offered with long or

LEFT: *A bulky, heavy-barreled rifle isn't always necessary for varmint shooting. In fact, most predator callers prefer the easier toting of a standard sporter rifle. In predator calling, firing more than a handful of shots consecutively is rare, and such rifles offer more than enough accuracy.*

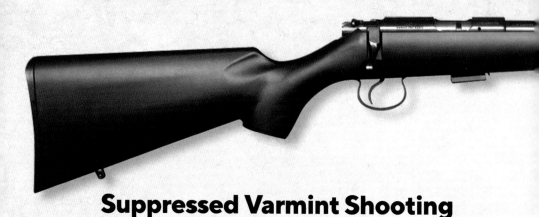

Suppressed Varmint Shooting

There's much to be gained from a suppressor, or a so-called silencer. They use a series of baffles contained inside a tube to reduce shot decibels considerably while also acting as a muzzle break, eliminating annoying muzzle jump. Unless shooting subsonic ammunition (rare in long-range varmint shooting), there's no real silence, as bullets produce sonic booms after breaking the sound barrier, though this normally occurs away from the shooter. But quality suppressors reduce .223 Rem. reports to .22 LR levels, and the thunderous .22-250 is reduced to .22 Mag. decibels.

So why doesn't every shooter own a suppressor? In portions of Europe, it's illegal to shoot a firearm without a suppressor, as it's considered intrusive noise pollution. The easy answer is suppressors, like "assault weapons" (whatever that means), scare gun-grabbing "progressives," so despite obvious positives, at this writing, owning a suppressor involves much red tape: a $200 tax stamp, application forms and a six- to nine-month approval period.

Congress recently introduced legislation, shrewdly labeled the SHUSH Act (Silencers Helping Us Save Hearing), aimed at eliminating most of the complications of purchasing suppressors. As of SHOT Show 2017, manufacturers were confident the bill would pass quickly, but the liberal mainstream media began a predictable propaganda program, labeling it the "assassin's act." Despite dominating the House, Senate and presidency, the typical RINO suspects caved to pressure, and the measure didn't have the votes needed to pass. As of this writing, there is still some hope, and should Republicans pick up some more seats during the 2020 elections, the bill could pass unimpeded.

The next hurdle is high-velocity centerfire suppressors, which start at around $650, running up to double that figure. Suppressors aren't complicated, but supply, demand and punitive taxes keep prices inflated. With relaxed regulations and more product moving, prices could come down.

With rimfire suppressors, it's important to purchase units that can be easily disassembled for cleaning, as ammo is inherently dirty. For centerfire use, purchasing, say, a 30-caliber "can" allows use on a wider variety of rifles, muffling varmint cartridge reports even more efficiently. A suppressor is easily traded between many rifles, and some manufacturers offer spring-loaded, quick-disconnect systems.

short, blued or stainless barrels. For those wanting more accuracy potential, the Mark II TRR-SR includes a heavy tactical stock with attached Picatinny rails, models with fluted bull barrels set in heavy tactical or thumbhole laminated-wood stocks, and even a short-barreled version threaded for a suppressor. The .22 Mag., .17 HMR and .17 WSM are also part of these lineups, with the dead-nuts-accurate Model 93 offered in multiple configurations.

■ Practical Auto-Loaders

The auto-loader is a .22 LR institution. Many varmint shooters wouldn't consider owning a semi-automatic centerfire rifle but choose an auto-loading .22 LR because those guns are fast handling and highly practical. They're also capable of surprising accuracy. The best deal in .22 LR self-feeders remains Marlin's tubular-magazine Model 60, with stainless, camo, synthetic-stocked, and laminated-wood-stocked versions available. They retail for less than $180, and the one I own is dead reliable and impressively accurate. Savage's A-Series has made its mark, holding ergonomic full-sized synthetic stocks and 10-round detachable magazines. They're offered in .22 LR, .22 WSM and .17 HMR. To others, Sturm, Ruger & Co.'s versatile 10/22 embodies everything auto-loading .22 LRs should be (see the sidebar "Customized Ruger 10/22s").

A SERIOUS VARMINT RIFLE

When you get serious about varmint shooting, even if only lowly burrowing rats are your target, you'll eventually crave a top-quality, highly-accurate centerfire rifle — real varmint iron. You'll want a heavy bull barrel. You'll want a tactical stock with barrel vents and a wide, steady forend. You'll likely be looking at a bolt rifle in something like Remington's 700 SPS or VTR (with a triangular barrel and built-in muzzle-break), Savage's Model 12 Varmint/Target Series or Model 10 Predator Hunter, Browning's X-Bolt Eclipse Varmint or Varmint Stalker, Ruger's Hawkeye VT (Varmint/Target), Howa's 1500 Heavy Barrel Varminter and newer Long-Range Rifle, or Mossberg's MVP Varmint. Regarding brands, you can get into those silly Ford versus Chevy versus Dodge-type arguments, but no one brand has the corner on accuracy today.

If you're tactically inclined, you might chose a new-style chassis rifle, bolt-actions with AR-like lines, such as Winchester's new XPC Chassis Rifle, the Savage 11/111 DOA Hunter XP (both of which start in .243 Win.), Ruger Precision Rifle (including 6mm Creedmoor), Mossberg's MVP LC or Howa HCR Chassis Rifle (all starting in .223 Rem.). Perhaps a first-quality single shot appeals to your sensibilities. The classic Ruger No. 1-V Varminter (currently in .223 Rem., with other chamberings floating around the used-gun market) or incomparable

AR-15s For Varmints?

AR-15s have become one of shooting's hottest commodities. But are they really viable for serious varmint shooting? At one time, I didn't believe so, until I shot my father's AR, enjoying it so thoroughly I requested a loner from Rock River Arms — a heavy varmint model with 24-inch bull barrel. That rifle was a shooter, assembling sub-¾-inch, 100-yard groups. I'd recently endured shoulder surgery, and the soft recoil allowed high-volume ground squirrel shooting without the painful bolt manipulation (my doctor had forbidden shooting any rifle, but it was spring and sage rats were frolicking). I became an instant fan. Before spring's end, I topped the gun with Trijicon's 5-20x50mm AccuPoint scope, and I'd laid untold ground squirrels low, including a Columbia at 405 laser-measured yards — a shot that would test a similarly chambered custom bolt rifle. After returning that test rifle, I had my own built, this one including a 20-inch bull barrel. Incredibly, it shots ½-inch groups. So yes, ARs are capable of fantastic accuracy (with the right barrels, which excludes light tubes attached to military-class ARs).

This past winter, that AR, topped with a Bushnell Elite 6500 4.5-30x50mm, became my predator-calling rifle of choice, mainly because I never trust coyotes to stand still, and the semi-auto platform is deadly effective on running targets. It's also fairly common to call in multiple dogs in my mountainous Idaho backyard. The first is often standing, but survivors definitely are not. Swinging with a sprinting, bouncing

coyote, concentrating on aiming, pulling the trigger (backed by 20- or 30-round magazines) and walking shots in makes running shots much easier than starting again after every bolt crank.

So the answer is yes, ARs are wonderful varmint and predator killing machines.

Thompson/Center Encore Pro Hunter Predator .204 Ruger, .223 or .22-250 Rem. offer accurate options.

Others look at a rifle they already own but seldom shoot and decide it's time for a custom rifle. A competent gunsmith can turn a rifle that has outlived its usefulness (in short action to accommodate standard varmint cartridges), or holding a barrel that's been washed out from too much shooting, into something useful and exciting. A crackerjack gunsmith can create a magic wand. Off comes the barrel, replaced by a quality custom number by Wilson, Krieger, Lilja, Douglas, Shilen, Criterion, E.R. Shaw and others (your gunsmith likely has a favorite), which specialize in uncompromising accuracy. Likewise, the cheap factory stock. Pore over catalogs from McMillan, H-S Precision, Bell & Carlson, Stocky's, Boyds or Hogue, seeking the lines, recoil pad and features that represent your ideal. Pistol grips, Picatinny rails, thumbhole configurations, custom colors, overmolded rubber and adjustable comb/length of pull? The custom market is there to serve any whim.

Suddenly, your factory trigger won't do (unless it's a Savage equipped with an AccuTrigger or Mossberg with LBA trigger). What you want is an adjustable model. Timney is a proven name (found on my .22-250 and .223 Remingtons), and Velocity Triggers is my new favorite (installed on my AR). There are others, but all are crisp, zero-creep triggers that break like a glass rod with a faster lock time and no overtravel after the shot. Be careful, though, as good triggers can ruin you. Return to a rifle you believed was fine before, and suddenly you'll find its trigger feels like a rusty screen-door hinge. Replacing the hidden magazine and floor plate with a detachable magazine has also become all the rage. You're paying for this. Make it your own.

The question then becomes to brake or not to brake? There are important gives and takes associated with muzzle brakes. I love them, and I hate them. Several of my varmint rifles wear brakes. Recoil didn't dictate that decision. It was muzzle jump in relation to high-power scopes. For example, squeezing off a .223 shot with the scope twisted up to 30-power generally resulted in losing the ground squirrel I was shooting at, leaving me clueless as to whether I'd hit or missed and how to correct my hold. With an Xtreme Hardcore Gear Slotted Hybrid Brake installed, shooting paper off a bench, my crosshairs

Modern Air Rifles
For Suburban Pests

There are situations in which shooting powder-driven projectiles is out of the question, including quiet .22 CB caps, shorts or subsonic rounds. In some settings, this could occasion a visit from local law enforcement. Air rifles are another matter, as they're not as apt to upset hand-wringing neighbors. Modern air rifles come in six basic styles: PCP (pre-charged pneumatic), CO2, multi-stroke, single-stroke, spring-piston and gas-ram. Of these, spring-piston, gas-ram and PCP prove superior for pest control and small-varmint shooting, offering the power and accuracy needed.

Spring-piston/break-action rifles are popular because of their lower cost. The mechanism is charged by "breaking" the gun on a hinge between the barrel and receiver or swinging a side or bottom lever (generally more accurate, barrels remaining stationary), which cocks a steel spring then triggered to push a column of air down the barrel. They're self contained and easy to maintain. Gas-ram rifles are like "springers," but instead of steel springs, they use sealed gas units pressurized during cocking. Pressing the trigger releases the compressed air and pushes a column of air down the barrel. Gas-pistons tend to last longer, retain consistency when left cocked for long periods and offer faster lock time and power, so they have become most popular. They can prove difficult to cock for weaker shooters. Both systems include considerable forward recoil, which requires specially designed scopes to avoid damage. Most are single-shots, though GAMO offers a 10-shot repeater.

PCP units are powered by removable cylinders of compressed air. They use spurts of expanding gas to move pellets down the barrel. They're accurate, recoil-free and power adjustable, and require no physical cocking. They often include repeating capabilities. They're also extremely quiet. The disadvantage is they require purchasing charging equipment or paying to have bottles filled, which means they aren't self contained. Exhausting a cylinder requires recharging or carrying a spare. Intricate internal parts also make maintenance more critical. Some PCP rifles — Airforce Airguns, for example — are offered in .25-caliber upward, generating enough energy to cleanly dispatch coyote-size animals, something to keep in mind in settled areas.

Power needs are largely dictated by how far you intend to shoot. Medium-powered rifles (say, 650 to 900 fps in .177, slightly slower in .22) are lethal to about 15 yards. "High-powered" models (more than 1,000 fps in .177, 900 fps in .22) normally extend range to 20 to 25 yards. Varmint size also factors in — starlings and doves versus squirrels and rabbits, for example. A moderately powered air rifle will knock invasive starlings, pigeons, English sparrows and ring-necked doves off backyard bird feeders at 15 to 20 yards. More powerful rifles are needed to snipe pigeons off a barn peak or power line or dispatch rabbits or ground squirrels raiding the family garden.

Standard calibers include .177 and .22. Modern .177-caliber air rifles generally post the fastest muzzle velocities, but .177 pellets (BBs are for children) weigh less so also bleed energy faster. If ranges exceed 20 yards, and especially on larger varmints, a .22-caliber is generally superior, starting slower but retaining more downrange energy, though I've killed ground squirrels to 30 yards with my .17 and head shots.

Pellet choice is important to lethality — Gamo Red Fire or Rocket, as examples, versus pointed Master Point target pellets. Also, lead-free pellets might provide sizzling muzzle velocities, but lead carries energy more efficiently for improved downrange punch. Air-rifle benchmarks include Gamo's break-barrel 10X Quick Shot Swarm Maxxim, pushing .22 pellets to 975 fps; Benjamin's Trail NP XL1500, a Nitro-Piston break-barrel in .177 producing 1,500 fps with alloy pellets, 1,200 with lead; Beeman's Mach 12.5 break-barrel in .117 (1,250 fps) or .22 (1,000 fps); and Crosman's Marauder, a quiet PCP rifle in .177, .22 and .25 calibers, with an eight-shot magazine and producing 1,000 fps in .177 caliber.

typically center the bullet hole after each shot. I easily watch shots in, adding to satisfaction and allowing instant adjustments to hold or scope turrets after missing.

The problem with brakes is noise — horrendous noise. When I pull out my compensated .22-250, it takes just one shot for companions to not-so-politely request I move down the road 100 yards. Shot concussion is perceivable 50 yards away, and muzzle blast is ear splitting, often raising dust and straw before my shooting position. When shooting my '250, I twist foam plugs into my ears and install muffs. But the crosshairs don't move when I cut a shot.

⊕ Chapter 8
Handgun Varmints

hooting small varmints and predators is obviously as much about having fun as vermin control. We use the control part to wheedle access into prime private properties, but high-volume, off-season shooting provides the fun and helps keep us sharp for fall big-game seasons. With that attitude, I shot New Mexico prairie dogs as a teen with true big-game rifles, bought into Remington's 5mm Rimfire early to address Southwestern rock squirrels and jackrabbits (adopting a .17 HMR as 5mm ammo dried up), made old new by loading light .22 Hornet pills to 3,000 fps via cutting-edge propellants and more recently developed an affinity for the economical .223 Rem., intriguing .17 Hornet and .204 Ruger. Small-varmint shooting eventually became a game of pushing envelopes — faster velocities while seeking dramatic impact and longer ranges within a reasonable hit-to-miss ratio via turreted scopes. It's what varmint shooting is all about, but for me, variety is the spice of life.

I can't remember a time when I wasn't enthralled by handguns, but it was well before I was allowed to own or purchase one. So it wasn't long before I began toting various pistols into high-volume varmint fields. I once shot a 90-yard New Mexico prairie dog with a Bryco .22 LR automatic pocket pistol. I've brought out a 1911 in the middle of a hot ground squirrel shoot, burning 200 handloads because it makes me happy. But that isn't exactly what I've in mind here.

My honest-to-goodness varmint handguns — those scoped handguns that'll hold their own with rifles within respective limitations (150 to 200 yards) — are where real handgunning fun comes in and the subject of discussion here.

Why Pistols?

Why handguns and not true varmint rifles? From a practical standpoint, handguns are just easier to stash, poke out a pickup window while making ranch or farm rounds and wear in a hip or shoulder holster while on walk-about forays.

LEFT: *The author loves his varmint rifles, but he's also long held a strong affinity for handguns. His Taurus Raging Hornet .22 Hornet revolver is one of his favorite varmint guns, and he used it to shoot this Oregon ground squirrel at more than 125 yards.*

But varmint shooting and predator hunting isn't really about practicality. So, the more honest answer is the added challenge of shooting a handgun well simply adds to my shooting enjoyment — something that doesn't take anything away from rifle shooting but instead serves as another facet to the shooting sports. For me, this enjoyment comes not in limited hope-and-poke, lucky-shot success (like that 90-yard Bryco kill) but in developing the degree of skill needed to create decent hit-to-miss ratios at longer ranges. This happens only with certain classes of pistols fed the right type of ammunition.

■ Scoped Revolvers

Revolvers have remained popular because of inherent accuracy and faster follow-up than the single-shot systems that typically constitute standard varmint pistols. The modern revolver includes strong actions that can withstand the high pressures of modern cartridges. One example is my treasured nine-shot Taurus Raging Hornet (built on the Raging Bull frame) chambered in the rimmed .22 Hornet. These were limited-edition revolvers and are found only by scouring the used-gun market, but they're a hoot of a good time when topped with a long-eye-relief pistol scope. I have my best luck within 100 yards, but with a good rest and a careful squeeze, I've taken many ground squirrels and prairie dogs at 150 to 175 yards. I've also cleanly killed several eating-size wild boars with carefully placed shots, as well as coyotes responding to calls.

Taurus also made the seven-shot Model 17 Tracker in .17 HMR, wearing a 6.5-inch barrel. Taurus temporarily ceased production of these revolvers, but word is

they are returning by popular demand. HMR revolvers can also be had from Ruger (New Model Single-Six) and Heritage (Rough Rider), though I'm uncertain about the possibility of tacking scopes to these. Perhaps that's a job for an experienced gunsmith. My .17 HMR Taurus Tracker shoots flat to 100 yards, and prints sub-½-inch groups at 50 yards. More

While on a varmint shooting road trip in western Wyoming, the author put his Thompson/Center .221 Rem. Fireball pistol through the paces on a colony of Richardson's ground squirrels at 80 to 125 yards.

Taurus offered a .17 HMR Tracker revolver for a brief time, discontinued production, and is bringing them back again. Paired with a long-eye-relief pistol scope, they are capable and fine accuracy — enough so to hit ground squirrel to 100-plus yards.

common are .22 Mag. revolvers, which easily match HMR ballistics, offered in the eight-shot Taurus Model 941 or nine-shot Model 992 Tracker .22LR/.22 WMR and Smith & Wesson Model 48 Classic, as examples.

Of course, .22 LR revolvers are common. The best for varmint applications include a barrel at least 6 inches long and scope adaptability, such as the Ruger GP-100 10-shot (6-inch barrel), Smith & Wesson Model 617 10-shot (6-inch), aforementioned Taurus 992 Tracker (6.5-inch) and 970 Tracker seven-shot (6-inch). Consult a gunsmith for scope-mounting options.

■ .22 LR Autoloaders

Another awesomely fun approach is an autoloading rimfire handgun wearing a compact scope, especially a fine-point, reflex-dot scope. The best pistol options include integral Picatinny-type rails, making it simple to clamp optics home. Within the respective range capabilities of a .22 LR pill spit from a short

The author's father enjoys shooting his customized Ruger Charger .22 LR while targeting ground squirrels. This pistol model, with attached scope, is capable of the accuracy of the Ruger 10/22, which the model is based on.

pistol barrel, the dot system makes a lot of sense, giving you a more precise means of directing shots into small varmints than iron sights. Prime candidates for this treatment are epitomized by the Beretta Model U22 Neos, similar Smith & Wesson 22A and Browning's Buck Mark Field Target and UDX series. All have long target barrels, 10-shot magazines and integrated Picatinny rails.

Ruger's Mark III Target also includes a mounting rail and 10-shot magazine, with 6.875-inch bull or slab-side barrel, the newest Mark III accepting a scope base and holding a stiff, 6.875-inch fluted barrel. Both Ruger designs are renowned for accuracy and reliability. Tactical Solutions offers aftermarket parts for those Rugers or similar designs made from the ground up. Another interesting option is Keltec's .22 WMR self-loader, the PMR-30, with a 30-round magazine.

Ruger's Charger is unique in .22 LR pistols. It's essentially a 10/22 rifle scaled into a pistol with an ergonomic pistol grip, 15-shot BX-15 magazine, scope rail and included bipod. It's offered with laminated-wood or black synthetic stock and in standard and take-down models. The 10-inch barrel is threaded for a suppressor, which would make it doubly fun to shoot. With a BX Ruger trigger installed, my father's Charger is a tack-driver and perfect truck-hood pistol.

■ Single-Shot Handguns

For more precise work on small or distant targets, single-shot centerfire pistols are the trusted choice. Warren Center revolutionized long-range pistol design in 1965 with the introduction of the Contender, now known as the Thompson/Center Contender. These break-action single-shots with interchangeable barrels pioneered the use of bottle-neck cartridges in pistols. Products such as Rossi's Matched Pair Dual Threat Performer, in .223 Rem. or .243 Win., and CVA's Scout, in .243 Win. and larger cartridges, followed. Newer systems, such as the Maximum Single-Shot, with falling-block-type action, in .22 Hornet to .375 H&H,

and Competitor Single-Shot, with a rotary cannon-type action in any chambering imaginable, have appeared since.

T/C's original Contender, now the Contender G2, has remained most popular, and original barrels are available in a huge variety of cartridges. Newer to the T/C lineup, the Encore Pro Hunter is designed to handle higher pressures and more powerful rounds. Older Contender barrels are floating around online auctions or can be ordered from companies such as SSL Industries in just about any round you can think of. Currently, Contender G2 barrels are available from T/C-Smith & Wesson in .17 HMR, .204 Ruger, .223 Rem. and others. In Encore pistols, they're available in .204 Ruger, .223 and .22-250 Rem., .243 Win. and others.

My Contender action wears a recently purchased 10-inch .221 Fireball or love-worn 14-inch .223 Rem. barrel with AR-style muzzle break installed so I can watch shots in. I also own 10-inch 7mm TCU and 14-inch .30-30 barrels. In varmint settings, the .221 Fireball with a Nikon Force XR 2.5-8x28mm scope provides reliable accuracy to 150 yards. My 2-6x32mm Bushnell-scoped .223 is a deadly ground squirrel iron to 200 to 225 yards (on a good day). I once killed a Texas coyote at a confirmed and witnessed 289 yards with the .223. I've also shot squirrels with the short-barreled 7mm TCU (.223 Rem. necked up) and 100-grain hollow-points, the

The author has long coveted a Remington XP-100 in .221 Rem. Fireball but settled for a T/C barrel in the same caliber. The T/C is easier to come by, cheaper and obviously quite accurate. These prairie dogs were sniped from a measured 90 to 160 yards.

lightest 7mm bullet offered. (I wish someone would make a 75- to 85-grain 7mm pill — hint, hint.) Further, I've shot squirrels with the 14-inch .30-30 Win. fed 100- to 110-grain soft- or hollow-points. The drop-in single-shot barrel allows loading streamlined pointed bullets, improving ballistics considerably from traditional .30-30 round-nose fodder designed for tubular magazines. The 7mm and .30-30 are especially useful while predator calling in wooded areas. The 100- to 110-grain hollow-points expand only little at pistol velocities and won't damage hides.

Bolt-action pistols are also part of this fun — models such as the sadly discontinued Remington XP-100 chambered in the highly efficient .221 Fireball (and others such as .223 Rem.) or Savage's old Striker. Some custom wares are floating around, too. Introduced in 1963, the XP-100 (eXperimental Pistol No. 100) includes a nylon stock with a highly ergonomic, thumb-rest-equipped, centrally mounted grip. Built on what would later become the Model 600 rifle action, the XP-100 has a reputation for extreme accuracy. Originally including 10.75-inch barrels (later released with a 14.5-inch barrel and more powerful cartridges), the .221 Fireball round was created by shortening the .222 Rem., allowing more efficient powder consumption in the short tube and muzzle velocities to 2,700- plus fps with 45-grain bullets. It's a pistol that's on my wish list, but for now, I'll have to remain content with my Fireball-chambered T/C barrel, which is much cheaper and easier to come by.

VARMINT-PISTOL PRECAUTIONS

Pistol cartridges useful for varmint/predator shooting must provide mild-mannered recoil for comfortable shooting during prolonged periods, accuracy capable of drilling small targets at reasonable ranges, and reliable bullet expansion on small rodents such as ground squirrels and prairie dogs at actual velocities produced by a particular cartridge and barrel length. The latter is vitally important, as without sufficient speed or the availability of bullets produced in a specific caliber and designed to expand at lower velocities, that pistol cartridge might as well be shooting full metal jackets.

Easy example: my T/C 7mm TCU with a 10-inch barrel. The cartridge was once the darling of metallic silhouette shooters, offering mild recoil and reliable plate knockdown combined with extreme accuracy. Its problem as a varmint cartridge isn't with the round but available 7mm bullets. I'm not aware of any 7mm bullets weighing less than 100 grains, and those designed to expand at standard rifle velocities. The popular 7mm-08 Rem., for example, starts at 2,900 fps with 100-grain pills. A 7mm TCU produces only 2,250 fps and only with 14-inch tube and maximum loads. My normal load pushes around 2,000 fps. I get no expansion on ground squirrels, even though it's accurate enough to center them regularly. The 7-30 Waters, a necked-down .30-30, can push 100-grainers to 2,600 fps, which would likely produce more reliable bullet performance.

Handloading is nearly mandatory for the varmint shooting pistolero. Factory ammo, loaded to rifle pressures, is rarely accurate from pistols, and a handloader can choose bullets that perform at slower pistol velocities.

By necessity, the pistol varmint shooter must become a handloader. Rifle ammo chambered in the same cartridges are simply too hot, resulting in generally poor accuracy, excessive muzzle flash caused by unburned powder and sometimes sticky cases or locked actions (especially in revolvers). Smith & Wesson's Model 53 in .22 Jet is a perfect example, with case setback after firing hot loads locking cylinders and leading to its commercial failure (though the round is viable in break-action pistols such as the T/C Contender). *Sierra Bullet's Edition V, 8th Printing of Rifle & Handgun Reloading Data* includes a section titled "Single Shot Pistol Reloading Data," and is an exceptional resource for modern handgun loaders.

I developed a novel test while working up loads for my Taurus Raging Hornet (because of a rash of sticky cases) I think is quite sound. From a published starting load (T/C Contender Reloading Manual, 1991), I loaded single rounds, adding .3 grains of powder in ascending charges (made more substantial because of the .22 Hornet's minuscule case capacity). I waited until sunset to wander outside and shoot each load in order, taking note of when notable flame began to belch from the muzzle. I then worked loads just beneath that level, discovering this also produced excellent accuracy. Unburned powder shotgunning the base of the bullet after clearing the muzzle doesn't promote dead-nuts accuracy.

My Hornet revolver also illustrates how pistol velocities affect bullet performance. Seeking a lighter bullet to produce flatter trajectories from that 10-inch-barrel, I

The author's T/C 7mm TCU barrel is accurate enough to hit ground squirrels, but the 100-grain bullets offered in 7mm don't open at pistol velocities (about 2,000 fps). This is a common problem when varmint shooting with handguns.

believed Barnes' 36-grain Varmint Grenade was the answer. Test loads proved quite accurate, and my father and I were headed to Montana for a prairie dog shoot in a couple of weeks. I loaded several hundred rounds. It only took a couple of prairie dogs to realize I'd made a grave mistake. Those bullets, designed for high-velocity rifles, acted like FMJs. Pulled and reloaded in my .223 rifle to 3,700 fps, the bullets live up to their label.

A final thought: To shoot any scoped pistol well, you must adopt a solid rest. Off-hand shooting is for iron sights and point-blank shooting with magnum handguns. If you want to hit a tiny ground squirrel at even 75 yards or a called-in coyote at 100, use a rest, no ifs, ands or buts — a subject we'll get into in great depth in Chapter 11, "Give It A Rest." Only by doing this will you realize the full potential of your short-barreled weapon, hitting the mark more often than missing and enjoying the full potential of these challenging but accurate weapons.

USEFUL VARMINT-PISTOL CARTRIDGES AND LOADS

■ .22 Hornet

The .22 Hornet makes an exceptional pistol round, producing little recoil and surrendering "minute-of-squirrel" accuracy and killing performance. When loaded for a strong action such as the Contender, the .22 Hornet loses only about 400 fps from a 10-inch barrel; not too shabby for pistol ballistics. In general, best results were realized in my Taurus Raging Hornet with 34- to 35-grain, light-skinned HP bullets, my father's Contender Hornet barrel preferring 40- and 45-grain pills. All listed loads will open on small varmints.

PET LOADS, .22 HORNET, TAURUS RAGING HORNET REVOLVER, 10-INCH BARREL

Bullet	Powder	Charge	Velocity	Primer
34-gr Midsouth Varmint	W296	10 grs	N/A	Rem. 7 ½ BR
35-gr Hornady V-Max	W296	10.5 grs	N/A	Same

The .221 Rem. Fireball was traditionally loaded with 50-grain bullets to knock down steel-plate targets, but the author finds polymer-tipped 40-grain pills provide more explosive impact when shooting small varmints such as ground squirrels or prairie dogs.

PET LOADS, .22 HORNET, T/C CONTENDER, 10-INCH BARREL

Bullet	Powder	Charge	Velocity	Primer
35-gr Hornady V-Max	Lil'Gun	12 grs	2,641 fps	Rem. 7 ½ BR
40-gr Sierra #1200 Hornet	H110	10.2 grs	2,198 fps	Win. WSR
40-gr Hornady V-Max	N-110	9.5 grs	2,140 fps	Rem. 7 ½ BR
45-gr Sierra #1210 Hornet	H4227	9.5 grs	2,150 fps	Same
45-gr Speer SP	H4198	10.5 grs	2,002 fps	Same

.22 K-HORNET, T/C CONTENDER, 10-INCH BARREL

Bullet	Powder	Charge	Velocity	Primer
40-gr Sierra #1200 Hornet	W296	11.3 grs	2,400 fps	CCI-400
45-gr generic Hornet	W296	11 grs	2,336 fps	N/A

■ .221 Fireball

The Fireball once held the distinction as the fastest, flattest-shooting pistol cartridge around when introduced in 1963 in the revolutionary Remington XP-100. The cartridge is capable of sub-MOA accuracy, even from pistols, and this shortened version of the .222 Rem. is easily capable of taking small varmints to 200 yards in capable hands. The .221 Fireball is extremely efficient, producing impressive speeds with little powder.

PET LOADS, .221 FIREBALL, T/C CONTENDER, 10-INCH BARREL

Bullet	Powder	Charge	Velocity	Primer
40-gr Hornady V-Max	H4198	17 grs	2,600 fps	Rem. 7 ½
40-gr Sierra #1210 Hornet	H110	13 grs	2,714 fps	Win. WSR
45-gr Hornady Hornet	IMR4198	18 grs	2,600 fps	CCI BR 4
45-gr Speer SP	H4198	16 grs	2,450 fps	Same
50-gr Hornady V-Max	RL-7	18.5 grs	2,600 fps	Same

■ .223 Remington

The popular .223 operates well in pistols, particularly the T/C Contender with a 14-inch barrel. The Remington XP-100 was also once chambered in .223 and with a longer 14.5-inch barrel. In pistol cartridges, fast-burning powders provide the best results, eliminating excessive muzzle blast and flame. The loads listed combine accuracy with huge splat factor on small varmints. Reduced-power .223 loads in Chapter 10, "Handloading To Needs" also make excellent pistol ammo.

PET LOADS, .223 REM., T/C CONTENDER, 14-INCH BARREL WITH MUZZLE BREAK

Bullet	Powder	Charge	Velocity	Primer
40-gr Sierra BlitzKing	RL-7	23 grs	2,900 fps	Federal 205
40-gr Hornady V-Max	H322	23.5 grs	2,700 fps	CCI BR 4
40-gr Hornady V-Max	H4198	22.5 grs	3,014 fps	Win. SR
42-gr Lead-Free Frangible (Rocky Mountain Reloading)	Benchmark	25.3 grs	2,875 fps	CCI BR 4
45-gr. Sierra #1210 Hornet	H322	23 grs	2,650 fps	Same

■ .243 Winchester

Thompson/Center's Encore is like the Contender but engineered to handle the increased pressures of larger-capacity rounds, such as Winchester's .243. CVA's new Scout is another stout break-action pistol chambered in .243 Win. Because the .243 is the smallest offering in the Encore lineup, the break-open action can be loaded fairly hot (relative to pistol rounds), though keep an eye on muzzle flame as an indication of when to back off for improved accuracy.

PET LOADS, .243 WIN., T/C ENCORE OR CVA SCOUT, 14- OR 15-INCH BARREL

Bullet	Powder	Charge	Velocity	Primer
55-gr Nosler Ballistic Tip	H380	46 grs	3,156 fps	Win. LR
58-gr Hornady V-Max	RL-15	41 grs	3,100 fps	Rem. 9 ½
60-gr Sierra #1500 HP	H380	48 grs	3,249 fps	Win. LR
65-gr Hornady V-Max	N-140	41 grs	3,170 fps	CCI 200
75-gr Sierra HP	A-2495	37.6 grs	2,900 fps	Federal 210

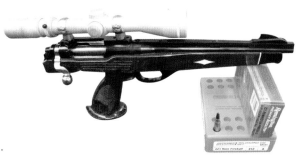

This is the author's dream pistol: Remington's futuristic-looking XP-100 (eXperimental Pistol 100), with a 10¾-inch barrel and chambered in the super-efficient .221 Fireball, which was designed for top performance from short barrels.

■ 7mm TCU

The 7mm TCU (Thompson/Center Ugalde) graduated from wildcat status in the late 1970s as a winning metallic silhouette cartridge. Cases are easily made by necking up the common .223 and then fire-forming. As stated, the 7mm TCU makes a poor small varmint cartridge, but I am including my most accurate loads here as excellent predator medicine assured to not damage pelts.

PET LOADS, 7MM TCU, T/C CONTENDER, 10-INCH BARREL

Bullet	Powder	Charge	Velocity	Primer
100-gr Sierra Varminter HP	H322	*25 grs	2,029	CCI BR 4
*Mild load.				
100-gr Sierra Varminter HP	H4198	24 grs (max)	2,176	CCI BR 4

■ .30-30 Winchester

It's difficult to think of the ancient .30-30 Win. and varmint shooting in the same sentence, but the T/C Contender, which allows pointed bullets to be dropped into its opened chamber and pushing light-skinned 100- to 110-grain bullets to 2,100-plus fps, does a respectable job on small varmints.

PET LOADS, .30-30 WIN., T/C CONTENDER, 14-INCH BARREL

Bullet	Powder	Charge	Velocity	Primer
100-gr Hornady Short Jacket	W296	17.7 grs	2,200 fps	CCI-200
110-gr Sierra #2110 HP	IMR4198	27.7 grs	2,200 fps	Rem. 9 ½
110-gr Sierra #2100 RN	W296	17.5 grs	2,100 fps	Same
110-gr Hornady V-Max	RL-7	32.3 grs	2,400 fps	CCI-200
*110-gr Barnes TAC-TX FB	Ramshot TAC	30.5 grs	2,400 fps	Same

*1-inch, 100-yard groups; excellent pelt-shooting and hog load.

⊕ Chapter 9

Varmint Scopes

remember when I considered a scoped .22 LR an abomination, an attitude forged by arrogant youth and better-than-average eyesight. Heck, I shot my first deer with an iron-sighted .243 Win., if you can imagine such a thing today. Reading Robert Ruark's seminal *Horn of the Hunter* while still too young to understand half of his heady vocabulary, when his scope became "possessed by demons," as professional hunter Harry Selby put it in a closing chapter, I wholly endorsed his decision when he "unscrewed the telescopic sight and threw it away."

Of course, that attitude seems ridiculous today, as I can't imagine directing projectiles with anything approaching precision without the aid of optics — something more pointed when targets are small varmints or predators coveted for their hides. Firearms scopes have evolved at a meteoric pace since I attached my first to a firearm. Although iconic gun writer Jack O'Connor's advice on firearms and cartridges still holds a lot of water to this day, anything he said about rifle optics is defunct. My first scope, a Bushnell 4-12x42mm, wasn't cheap by late 1970s standards. But though it held up to years of abuse, I'd wager I could buy a scope for fewer current dollars that would prove superior in every way — though that old scope was likely made in the United States or at least Japan, not communist China.

Still, especially in the world of varmint or tactical scopes, you get what you pay for, at least in terms of rugged construction, optical quality and protective/anti-reflective coatings. And coatings can really be what makes a scope and ultimately dictates cost — cheaper scopes generally include thin coatings applied in days, top-quality wares having coatings applied through months. The former are much more prone to scratches while doing things like, say, swabbing away accumulated dust with a shirt-tail corner, which by the way, should be avoided when possible.

. . . .

LEFT: *You can't hit what you can't see This is the reason many varmint-dedicated scopes include high magnification. Investing in the best optics you can afford also assures crisp views during demanding conditions.*

A LensPen or individually wrapped optical wipes should always reside in your range bag. Best-quality coatings are also engineered to allow better light transmission for brighter, crisper views, and often include corrective measures to assure truer color fidelity. The exceptions to these rules normally revolve around warrantees. Vortex optics, for example, offers no-questions-asked product replacement no matter how an optic is damaged and for the life of the scope, not just the owner. It offers this coverage on even entry-level models.

Like the varmint cartridge and varmint rifle labels, the term varmint scope can mean different things to different shooters. The easiest designation is made between big-game scopes and those used for true varmint shooting (predators often welcoming parallels to big-game needs). For many years, I believed no big-game hunter needed anything more than a straight 4X or 6X scope (begging the pardon of the extreme long-range crowd). I shot deer at incredibly long ranges with such scopes and saw no need for more magnification. The near-standard 3-9x40 configuration is a great compromise to this conviction, though when I owned my .243 Win. topped with a Bushnell 4-12x42mm scope, it most often sat on 6-power. Big game is called big for a reason.

Varmint shooting is another matter, obviously. An average ground squirrel is no larger than a 12-ounce soda bottle, and many are no larger than an average cellular flip-phone. Prairie dogs aren't much bigger. And even the larger varmints like the

Most varmint shooters prefer a variable scope for the versatility afforded. The author kept a Bushnell Elite 6500 4.5-30x50mm attached to his AR predator-calling rifle all winter for this kind of versatility.

chucks are sometimes — of course, not always — shot at ranges that would cause the average deer hunter to balk (at least before it became fashionable to see how far the envelope could be pushed via American Sniper delusions). I often say you can't hit what you can't see. Sticking to the standard configurations is good, but you'll never extend your maximum effective range when you're shooting at an indistinct blob instead of placing shots carefully on a clearly defined critter. Besides, seeing rodent hide to each side of a finer cross-hair provides confidence, a commodity sometimes more valuable than pure skill.

So the true varmint scope is typically one with higher power for longer reach and finer detail on smaller targets, and wearing a higher objective to provide more latitude to separate lighted and shadowed areas within the field of view. Just as an overview, some of the varmint scopes I own or have recently enjoyed include Leupold's VX-3i 8.5-25x50mm CDS Target (Remington 700 VTR, .223 Rem.); Meopta's MeoPro 6.5-20x50mm HTR (Mossberg MVP Varmint, .204 Ruger); Bushnell's Elite 6500 4.5-30x50mm (customized .223); Trijicon's 5-20x50mm AccuPoint (custom .223 AR); Vortex's Viper PST 6-24x50mm (Savage .17 Hornet and custom .22-250 Rem.); and Leica's ER-LRS 6.5-26x56mm. These scopes range from reasonable to extreme.

Lines blur considerably when contemplating a dedicated predator calling gun, where big-game rifle configurations serve just fine, though cranking the big glass to lower powers also gets the job done, with added carrying weight but better overall resolution. The object, after all, is to call predators as close as possible before taking the shot, and even the diminutive fox is considerably bigger than the average small varmint.

Let's have a look.

Styrka's S5-Series 4.5-14x44 SH-BDC might be considered a perfect fit for this Savage A17 auto-loading .17 HMR, providing plenty of power to stretch range but proving not too heavy, which makes it easier to tote on walk-about hunts.

■ Rimfire Glass

I've attached standard centerfire scopes to .22 LRs and got along just fine much of the time. The problem you'll sometimes encounter is one I discovered this past spring. After completing tweaks to my customized Ruger 10/22, I stole the quality Leupold "straight-six" from my .25-'06 and installed it in high rings. I liked the scope's clarity, familiarity and 42mm objective, which I thought might come in handy during nighttime jackrabbit shoots. The problem I soon discovered is that targets within 50 yards remained fuzzy, with no way of correcting for focus. Addressing ground squirrels that appeared at point-blank range meant shooting at indistinct blobs. I then tried a Leupold 2-7x40mm variable that once lived on a 7mm Rem. Mag. With the high mounts chosen to accommodate the prominent cheekpiece on my Hogue Tactical Thumbhole stock, the scope didn't provide enough downward adjustment to sight at 50 yards. Becoming frustrated, I finally ordered Bushnell's Rimfire Optics A22 with Drop Zone-22 BDC Reticle in 3.5-10x42mm configuration, including front parallax focus from 25 yards to infinity. It proved a perfect fit.

RIGHT: *Pistol optics are different than those attched to rifles, including long relief to allow arm's-length sighting. Many shooters mount standard scopes on light-recoiling pistols, but this has always felt odd to the author.*

The newest fad are rimfire scopes regulated to specific cartridges, such as my Bushnell Drop Zone-22 BDC Reticle for standard-velocity (1,250 fps) .22 LR, to those made for .22 WMR or .17 HMR. These include internal cross-hair hash marks for point-on aiming at 50 through 150 yards or elevation turrets calibrated to set ranges while shooting ammo with specific ballistics. They lend new precision to rimfire shooting often missing from standard rimfire setups and help extend maximum effective range without using "Kentucky windage."

Worthwhile rimfire-dedicated optics include the Bushnell already mentioned, Nikon's turreted P-Rimfire 2-7x32mm and Prostaff Rimfire II in 3-9x40 and 4-12x40mm, Leupold's VX-1 2-7x28mm .22 Caliber Rimfire, the Vortex Diamondback 2-7x35mm with V-Plex reticle, Weaver's Rimfire 3-9x35mm with Dual-X RV-9 reticle, the BSA Sweet 22 and Sweet 17 with calibrated .22 LR and .17 HMR turrets, Simmons' .22 Mag. 3-9x32mm Rimfire and Barska's 2-7x32mm AO .17 Hot Magnum 6-18x40mm.

■ Pistol Scopes

Pistol-dedicated scopes include long eye relief to accommodate arm's-length cross-hair sighting. This means when a pistol is held well away from the eye while rested over shooting sticks or atop a rest, you receive an edge-to-edge field of view, and the cross-hairs remain sharp. Dot scopes make excellent pistol options to a point because they're not critical of eye relief, though they usually include zero or very low magnification, limiting their usefulness to close-range work.

There's no such thing as an AR scope. ARs are just like any other rifle and can be shot with whatever you might prefer on your favorite bolt rifle. A single-piece cantilever mount is normally best to keep the charging bolt clear, easily clamping onto standard Picatinny rails. Fred Eichler photo.

Trijicon AccuPoint 5-20x50mm

Many pistol scopes, such as the Leupold M8-2X on my Taurus .17 HMR and Swift 4x32mm on my .221 Rem. Fireball, are fixed power, usually no more than 2 to 4 power, which is effective to about 125 to 150 yards, depending on magnification. Quality fixed models include Swift's Reliant and Premier Series 4x32mm, Nikon's Force XR 2x20mm, Simmons' Prohunter 4x32mm and Leupold's FX-II 4x28mm.

Many of my varmint pistols, such as my Taurus Raging Hornet in .22 Hornet or especially my T/C Contenders in .223 Rem., hold variable-power models. My Hornet, for example, holds a Tasco 1.25-4x28mm, allowing quicker target acquisition when ranges are intimate and a bit more reach on longer ground squirrels or prairie dogs when needed. My .221 Fireball and .223 Rem. hold more powerful variable scopes, the .221 a Nikon 2.5-8x28mm and the .223 a 2-6x28mm Bushnell. I sometimes yearn for a bit more in the .221 and .223, such as Burris' 3-12x32mm with the adjustable-objective Ballistic Plex Reticle, as I believe this would also improve my maximum effective range, as even at 6-power ground squirrels beyond 200 yards turn into specs — but then at those kind of ranges, perhaps a rifle is warranted.

Prime examples of high-quality variable pistol scopes include Nikon's Force XR 2.5-8x28mm with BDC Reticle, Simmons' Prohunter 2-6x32mm Handgun, Swift's Reliant and Premier 2-6x32mm, Weaver's Classic Pistol 2.5-8x28mm with Dual-X Reticle, Burris' 2-7x32mm and Leupold's VX-3 2.5-8x32M D.

Long-range scopes normally include higher-than-average magnification and large objectives to cut through glare, heat shimmer and dim light. This relatively affordable Leupold VX-3i 8.5-25x50mm CDS Target includes covered turrets.

■ Centerfire Varmint Optics

Centerfire scopes are offered in fixed and variable configurations, both available in high-powered bench-rest options in powers as high as you dare. There's nothing wrong with fixed, high-magnification scopes if you're dedicated to only the longest shots on the smallest varmints or larger targets such as hogs. They tend to be lighter and are simpler, but they can hinder shots at closer ranges. I prefer a top-quality variable-power model. They simply prove more versatile. For example, my .223 AR now wears a Trijicon 5-20x50mm AccuPoint. When I'm in eastern Oregon sniping distant ground squirrels or Montana shooting prairie dogs, it's safe to say that scope never comes off 20-power. But that AR also doubles as a dedicated predator calling rifle, for reasons discussed in Chapter 7, "Varmint Rifles." When I'm calling and might have an eager coyote or sneaky bobcat in my lap, it stays dialed down to 5 power. Should a coyote hang up past 150 yards, I'll likely want a setting somewhere in the middle, depending on how steady my rest is — fence post versus off a bent knee. That scope keeps me covered in every conceivable situation.

As another example, the 15-60x52mm Vortex Golden Eagle on my custom .22-250 Rem. allows me to reach out there and touch someone, as well as providing startling clarity on small or distant targets. But as the season progresses, you can bet there comes a hot day in June when the highest 60-power setting will do nothing but gather dancing heat-shimmer and obscure targets annoyingly. It's easy enough to dial down, still receiving high-end magnification but also a cleaner view. Just for comparison, I've seldom experienced heat-shimmer issues with scopes set to 24- to 30-power magnification.

Most scopes include ¼-inch-per-click, or ¼-MOA, adjustments, which means adjustments move crosshairs ¼ inch at 100 yards, 1/2 inch at 200, 1 inch at 400 yards

■ Focal-Plane Decisions

Confusion is common when pondering a high-end varmint scope and the business of front/first versus rear/second focal plane, usually listed in spec sheets as simply FFP (first focal plane) or SFP (second focal plane). The easy answer is with FFP (the reticle situated in front of the erector tube), the size of the cross-hairs changes as power is increased or decreased. With SFP (the reticle sitting behind the erector tube), cross-hairs remain the same size as magnification changes. Why is this important? With SFP, any system the scope uses to help judge the range and speed of an object (represented by outer hash marks in MOA or mil-spec graduations) are only accurate at one power setting, normally the highest. With FFP scopes, such reticles are always dead-on accurate at any power, an advantage in fluid military or extreme long-range settings. These graduation marks allow mapping your scope's gradient marks against objects of known dimensions or something common to an area and generally the same size (a fence post or the more symmetrical wheels of a center-pivot irrigation system, for example). Comparing how such objects fit into known gaps gives you almost instant range estimation, but only at the SFP's highest setting but at all settings with FFP scopes. This is hugely simplified, of course, but it gives you insight into how such reticle graduations are designed to work.

Now, from a personal perspective, I don't need to judge range via MOA or mil graduations, nor am I quick enough to do the math ultimately required to make those systems sing. I own dead-nuts Bushnell range-finder binoculars that give me the laser range with the push of a button. Perhaps more importantly, SFP scopes maintain the finest cross-hair aiming point possible at the highest powers. It's not that the cross-hairs actually change size in a FFP scope at higher powers, but they appear to grow thicker as they maintain their relative relationship to objects in the field of view. When shooting tiny ground squirrels or prairie dogs way over yonder, I want the finest aiming point possible — one that obscures the smallest amount of target area.

■ Useful Configurations

Again, magnification options really depend on what you shoot at most — .75-pound ground squirrels versus 10-pound woodchucks — and at what ranges — to a certain extent, how much you can afford to spend. I shot New Mexico prairie dogs with standard 2-7X to 4-12X configurations for decades without complaint — until I discovered high-magnification scopes and really began to severely stretch my maximum effective range. As I've pointed out, you can't hit what you can't see, and I can't see a ground squirrel beyond, say, 400 yards with a 9- or 12-power scope. I've already discussed many of the scopes attached to my favorite varmint guns. If I was being completely honest, I'd call the 6-24x50mm the most practical configuration possible for everything from ground squirrels to coyotes, pretending you're allowed only one choice. Though fairly large and relatively heavy (compared to the average big-game scope) Bushnell's 6500

Exposed turrets are handy while shooting small targets at long ranges, providing more precision than cross-hair hold-over marks. The shooter who creates careful ballisctic charts can generally extend effective range considerably while using a turret scope.

4.5-30x50mm arrangement is pretty tough to beat, too, with plenty of positives at both ends of the magnification spectrum. Fair warning, though: As with installing a top-quality replacement trigger in your favorite varmint rifle, when you become accustomed to the highest magnification scopes, it becomes incredibly addicting.

Rifle scopes come with standard screw-capped elevation and windage adjustment knobs manipulated with ¼-MOA clicks (one click equals .25 inch at 100 yards), covered graduated/numbered tower adjustment knobs and exposed, or "true turret" adjustment knobs. We're all familiar with standard scope adjustments, many with top screwdriver slots for adjustments (a penny normally works best), others with knurled finger knobs. Adjustments are made, the caps returned and zero set until adjusted again. Aiming sometimes involves using reticle marks outside the actual cross-hairs center or holding high and low according to range. Covered but graduated tower knobs can be manipulated like exposed turrets, allowing in-field cross-hair adjustments, but are not dust and weatherproof without covers in place.

Bushness Elite 6500 4.5-30x50mm.

■ Twisting Turrets

True turret scopes include interior rubber O-rings that make them impervious to elements. They allow dialing cross-hairs according to range and wind direction/velocity almost instantly. I've heard serious varmint shooters say children hold over with fixed cross-hairs, but adults dial turrets. In serious varmint shooting,

I tend to agree. During shooting practice at marked shooting ranges, turret hash marks are color coded with permanent markers for various ranges, but some companies, such as Kenton Industries (milled caps) and Custom Turret Systems (printable stickers), offer custom options for popular scope models with dials dedicated to your cartridge and load.

Turrets open a new world of shooting precision. They've let me push my maximum effective range by offering pinpoint, spot-on aiming instead of educated hold-over guesstimates. Take a laser pop, dial the range and give it a whirl, making small adjustments as needed. Perhaps most important, turrets allow dialing out wind, because although most of us likely grew up applying vertical Kentucky windage, it's counterintuitive to aim sideways. Turrets also turn low-power cartridges into long-range fun, as a .17 HMR at 350 yards or .17 Hornet at 400 offer the same challenges as dropping in a 1,000-yard

Xtreme Hardcore's TRU Level Long Range Picatinny Base and Ranger rings might be considered overkill on a .223 Rem., but the author doesn't think such a thing exists when assembling a precision varmint/predator rifle.

shot with a .338 Lapua. They make something like a .22-250 Rem., .220 Swift or .243 Win. pretty dangerous.

Another part of the turret discussion includes tube size, as in standard 1-inch, 30 mm or "magnum" 32 mm diameters. Although an argument could be made around light transmission, in reality, a larger tube simply translates into a wider range of elevation adjustments (technically also windage). Which diameter you choose really depends on cartridge capabilities. A .22 LR, for example, does not need more than a 1-inch tube. A 30mm is sufficient for most varmint shooting, and the 32 mm — found in expensive brands such as NightForce — is useful for the longest shots you can imagine (often combined with 10, 20 or 30 MOA bases, which I'll touch on later).

I'm pretty proud of a 468-yard shot I made on a ground squirrel with my .17 Hornet, so I'll tell you about it. This unlucky squirrel occupied the lip of a sandy wash at the top of a vertical sand face. I'd been working on some squirrels at 338 yards, so I made a quick guesstimate, spun the elevation

A scope-mounted or base-integral bubble level is a welcome addition to any varmint shooter's optics setup. Slight rifle/ scope tilt can turn into big misses when ranges stretch beyond 350 yards, and a quick glance at the bubble assures that you are plumb.

turret and gave it a try. There was a small flick of sand well below the squirrel, maybe 3 feet low. I made some calculations, added some more clicks and tried again, hitting 1 foot low and 8 inches left. The slightest breeze was blowing right to left. Then, I was dealing in increments I could wrap my head around. I made some more adjustments, squeezed off another round and the little fellow fell backward, kicking his tiny feet before spinning in circles and tumbling over the ledge. I started walking. My father wanted to know what I was up to. I needed confirmation. The squirrel was lying at the base of the

sand face, dead as fried chicken. I ranged back to the truck with my Bushnell Fusion 1 Mile laser range-finder binos: 468. It would never have happened without Vortex Viper PST turrets.

Turret cons? I've forgotten to reset turrets after shooting at a different range and missed easy shots. The best turret systems, such as Vortex's top-end wares or Nightforce's models, include zero stops at the shortest range sighted, allowing faster resetting after longer shots. All turrets scopes include physical horizontal hash marks, which can be marked with red indelible ink for an instant bottom reference mark. The only problem with ink-marked or dedicated turrets is changing loads means settings become null and void. The biggest con, of course, is quality turrets scopes invariably cost more than comparable covered-adjustment models.

■ Lighted Reticles

Many of my top-end rifle scopes and one of my pistol scopes include rheostat-controlled lighted reticles. They would prove useful for hunting predators or wild boars by night with artificial light or at the edges of legal shooting hours in heavy cover or during an overcast day, but for small-varmint shooting, they serve little purpose and add to overall costs and clutter. I can take them or leave them, but it's there if, say, a coyote runs in the headlights while I'm returning to camp one evening.

■ Mounts, Rings and Accessories

A quality varmint scope deserves quality anchoring hardware. While working retail, it never ceased to amaze me how a customer would spend a bunch of money on a top-grade firearm and expensive scope but approach mounts and

The predator caller can normally get along well with a standard big-game scope in 3-9X or 4-12X configurations, as the object of calling is to bring predators closer.

rings with indifference. Bases are bases, and rings are rings, you might insist, and in the case of rimfire or sporter rifles holding standard-issue scopes, I might agree. Though varmint rifles don't kick like big-game cartridges and rifles, they get shot much more, meaning a lot of heating and cooling and slow but sure battering. They also tend to hold larger, heavier scopes. With the full forces of opposite and equal physics in play, big glass is harder on bases and rings. So my advice is to be better safe than sorry.

Two-piece Weaver-type bases and clamp-on rings have been getting the job done for decades, and although even some of my favorite varmint rifles wear them out of necessity (no other options offered), when parts are available, I prefer a one-piece Picatinny-style bases or one-piece base/ring assemblies. Such options make slight misalignments less likely and prove much stouter during the long haul. My favorite, Xtreme Hardcore Gear's XHCG Tru Level Picatinny Mount, serves as an example of what to look for. It's offered for the most popular rifle brands and models, in 0 and 20 MOA (I'll explain momentarily) and includes incorporated, rear-facing bubble levels. It's milled from 7075 T-6 aluminum with MIL-STD 1913 cross slots and given a Mil- Spec 8625 Type 3 hard-coat, and anchored with .225-inch torx-head screws. Every facet of this base speaks precision and ruggedness. Warne Tactical and Weaver's Multi-Slot bases are other examples. Bases labeled 10, 20 or 30 MOA are angled to point the scope downward, which in turn pushes the rifle barrel upward, affording more scope travel for extreme long-range shooting, something I'll go into in greater detail in Chapter 13, "Long-Range Primer."

After installing a rock-solid base, choose nail-tough rings — something with at least four-screw clamping, though six-screw clamping is welcomed. Xtreme Hardcore, again, makes my favorite. Six-hole Ranger Tactical Long Range Rings are machined from highest-quality aluminum and matched to within .001 inch, the clamping system including twin cross-slot bolts and twin stainless-steel guide rails that press into the ring base. XHCG Force Recon Tactical Long Range Rings are similar but include built-in bubble level on the rear ring base to keep rifles dead level to eliminate left-right misses. Six-screw Warne AngleEye Extreme Long

Range, Vortex Precision Matched, Weaver Six Hole Tactical and Burris all-steel, four-screw Zee Rings are also welcomed on my rifles.

In the AR world, single-piece cantilever mounts provide distinct advantages, offering not only a solid anchor but also setting the scope out of the way of charging handles for easier loading. Many include miniature Picatinny rails atop the predominantly six-screw ring caps for adding accessories such as lasers or lights for activities such as nighttime wild boar or predator hunting. Look to Burris' AR-P.E.R.R., Weaver's SPR 30mm, Vortex's Viper Cantilever and Warne's R.A.M.P. as prime examples.

For serious long-range shooters (who haven't purchased Xtreme Hardcore bubble-level base or rings), a clamp-on level is a good investment toward precision shooting, helping detect and eliminate rifle cant that can ruin accuracy. Look to Vortex's LO Pro Bubblevel or Burris' Bubble Level Ant-Cant Devise. Other welcomed accessories are clamp-on throw levers that clamp onto variable-scope adjustment rings for effortless magnification adjustment. They're available from Warne, Leupold, Vortex, Nightforce and others. And again, if you purchase no other scope accessory, buy a LensPen to keep your investment clean and scratch free.

Leupold VX-3i 8.5-25x50mm CDS Target.

⊕ Chapter 10
Handloading To Needs

Handloading is largely integral to varmint shooting for many reasons, not the least of which is high-volume shooting becomes cost prohibitive when depending on factory ammunition. It's also difficult to ignore the fact varmint medicine can prove fairly specialized, holding distinctive bullets or loaded especially hot; combinations not always available in factory-loaded packaging. More pressing to many varminters, handloading lets you tailor loads to wring maximum accuracy from specific rifles. My .17 Hornet, for example, shoots exceptionally well with Hornady Superformance factory ammo, but I shrunk groups to one ragged hole by fine-tuning handloads. And although it's true factory ammo has become increasingly accurate through the years, it's also true ammo makers must serve the greatest cross-section of firearms possible in relation to magazine length (that is, bullet-seating depth) and safety concerns for ammo fired from older guns.

Handloading opens more options, allowing, for example, coaxing a little more from a round, always watchful for obvious pressure signs such as sticky actions or flattened or firing-pin-pierced primers. It's commonly accepted among many handloaders that maximum velocity automatically equals poor accuracy. This can hold true if loading for velocity for velocity's sake, but it certainly isn't the rule. When working loads for lighter varmint rounds, such as the .22 Hornet and .223 Rem., the tendency is to push for maximum performance within standard working pressures (some powders offering lower pressures than others) combined with maximum accuracy. I have three .223 loads that deliver one-hole groups at maximum velocity, providing the dramatic impacts and quick kills I seek. But handloading might also create quieter, more pleasant reduced-power loads that are also less costly to assemble.

Saving money is what got me into handloading while still a teen, when a box of factory centerfire ammo cost one-quarter to half of what it does today. So in relation to component costs in the late 1970s and early 1980s, that's really saying

....

Handloading lets you tweak ammunition for maximum accuracy most of all, but also lets you choose the exact bullet needed for specific jobs and maybe get a bit more performance than offered by factory rounds.

For most serious varmint shooters, handloading is necessary from a standpoint of economics. The author easily burns 300 to 500 rounds on an average weekend outing — a quantity that would prove cost prohibitive with factory loads multiplied by a dozen trips annually.

something. But then again, handloading also let me shoot bullets that just couldn't be touched in factory offerings, like those 6mm 60-grain Sierra hollow-points with which I exploded small varmints. That has changed, too, as a wider array of factory loads meet more specialized needs. Hornady Superformance Varmint is a perfect example, sometimes providing unmatched velocities from modern rifles in good working order. Nonetheless, in terms of pure costs, premium .223 Rem. ammo costs from $20 to $23 per 20 rounds, or about $1 a shot, but I can easily assemble ammo including best-quality varmint bullets for as little as 25 cents per round. Now, multiply 75 cents by the 350 to 400 rounds of .223 regularly burned during a weekend in target-rich ground-squirrel habitats — in addition to other ammo.

Taking just the .223, its popularity hinges largely on cost — with once-fired military brass so cheap the 10 or so loadings you get from each translates into pennies — though I seem to pick up all the free .223 brass needed. Another option for saving money is overstock or blemish outlets such as Shooter's Pro Shop or outfits trading in pulled, blemished or discontinued bullets, such as Rocky Mountain Reloading. For example, RMR has relinquished website deals such as premium-grade 50-grain JHPs (which my .22-250 loves) for $17 per 100, 50-grain Lead-Free Frangible (one of my AR's favorites) for $30 per 250, or 42-grain Lead-Free Frangible (creating one of my best .223 T/C Contender loads) for $30 per 250. RMR also carries brass, often factory primed (the cases those pulled bullets came out of). That's just an example of how scouring the Internet can save additional money.

One quick note on bullet selection: Bullets for big-game hunting or target shooting can vary greatly in construction and performance from varmint projectiles. Big-game bullets must hold together and drive deep, meaning they might not expand sufficiently on small varmints. Many match-grade bullets — though not all — are designed only for accuracy. Designers don't care if they open. They're only interested in tiny groups. These bullets can actually act like FMJs on even big game and especially varmints. There are exceptions. The

Some examples of varmint and predator bullets in .224 caliber, left to right, lightest to heaviest: 35-grain Hornady V-Max, 36-grain Barnes Varmint Grenade, 40-grain Sierra Hornet, 40-grain Sierra BlitzKing, 40-grain Cutting Edge Raptor, 45-grain Hornady Bee, 45-grain Sierra Hornet, 50-grain Speer, 55-grain Speer HP, 50-grain Hornady V-Max, 50-grain Hornady GMX, 50-grain Cutting Edge Raptor, 50-grain Lead-Free Frangible, 52-grain Hornady ELD Match, 65-grain Sierra SBT and 69-grain Rocky Mountain Reloading 3-Gun Hunter.

true varmint bullet is designed to fly to pieces on impact, providing terminal performance assuring even marginal hits kill small varmints instantly, as ranges are often long and targets small, and stuff happens. While shooting hotter varmint rounds with highly frangible bullets, for example, I've killed the ground squirrel I was aiming at and his buddy a few feet to one side.

Finally, lead-free bullets are making inroads as environmental awareness make them increasingly politically correct. Some homogeneous-alloy pills — such as Barnes' original X-series, Hornady's GMX or Nosler's E-Tip — aren't varmint bullets, though they're excellent predator pills, inflicting minimal pelt damage (see Chapter 11, "Pelt Shooting") and ideal hog fodder. But lead free designs — such as Nosler's Lead-Free Ballistic Tip Varmint, Cutting Edge's milled-brass/segmented FB Raptor, Sinterfire's pressure-molded zinc-copper-powder designs or Barnes Varmint Grenades — represent explosive varmint sedatives.

PET LOADS, SMALL-VARMINT VERSION

A couple of notes before we begin: Results in your rifles might vary, so consider these starting points, and work from there, fine tuning for tighter groups (see the next chapter for Pelt-Shooting options).

Some cartridges and rifles are touchier than others. If these loads synchronize with you rifle, sweet. Also, many of these loads are pretty hot, so always start 10 to 20 percent below the suggested charges and work up while watching carefully for signs of excessive pressures. Your guns or cases might be slightly different from mine. Last, velocities provided are often best-guess estimates based on available information, so don't take them as gospel.

■ .17 Hornet

Like its parent cartridge, the .22 Hornet, the .17 Hornet requires careful attention to detail. With loads ranging from a wee 10 grains to measly 13 grains, small powder increments make a big difference to accuracy and working pressures. Unsafe pressure spikes can occur with as little as a half grain of powder. My .17 Hornet is one of those rare rounds for which I shoot only one load: the Western Powders A1680 load listed below.

My goal while working up a .17 Hornet load was to duplicate Hornady's factory ballistics. The company developed it after all, and those guys know what they're doing. This proved a wise move, as with a little tweaking, I improved on the ½-inch groups factory loads printed, turning my .17 Hornet into a single-holer. My tests with W296 — my favorite .22 Hornet propellant — proved disastrous, printing 4-inch 100-yard groups (your results might vary). I experienced worthwhile results with Lil'Gun, but "only" ¾- to 1-inch groups. More experimenting would likely yield better results, but it's difficult to invest further investigations when an established load stamps one hole.

PET LOADS, .17 HORNET, SAVAGE 25 WALKING VARMINTER, 22-INCH BARREL

Bullet	Powder	Charge	Velocity	Primer
*20-gr Hornady V-Max	A1680	12 grs	3,650 fps	Rem. 7 ½ BR
20-gr Hornady V-Max	Lil'Gun	10 grs	3,629 fps	Same

*One-hole groups.

■ .17 Fireball

The .17 Fireball (and ballistically identical .17 Mach IV), like its parent .221 Fireball, is a highly efficient cartridge giving varmint shooters a lot for so little. It easily surpasses 4,000 fps with 20-grain bullets and only 14 to 20 grains of powder, with explosive results on small varmints. Shooting my father's .17 Fireball is a joy — which doesn't happen often, as he's usually shooting it. Loaded with a 25-grain pill, it makes an acceptable predator round, providing adequate penetration and seldom exiting. Limited case capacity requires diligence, as half-grain increments can produce 100 fps jumps in velocity and unsafe pressures. The .17 Fireball, in general, shoots best with maximum loads.

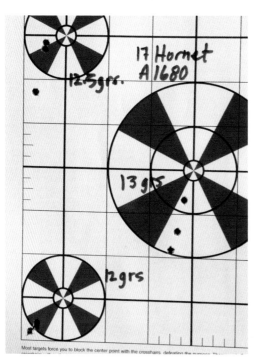

. . . .

Accurate 1680 has been the magic powder for the author and his .17 Hornet. It's the only powder that allows matching Hornady factory velocities and has proven quite accurate, eventually tweaked into consistent one-hole groups.

Most targets force you to block the center point with the crosshairs, defeating the purpose. Th...

Bullet	Powder	Charge	Velocity	Primer
20-gr Hornady V-Max	X-Terminator	19.5 grs (max)	4,050 fps	Rem. 7 ½
20-gr Hornady V-Max	IMR8208 XBR	20 grs	4,150 fps	Same
20-gr Hornady HP	H335	19.5 grs	3,915 fps	CCI 400

■ .204 Ruger

The sizzling .204 Ruger is fairly trouble-free for handloaders. Like the loosely related .223 Rem., it isn't that finicky and is capable of fantastic accuracy with multiple powders and bullets. For small varmints, I prefer 32-grain pills, as they easily surpass 4,000 fps without pushing maximum pressures, a rifle sighted point-on at 200 yards hitting only about 15 inches low at 400. I've been unable to duplicate Hornady's stated 4,225 fps factory Superformance Varmint velocities with available powders. The closest you'll get to this is with Vihta Vouri N-140, which also relinquishes fantastic accuracy. Heavier 40-grain pills provide more punch on coyote-sized game and superior ballistic coefficients, which are welcomed in breezy conditions and at extreme ranges.

PET LOADS, .204 RUGER, MOSSBERG MVP VARMINT, 24-INCH BARREL

Bullet	Powder	Charge	Velocity	Primer
*32-gr Nosler Varmageddon Tipped	N-140	28.5 grs	4,100 fps	CCI BR 4
32-gr Hornady V-Max	H322	25.5 grs	3,996 fps	Same
32-gr Sierra BlitzKing	X-Terminator	27.5 grs (max)	3,960 fps	Same
32-gr Hornady V-Max	TAC	27.5 grs	4,100 fps	Same

*(5-shot/one-hole groups)

PET LOADS, .204 RUGER, BROWNING X-BOLT VARMINT, 22-INCH BARREL.

Bullet	Powder	Charge	Velocity	Primer
32-gr Nosler Ballistic Tip	Varget	28 grs	3,875 fps	CCI 400
32-gr Hornady V-Max	Benchmark	27 grs	4,050 fps	Same
32-gr Sierra BlitzKing	Varget	29 grs	3,950 fps	Same

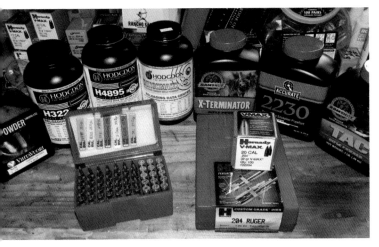

The .204 Ruger isn't a particularly picky cartridge, and good accuracy is provided by a variety of powders. So far, Vihta Vouri N-140 and 32-grain Nosler Varmageddon Tipped have provided the best groups — five-shot/one-holers, in fact.

■ .22 Hornet (and K-Hornet)

The .22 Hornet is a tricky little bastard. Its tiny case makes small powder increments substantial, yes, but it has other problems. One gun writer of note cannot type "22 Hornet" without first adding an "inherently inaccurate" modifier. It's more truthful to say loading the Hornet is delicately tedious. The .22 Hornet can be made to shoot MOA groups in quality bolt or single-shot rifles, but seldom without extensive experimentation. The Hornet is touchy, even in details as seemingly mundane as primers. One load likes a plain-Jane small-rifle primer, another a small pistol cap and still another benchrest grades. Powder is monotonously measured to the tenth of a grain, and that tenth can make or break your results. The thin-walled bottleneck cases "flow" after repeated firings, so each piece of brass must be frequently inspected for split necks and precisely trimmed to length. Seating depth can also prove hyper critical, the case head-spacing off the prominent rim. Often, you need bullets that just touch the lands to assure they point straight down the barrel instead of ever so slightly cocked. Finally, you must carefully match case brands, as volume can vary considerably — Remington and Winchester generally offering the highest volume, and Hornady and PPU normally less (not necessarily a bad thing, as that indicates thicker walls likely to provide longer life).

Handloading the .22 Hornet is essentially mandatory today, unless you consider $1.50 a pop for factory rounds acceptable. Which brings to mind another modern

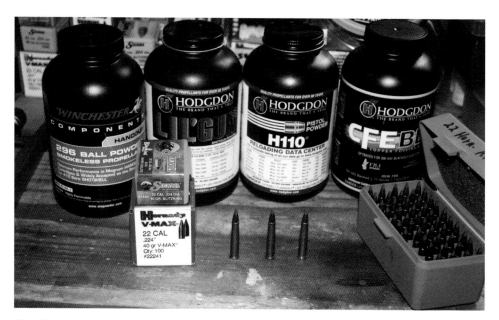

The .22 Hornet is tedious to load, touchy to small changes in powder charge and demanding attention to small details. Polymer-tipped 40-grain pills and Winchester W296 provide the author his best accuracy.

.22 Hornet bane: the 35-grain pills (sometimes lighter) that have become a new factory-load standard in the interests of breaking the magic 3,000 fps threshold. Although that might appear a plus at first, real-world ballistics tells a different story. The classic 45-grain Hornet pill also poses setbacks. A streamlined 40-grain bullet, such as Hornady's V-Max, is where it's at with the .22 Hornet, turning lackluster ballistics into something more impressive.

Let's look at the numbers: A 35-grain Hornady V-Max/Nosler Ballistic Tip launched at 3,100 fps clocks only 1,127 fps and drops 17.5 inches at 300 yards (about the Hornet's maximum effective range). A 45-grain Hornet soft-point leaving the barrel at 2,690 fps slows to 1,128 fps and drops nearly 19.5 inches at 300 yards. The 40-grain Hornady V-Max, departing at 2,800 fps (I get a bit better than this with my favorite load, listed below) is still stepping along at 1,698 fps and drops slightly less than 11 inches at 300 yards. With a cartridge of this class, 7 to 9 inches less drop is significant.

I get my best results from W296, H110 and Lil'Gun — with newer CFE-BLK showing great promise.

PET LOADS, .22 HORNET, SAVAGE 340 SERIES E, 22-INCH BARREL

Bullet	Powder	Charge	Velocity	Primer
40-gr Hornady V-Max	*W296	11.3 grs	2,875 fps	Rem. 7 ½ BR
	Lil'Gun	13.2 grs	2,800 fps	CCI 500 Mag
	H110	11.5 grs	2,850 fps	CCI 450 SP
	CFE-BLK	13 grs	2,625 fps	Rem. 7 ½ BR

*Generally most accurate.

PET LOADS, .22 HORNET, SAVAGE 25 WALKING VARMINT, 22-INCH BARREL

Bullet	Powder	Charge	Velocity	Primer
40-gr Nosler Varmageddon HP	Lil'Gun	13 grs	2,780 fps	CCI 400
45-gr generic Hornet	W296	11.3 grs	2,700 fps	Same
	H4227	11.5 grs	2,650 fps	Same

PET LOADS, .22 K-HORNET, T/C ENCORE, 24-INCH BARREL

Bullet	Powder	Charge	Velocity	Primer
40-gr Hornady V-Max	Lil'Gun	13 grs	3,050 fps	Win. WSR
45-gr generic Hornet	A1680	15 grs	2,875 fps	Same

■ .221 Fireball (rifle)

The efficient .221 Fireball really comes into its own in rifle-length barrels, easily breaking 3,000 fps with even fairly mild loads. It's also pleasant to shoot and incredibly accurate, the reason I enjoy shooting my father's Fireball Contender rifle whenever we get together for varmint shoots.

PET LOADS, .221 FIREBALL, T/C CONTENDER, 21-INCH BARREL

Bullet	Powder	Charge	Velocity	Primer
40-gr Hornady V-Max	RL-7	18.6 grs	3,150 fps	CCI 400
40-gr Hornady V-Max	A1680	18 grs	3,275 fps	Same

H4198 and Reloader-7 are excellent starting points when seeking maximum accuracy from the .221 Rem. Fireball shot from rifles. The .221 Fireball is an efficient cartridge, and a little powder goes a long way.

■ .222 Remington

Admittedly, I've limited experience with the .222 Rem., but a friend I shoot varmints with regularly does, being an early and enduring fan. The .222 has slightly less hop than the more popular .223, giving up 200 to 300 fps to the latter. This also makes the .222 a quieter round, a plus in populated areas when sniping, say, Eastern woodchucks or calling predators on small properties.

PET LOADS, .222 REM., SAVAGE 25 WALKING VARMINTER, 22-INCH BARREL

Bullet	Powder	Charge	Velocity	Primer
40-gr Hornady V-Max	A2015	23 grs	3,550 fps	Rem. 7 ½
40-gr Nosler Ballistic Tip	Benchmark	23.5 grs	3,100 fps	N/A
45-gr generic Hornet	H322	24 grs	3,275 fps	Rem. 7 ½
50-gr Sierra Spitzer Varminter	W748	26.5 grs	3,100 fps	Same

■ .223 Remington

Other than my cantankerous but accurate .22 Hornet, I've probably invested in more load development with the .223 Rem. than any other varmint cartridge. Maybe that's because those efforts are generally rewarding. I'm fairly certain I could pick any suitable .223 powder and find a load printing at least sub-1-inch groups from my customized Savage rifle, if not one-hole groups. The .223 is forgiving, as my .223 bolt rifle assembles one-hole groups from at least three loads. More remarkable, I might shoot a mixed bag of handloads in everything from hot 36-grain Barnes Varmint Grenades to my favorite 40-grain loads to 55-grain FMJs, and the impact will generally remain within reasonable parameters or, more pointedly for our discussion, print minute-of-squirrel within 250 yards. That's not something I can say for my fussy .22-250, which prints to different spots with same-weight bullets of various brands and equal charges of powder. My favorite .223 powders are Benchmark, H4198 and Ramshot TAC. My favorite bullets are in the 36- to 40-grain range, providing flat trajectories to 350 to 400 yards and impressive splat factors.

PET LOADS, .223 REM., CUSTOMIZED SAVAGE 10, 20-INCH BARREL WITH MUZZLE BRAKE

Bullet	Powder	Charge	Velocity	Primer
36-gr Barnes Varmint Grenade	Benchmark	27 grs	3,700 fps	CCI BR 4
x40-gr *Polymer-Tip	Ramshot TAC	27.3 grs	3,600 fps	Rem 7 ½ BR
x40-gr *Polymer Tip	H4198	22.5 grs	3,500 fps	Same
x40-gr *Polymer Tip	W748	27.7 grs	3,400 fps	Same

*Hornady V-Max/Nosler Ballistic Tip/Sierra BlitzKing

x(One-hole, 100-yard groups)

PET LOADS, .223 REM., REMINGTON 700 ADL, 26-INCH CUSTOM BARREL

Bullet	Powder	Charge	Velocity	Primer
40-gr Nosler Varmageddon HP	Varmint	27 grs	3,300 fps	Rem. 7 ½
40-gr Barnes Varmin-A-Tor	A2460	27 grs	3,700fps	CCI 400
50-gr Speer TNT	W748	26.5 grs	3,200 fps	Same
50-gr Midway Dogtown	H4895	27 grs	3,300 fps	Same
*52-gr Nosler Match HP	H4895	25.5 grs	3,300 fps	Same

*(will expand on small varmints)

*52-gr Sierra BTHP	W748	27 grs	3,300 fps	Rem 7 ½ BR

*(5-shot, ½-inch, 200-yard groups)

Some of the author's most accurate .223 Rem. loads, left to right: 40-grain Hornady V-Max over 27.3 grains of Ramshot TAC, 40-grain Nosler Ballistic Tip and 22.5 grains H4198, 36-grain Barnes Varmint Grenade and 27 grains Benchmark, and 40-grain Cutting Edge Raptor and 27.7 grains W748.

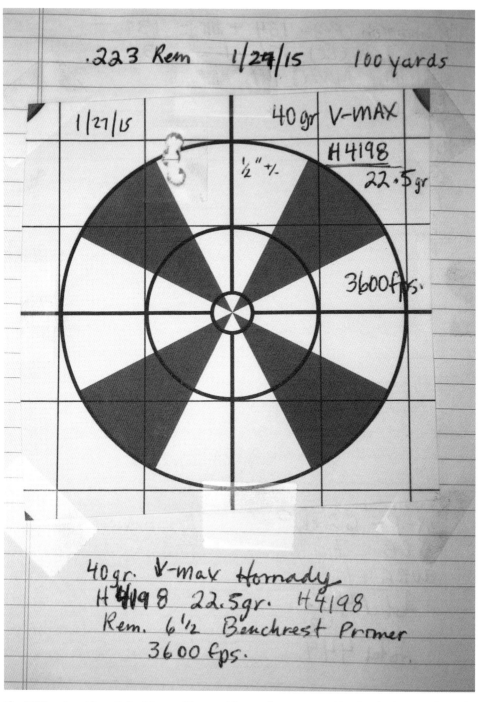

The .223 Rem. is an inherently forgiving cartridge, providing excellent accuracy with various loads. Here's the result of the author's preliminary test loads with H4198 and 40-grain polymer-tipped bullets.

PET LOADS, .223 REMINGTON

Quiet and accurate reduced-power loads for shooting near civilization, duplicating .22 LR and WMR ballistics. Note: Also excellent in T/C Contender pistols.

Bullet	Powder	Charge	Velocity	Primer
40-gr generic soft-point	IMR/H4895	16 grs	1,586 fps	Rem. 7 ½
*45-gr generic Hornet	SR4756	10.5 grs	1,800 fps	Same
*(1/4-inch, 100-yard groups).				
55-gr generic soft-point	Trail Boss	4 grs	1,074 fps	CCI 400
55-gr generic soft-point	Titegroup	3.1 grs	1,064 fps	Same

PET LOADS, .223 REM. AR, ROCK RIVER ARMS V4, 24-INCH BULL BARREL, 1:8 TWIST

Bullet	Powder	Charge	Velocity	Primer
50-gr Barnes Varmint Grenade	H322	24.5 grs	3,200 fps	CCI 400
50-gr Lead-Free Frangible/	W748	26 grs	3,200 fps	Same
55-gr Midsouth BTSP	CFE-223	27 grs	3,000 fps	Same

*(See sidebar below for ideas on viable .223 AR wild boar loads)

■ .22-250 Remington

I'm admittedly limited on what I can do with my .22-250, as its custom barrel holds the 1:14 rifling twist commonly given that cartridge. This became standard factory rifling early in the quest for speed, meaning it's suited only to the lightest bullets. My .22-250, for example, keyholes 50-grain Barnes Varmint Grenades at only 50 yards, a bullet requiring minimum 1:10 rifling to stabilize. I receive top-notch accuracy from 50-grain polymer-tipped and lead soft- and hollow-points from this rifle. My .22-250 is fairly picky, a trait of most 250s I think, and accuracy is realized only with spot-on powder loads and typically a limited number of bullet models. Vihta Vuori N-140, W760 and CFE-223 have emerged as my favorite 250 fuels.

PET LOADS, .22-250 REM., CUSTOM 98 MAUSER, 26-INCH CUSTOM BARREL

Bullet	Powder	Charge	Velocity	Primer
40-gr Hornady V-Max	N-140	37.8 grs	4,140 fps	CCI 200
50-gr Sierra BlitzKing	H4895	34.5 grs	3,725 fps	Same
x50-gr Speer Soft-Point	N-140	36 grs	3,680 fps	Same
x50-gr Sierra BlitzKing	CFE-223	39 grs	3,900 fps	Same

PET LOADS, .22-250 REM., MOSSBERG 800-CV, 26-INCH BARREL

Bullet	Powder	Charge	Velocity	Primer
40-gr Nosler Varmageddon HP	IMR3031	35.5	4,000+ fps	CCI 200
50-gr Midway Dogtown	H4895	34 grs	3,800 fps	Same
x52-gr Nosler HPBT	W760	41 grs (max+)	3,800 fps	Same

PET LOADS, .22-250 REM., MARLIN X-7 VH, 26-INCH BARREL

Bullet	Powder	Charge	Velocity	Primer
x40-gr Nosler Varmageddon HP	CFE-223	40 grs	4,000+ fps	CCI 200
40-gr Nosler Varmageddon HP	CFE-223	43 grs	4,300+ fps (max)	CCI 200
x(one-hole groups)				

The author's custom .22-250 caused many moments of hair pulling. This was the hectic start. He was just about to concede this was the best the rifle could do when he started making progress, finally finding combinations resulting in sub-½-inch groups.

■ .220 Swift

Enough time has passed since I owned a Swift that I've misplaced my handloading notes. Pity, as I had some nice loads worked up for that straight-shooting Ruger M77 Varmint, though I still recall the basic velocities I was working within for certain bullet weights. So for this listing, I'll rely on my father, who would rather shoot a ground squirrel than all the big game in North America and is a big fan of the .220 Swift. The Swift suffers the same fate as most .22-250s. It's rifled too slow (1:14 to 1:12) for bullets weighing much more than 50 to 55 grains, as manufacturers sought to break the magic 4,000 fps mark — an easier task today with the development of new powder formulas, such as N-140, and Hodgdon Extreme powders such as Varget.

PET LOADS, .220 SWIFT, RUGER M77 HAWKEYE VARMINT, 26-INCH BARREL

Bullet	Powder	Charge	Velocity	Primer
40-gr Sierra BlitzKing	H380	44 grs	4,150 fps	CCI 200
50-gr Hornady V-Max	Varget	36.5 grs	3,700 fps	Same
—	IMR4895	36.9 grs	3,900 fps	Same
—	IMR4350	42 grs	3,850 fps	ame
50-gr Speer TNT Green	RL-15	37 grs	3,800 fps	Federal 210
*52-gr Nosler Match HP	IMR4064	38.2 grs	3,900 fps	CCI 200

*(will expand on small varmints)

■ .243 Winchester

I loaded so many .243 Win. shells in my youth that my favorite 60-grain Sierra No. 1500 hollow-point load (see below) is permanently branded on my brain. H380 was my favorite then, with newer powders such as N-140 providing the medium-slow burn this round needs for maximum performance. As a small-varmint cartridge, the .243 is at its best with the lightest 6mm pills. Winchester was intuitive enough to understand this round would be used as a cross-over varmint/light big-game round and settled on a middle-ground 1:10 twist that became standard for rifles chambered in the cartridge (some Remington rifles include 1:9 twists), a good compromise for the light bullets we'll look at. The .243 is capable of top-rate accuracy across the board.

PET LOADS, .243 WIN., REMINGTON 700 ADL, 24-INCH BARREL

Bullet	Powder	Charge	Velocity	Primer
55-gr Nosler Ballistic Tip	Varget	45 grs	3,975 fps	CCI 200
55-gr Sierra BlitzKing	H4895	42 grs	3,850 fps	Same
58-gr Hornady V-Max	N-140	43 grs	3,700 fps	Same
*60-gr Sierra Varminter HP	H380	45 grs	3,525 fps	WSR
*The jackrabbit and prairie dog load of my youth and still a dandy.				
65-gr Hornady V-Max	RL-15	40.8 grs	3,550 fps	CCI 200
90-gr Sierra FMJ-BT	A4350	42 grs	2,900 fps	Same

PET LOADS, .243 WIN., T/C ENCORE RIFLE, 24-INCH BARREL

Bullet	Powder	Charge	Velocity	Primer
55-gr Nosler SP	H4895	40 grs	3,650 fps	CCI 200
70-gr Nosler Ballistic Tip	W760	45 grs	3,500 fps	Same
75-gr Hornady V-Max	Varget	40.5 grs	3,450 fps	Same

The .243 Win. is capable is extremely good accuracy and normally doesn't require a lot of tedious trial and error to get there. A 60-grain Sierra hollow-point over 45 grains of H380 was the author's favorite varmint load as a teen and remains viable today.

■ .257 Roberts

The .257 Roberts was loaded with 87-grain bullets on its introduction, looking, again, to break a velocity barrier marketing types believed would grab headlines — in this case, 3,000 fps. It just managed — some would argue it just missed — to hit that mark with the powders and rifle actions available at the time (1934). So, although the 87-grain benchmark might have missed the mark as a big-game rifle, it serves varminters well. With modern powders and actions built to handle +P loads, the Roberts delivers its best performance via reloading, as factory loads are normally pretty tame in diffidence to older guns. Larger case capacity means the .257 Roberts is seldom picky, relinquishing good accuracy with a wide variety of loads and bullets.

PET LOADS, .257 ROBERTS, MOSSBERG 800, 24-INCH CUSTOM BARREL

Bullet	Powder	Charge	Velocity	Primer
*60-gr Hornady Flat Point	H4898	44 grs	3,500 fps	CCI 200
*Mild-recoiling, moderate-range small-varmint load.				
70-gr Sierra BlitzKing 210M	RL-15	45 grs	3,225 fps	Federal
75-gr Hornady V-Max	H4350	48 grs	3,400 fps	CCI 200
87-gr Sierra #1610 Varminter	IMR4895	41.9 grs	3,350 fps (max)	CCI 200

■ .25-06 Remington

Though I consider this necked-down '06 a bit much for small varmints, I share varmint forays with friends who shoot little else (those obviously less recoil sensitive than I am) and prove murderous with it. I own a .25-06, a tack-driving Brown Precision a giddy client gifted me in my guiding days after tagging a Booner New Mexico elk. Friends borrow that Brown more often than I shoot it. It mostly languishes in the gun safe, occasionally coaxing me to work true varmint loads and give it the occasional workout. Although this .25-06 shoots one-hole groups with 117- and 120-grain pills, it supplies only minute-of-squirrel accuracy with the lightest .257 pills, likely a result of too-fast rifling overstabilizing those shorter bullets. Hence, I was forced to back off a tad to assemble better groups. This is the best I can do with what I have to work with, though accuracy improves with common 87-grain offerings.

PET LOADS, .25-06 REM., BROWN PRECISION RIFLE CIRCA 1985, 24-INCH BARREL

Bullet	Powder	Charge	Velocity	Primer
75-gr Hornady V-Max	W760	52 grs	3,400 fps	CCI 200
—	IMR 4350	53.5 grs	3,400 fps	Same
87-gr Sierra #1610 Varminter	IMR 4831	56 grs	3,375 fps	Same
100-gr Nosler Ballistic Tip	RL-22	58 grs	3,275 fps	Same
100-gr Speer HP	IMR4350	51 grs	3,150 fps	Same

The author considers the .25-'06 a bit much for small varmints — even long-range coyotes — but many of his shooting partners disagree. His rifle relinquishes its best accuracy with 117- and 120-grain bullets but shoots minute-of-squirrel with lighter 75- to 87-grain pills.

Hogs, AR-15s and the .223 Remington

The .223 Rem. is the modern do-it-all rifle, especially with the advent of more reliable controlled-expansion bullets. Many would argue the .223 isn't an ideal hog round, and I agree to a point, but it really comes down to shot placement, not brute force. Besides, the real misconception comes from the notion all wild hogs weigh 200-plus pounds and are intent on murdering you. Ninety percent of hogs you'll encounter weigh 90 to 125 pounds, and at the close ranges presented during nighttime shoots (in particular) or in wooded areas, precise shot placement is easy to achieve. The AR platform has made the .223 a popular hog rifle, the latest heavy/long-for-caliber bullets making this "varmint cartridge" deadlier on game up to hog (and deer) size.

From a bolt or single-shot, the obvious question is rifling twist, as longer projectiles require minimum 1:10 rifling twist to stabilize the lightest of those offerings, and most true varmint rifles in-

The author didn't find his .223 Rem. AR wanting on this blond Texas hog. He used 69-grain Rocky Mountain Reloading 3-Gun Hunter topping 25 grains of CFE-223 powder.

clude a 1:12 twist. Faster 1:8 to 1:7 twists are required to accurately shoot effective hog medicine, a common configuration in ARs.

In relation to wild hogs, ARs make ideal platforms, handling well and wearing rails necessary for popular nighttime hunting paraphernalia, such as rail-mount lasers, predator lights and night-vision or thermal-imaging optics, all of which are welcomed while operating in darkness. The light keeps you from stepping into holes or tripping over cactus and rattlesnakes while recovering downed hogs, with the laser zeroed point-blank should you arrive after tipping a hog over to discover a spine-shot beast thrashing and gnashing and requiring a from-the-hip coup de grace.

PET LOADS, WILD BOAR VERSION, CUSTOM AR-15, 20-INCH BARREL, 1:7 RIFLING TWIST

Bullet	Powder	Charge	Velocity	Primer
55-gr Cutting Edge Raptor FB	Ramshot TAC	25 grs	3,000 fps	CCI No.41
60-gr Nosler Partition	Benchmark	22.5 grs	2,880 fps	Same
62-gr Barnes TTSX BT	Varget	24.5 grs	2,900 fps	Same
65-gr Sierra SBT	Ramshot TAC	25 grs	2,880 fps	Same
69-gr RMR 3Gun Hunter	CFE-223	25 grs	2,900 fps	Same
70-gr Hornady GMX	CFE-223	22.5 grs	2,650 fps	Same

The .223 Rem. gets the job done on hogs with select handloads. Four bullets the author has used successfully, left to right: 55-grain Cutting Edge Raptor, Cutting Edge 65-grain MTH (Match/Tactical/Hunting), 65-grain Sierra SBT and 50-grain Hornady GMX.

⊕ Chapter 11
Pelt Shooting

While still a brace-faced, freckle-nosed, just-barely teen, I developed a burning obsession with predator calling. I read everything I could find regarding the subject (in those days, mostly Eastern magazine writers detailing red fox strategies) and spent much of my free time putting accumulated knowledge to the test. This newfound passion might have had something to do with the raw-fur market in the late 1970s and early '80s: plentiful and sometimes foolish gray foxes fetching $50 apiece; coyotes averaging $35 to $65, depending on color and fur thickness; bobcats starting at $175 and going up from there. For two years after my escape from the drudgery of high school and my parent's clutches, I made my way in the world trapping and calling predators, with a little big-game guiding tossed into the mix. The fur market held up well into my first couple of years of college, fluctuating wildly thereafter. So from my early teens into my mid-20s, and for a few years in the early 2000s, I spent lots of time shooting fur not for sport and relaxation but with a keen eye on profit margins. Today, that obsession continues, though decidedly for sport and all-important relaxation. But even during years when fur prices tank, I can't tolerate seeing a prime winter pelt go to waste (prime raw fur is always worth something). When fur prices bottom out, you won't make any money, but it can help pay for the gas burned while enjoying yourself — something that can't be said of other varmint shooting pursuits.

This is in no way meant to establish credentials but rather to illustrate that during several periods in my life, predator hunting served as a means to earn extra cash that let me buy expensive toys I wanted badly or, early on, keep a roof over my head and the lights on. That early urgency has never entirely left me, and even after I began to make a better living in many other ways, I've continued to approach varmint hunting with the same enthusiasm of my younger days. Where dead predators previously translated directly into dollars and cents, today they more often provide a welcomed respite from tedious toil.

Furbearers, such as this prime winter bobcat shot by Fred Eichler, are valuable commodities. Top prices don't go to hides with gaping holes blown through them. Handloading or careful ammo selection assures minimal pelt damage. Fred Eichler photo.

In those early days especially, that also meant that although hitting and recovering gray foxes, coyotes and bobcats was imperative to turning a profit, it was just as important that my bullets not inflict undue damage to valuable pelts. From the beginning, given a shot opportunity, killing varmints was easy enough using my familiar Remington 700 in .243 Win. — assuming I could hit them, which is another subject. But top fur prices don't go to pelts with fist-sized holes through their middles, and staying up late to tediously apply needle and thread to disguise the evidence cut into much-needed sleepy-time.

The continual challenge is to balance the need to drop predators in their tracks without shredding valuable pelts. This can prove hit and miss for shooters who depend on factory loads to feed their rifles, but a handloader can easily choose proper bullets and load recipes that get the job done without explosive results. It's important to point out that many mild-mannered cartridges — or reduced loads — assure minimal pelt damage, but there's no need to worry about shredding hides if you can't first hit them or, if you hit a predator, only to have it limp into the weeds where it won't be recovered. A .22 LR will kill a fox or bobcat hit just right and with zero damage — heck a coyote, as far as that goes. But you can't depend on the small rimfires to produce killing results every time. How about a .22 Mag.

Predator calling is the rare outdoor sport that can actually pay for itself. Predator Nation television host Fred Eichler poses with a season's take of fur — a collection representing a handsome payday. Fred Eichler photo.

To assure your bullets do not spoil prime fur, choosing the right cartridge or bullet for that cartridge is highly important. There are many ways to accomplish this, from no expansion to violent expansion that does not exit the animal. Fred Eichler photo.

or even the hot .17 rimfires? Again, when they hit just right, magnum rimfires will do the job (I've killed coyotes with my HMR, typically as targets of opportunity when no other weapon was available), but predator calling and hunting seldom offer ideals, with ranges stretching, targets fleeing, angles wrong, brush or grass intervening or darkness complicating extensive trailing.

Cartridge and load selection is dictated chiefly by terrain and vegetation density and how that influences shot ranges, and by the animals themselves — relatively delicate foxes and bobcats versus innately tough coyotes. At one end of the spectrum are Eastern red or gray foxes taken in wooded areas or on small farm fields, sometimes near civilization, where loud rifle cracks aren't appreciated (hey, I'm a gun guy, but don't embrace loud shooting in our rural neighborhood). At the other end of the gamut are Great Plains and Western coyotes in wide-open spaces where shots generally run longer and you'll disturb no one with the loudest, hottest varmint cartridges.

Come along as we investigate some of the insights I've gleaned after almost 40 years of hard-knocks experience.

SMALL VARMINT CARTRIDGES

During those lean years immediately after high school — when a dead coyote translated into cash to put toward truck fuel, rent and groceries, and a $400 high-country bobcat meant I was set for a month — my Savage 340 Series E .22 Hornet was the only rifle I used to collect fur. I invested in this inexpensive but fine-shooting rifle after too many monotonous evenings sewing the sporadic results of shooting 85- and 100-grain bullets from my love-worn .243 Win. The Hornet also had the obvious advantage of mild report, meaning when I called in multiple coyotes (or I missed), I typically received a second standing shot. The Hornet proved deadly on smaller predators such as gray foxes and bobcats at moderate ranges, even when marginally hit, but if I failed to plant bullets directly into the boiler room of a coyote, I typically had some tracking or a spirited chase ahead.

Initially, I fed that Savage 45-grain factory ammo fished from green-and-yellow boxes. Those soft-nosed bullets mushroomed well for knockdown kills and seldom produced exit wounds larger than a quarter, even after quartering-to shoulder hits so common on predators responding to calls. After accumulating enough brass, I purchased RCBS dies and began seating 45-grain Nosler Solid Base bullets atop 9.5 grains of Hodgdon H110 — pretty much the all-around standard Hornet load of the day. Never, other than basic sighting, did I print that load for groups, but it became my go-to varmint load and laid many predators to rest — by conservative estimates, a few hundred coyotes during a 20-year period. With that well-made bullet, now unfortunately discontinued, I could pretty much expect a nickel-sized exit wound every time I pulled the trigger, no matter which direction an animal faced.

I still shoot that battle-scarred Hornet regularly but seldom while calling predators. The .22 Hornet has a glaring issue, especially as a coyote rifle: It's a 200-yard cartridge, its maximum effective range on critters the size and tenacity of common predators. Sure, I've killed coyotes with my Hornet to 350 yards, only because I lived with that rifle and knew it well, but that's pushing the absolute limits of this archaic cartridge, especially while shooting squatty 45-grain bullets. On running shots, the .22 Hornet is maddening. I recall taking my Hornet on a December archery deer hunt on Colorado's Eastern Plains. The landowner related daily coyote sightings and didn't mind me taking pokes at them. He wasn't blowing smoke. I saw dozens of coyotes that week, all from the truck while coming and going. I killed one. All were well within range, but they were also running full tilt (the cowboy/landowner had been taking potshots at them with his .30-30 lever-gun while feeding cattle). I just couldn't hit them, leading them by five or six lengths but still coming up short, or more often, the dogs simply zigging instead of zagging. That's a big factor with leads that substantial.

More recently, I acquired a Savage 25 Walking Varmint in Hornady's sweet .17 Hornet, the company's variant of P.O. Ackley's wildcat of the 1950s. Loaded with 20-grain pills (the cartridge's optimal bullet), it's murderous on smaller varmints such as foxes and thin-skinned bobcats to 300 yards, if a little light for tougher coyotes. I have killed coyotes with my .17 Hornet and 20-grain bullets, but shot placement becomes hyper critical, and I suspect if I made a regular habit of it, I would eventually lose a dog or two. I might choose a 25- (Hornady V-Max) or 30-grain (Berger) bullet for added reliability, but then the cartridge's super-flat trajectory would be lost, sacrificing 500 to 750 fps in velocity and returning to

Small predators don't require a lot of killing, and further, powerful cartridges can inflict undue damage. The author took this Southwestern gray fox while shooting his love-worn .22 Hornet — a round perfect for smaller foxes and bobcats shot at moderate ranges.

a .22 Hornet pace. Again, ballistics perfectly suited to Eastern predator calling fields where ranges are shorter, but a recipe for disappointment on the Plains or Out West.

Besides the Hornets, the most obvious choices in mild-mannered predator cartridges are the .222 and .223 Remingtons. Of these, the .223 emerged as the undisputed winner in the sometimes logic-defying popularity contest determining which cartridges whither on the vine and which are accepted and flourish. The .223 is, of course, the U.S. military's cartridge of choice, making reloading brass super abundant and factory ammo highly affordable. I've shot plenty of coyotes with the .223 and find it a happy medium of affordable reloading (it uses half the powder of larger .224 rounds, a real consideration in the days of intermittent component shortages), relatively flat trajectory, mild recoil and report, and adequate knockdown energy to 300 or 350 yards. The standard load of a 55-grain bullet pushed to about 3,000 fps has accounted for untold numbers of dead 'yotes, using standard soft-nose bullets and full metal jackets (see the sidebar "A Case For FMJs") and seldom seeing an exit wound larger than a half-dollar.

I've also pressed my standard small-varmint loads into service: 36-grain Barnes Varmint Grenades and 40-grain polymer-tipped pills pushed to maximum velocities — 27 grains of Hodgdon Benchmark launching VGs to 3,700 fps and producing sub-1-inch groups, and 27.7 grains of Ramshot TAC producing slightly slower velocities but one-hole groups from my customized Savage 110. Note: Those are pretty hot numbers and should be approached with caution. During ideal conditions — broadside shots — those highly frangible bullets combined with such velocities result in bullet noses blowing away on impact, imparting maximum shock and knockdown energy, the base occasionally exiting to create dime-sized holes, and bullets more often failing to exit. That would be considered model performance. The problem is that such loads also occasionally create nasty gaping holes on raking, quartering-to or quartering-away shots, especially after encountering a shoulder or hip point. They're coyote killers and too much of a good thing for

The trick when shooting fur is choosing a cartridge balance with enough energy to put predators down convincingly but that shoots flat enough to hit them initially, without shredding hides. This obviously involves compromises.

smaller predators such as foxes and bobcats, but they will eventually result in damaged pelts.

A safer .223 coyote killer discovered recently is Cutting Edge Bullet's 40-grain (50 grains also offered) RS Raptor. These are precision milled-brass pills with deep hollow-point recess holding a prominent snap-in polymer top. What makes them unique, other than being milled from solid brass, is the large hollow point is scored internally, causing the tip to break off into four segments on impact. These segments act like tiny razors — cutting edges — that shred lungs but seldom exit, the solid base punching through and creating an exit wound slightly larger than .22 caliber. Cutting Edge bullets are match-grade accurate but cost more than standard-issue projectiles. They're also somewhat long for caliber, but milled grooves, which reduce friction and eliminate pressure spikes, mean they can be loaded using standard for-weight data. The 50-grain version requires minimal 1:10 rifling.

THE NEED FOR SPEED

Raw speed holds many attractions and real-world advantages while predator hunting, especially when shooting shifty coyotes in wide-open habitats. Although I've shot darned few — or maybe no — foxes or bobcats beyond 150 yards (most well within that range), coyotes are a different beast, especially in areas with the smallest amount of hunting pressure, which can include seemingly innocuous shooting such as ranchers sniping at them from pickup windows with often inadequate ranch rifles (like that Colorado landowner's .30-30 lever-gun). While predator calling, it isn't uncommon for coyotes to hang up at 350 to 400 yards

The Case For FMJs

Many serious varmint hunters forsake full metal jackets, believing they're ineffective on predators, especially tougher coyotes. Don't believe it. I've shot many coyotes with inexpensive 55-grain FMJ military ball ammo, especially after first acquiring a .223 Rem. and building my brass collection for handloading. Almost all rolled over on the spot. None were lost because of the nonexpanding bullets. Obviously, those shots resulted in minimal pelt damage, though holes are normally larger than .224, pushing fur and bone before them.

Military-surplus ball and bargain-priced FMJ ammunition is abundant in .223 Rem., as well as .308 Win. and .30-'06 Springfield, the latter welcomed for those who own a good deer rifle with which they want to shoot the occasional predator—though understand there will be additional recoil and noise to endure.

The reloading buff has a few options, but surprisingly not the endless supply offered by conventional designs, as true FMJs are rare outside .224 and .308 dimensions. Hornady offers FMJs in 55- and 62-grain

From the .223 Rem./5.56mm NATO, FMJ ammo is quite common and usually inexpensive. It makes perfectly acceptable predator-calling fodder, and knocks coyotes down convincingly.

.22-caliber, and 110-, 125- and 150-grain in .30-caliber (174-grain in .303). Sierra has a 90-grain 6mm, which I used extensively when younger, and 110 round nose and 150 FMJBT for .308. And that's pretty much it.

In the case of .257, .264/6.5mm, .277 (.270 Win.) and .284/7mm, which are common big-game calibers, the lack of true FMJs can often be substituted with target/match bullets, such as the Sierra MatchKing, Berger Target, Cutting Edge MTAC or Hornady Match, which typically perform much like FMJs on light-framed targets such as predators, especially at longer ranges and the slower velocities resulting. There are exceptions, especially when velocities exceed about 3,300 fps, so it's a good idea to test models and brands on something like a block of modeling clay or a jackrabbit before trusting

For the predator caller who wants to use a familiar deer rifle, full metal jackets or tough controlled-expansion bullets make a good choice. Tom Drumme used an all-copper Barnes X to shoot this 'yote with a .25-'06 Rem.

them on valuable predator hides. If they push through without explosive results, you're good to go. If they turn such targets inside out, you can bet the results on fur won't be pretty. You can purchase relatively cheap bulk .224- and .308-caliber FMJ bullets from discount outfits such as Rocky Mountain Reloading, and many are rugged military-contract pills.

One alternative to straight full metal jackets are quality controlled-expansion, mono-metal bullets designed for big game. Prime examples include, left to right: 50-grain Hornady GMX, 50-grain Cutting Edge Raptor and 55-grain Cutting Edge MTH (Match/Target/Hunting).

after approaching a meadow or clearcut edge, surveying the situation endlessly. A heavier pill pushed on a flatter trajectory is more likely to stay the course at such ranges, especially in even moderately breezy conditions.

And running shots are all too common on Wily Coyote. The difference between a 3,000- and 3,600-fps round is holding on a coyote's head or shoulder (depending on range) instead of at the open space before a quickly departing dog. Those velocity examples are also at actual range, not misleading muzzle velocities, remembering also that a heavier bullet with superior sectional density maintains velocity over a longer distance than lighter, stumpy bullets. And let's face it, in prime Western habitats, incidental shots at coyotes spotted from the vehicle while driving between calling spots or conducting other business are always running and often at extreme distances. Honestly, I'll always shoot at such coyotes until they're out of sight, holding them in the bottom of the scope if that is what's required. This might also be why some of my most impressive shots have been on coyotes. Passing any shot at any coyote (when and where legal, of course) isn't an option, a sentiment shared by many Western acquaintances. Another ugly reality: Faster, heavier bullets provide better odds of anchoring such dodgy dogs after marginal hits.

When talk turns to speedy predator rounds, you can bet the wildly popular .22-250 Rem. and venerable .220 Swift will dominate discussions, with the odd .224 Weatherby Mag. or .223 Win. Super Short Magnum tossed into the mix by those who gravitate to novelties. The '250 and Swift can push 50- to 55-grain bullets 3,600 to 3,800 fps, with modern powders such as Hodgdon's Varget and CFE-223, Accurate's 2520, Alliant's RL-15 and Vihta Vouri's N-140 helping move things along. I owned a Ruger M77 in .220 Swift for years and now have a custom .22-250 Rem., and these cartridges accounted for a couple of pickup loads of prairie yodelers. I've also accumulated a lot of painful lessons in the process. The first was that most factory ammunition reaps havoc on fur from these hopped-up rounds, especially when bullets find bone.

In my Swift, I found a solution by pushing a 52-grain Nosler Solid Base at about 3,850 fps, using H380 when it was a more fashionable propellant than it is today. The nose was shed on impact, with just the solid base exiting in a neat little .224-caliber hole most of the time. That bullet is no longer available, but newer controlled-expansion models — such as the Barnes 45-, 50-, 53- and 55-grain TSX FB (hollow-points); 50- and 55-grain TTSX FB (polymer-tipped); 55-grain TAC-X; 50- and 55-grain Hornady GMX (tipped); and Nosler 55-grain E-Tip — offer superior substitutes, with solid copper construction peeling to a solid core and expansion checked there. Early in Barnes' X-bullet development, some pressure spikes were witnessed because of the longer bearing surface, but milled groves quickly remedied the situation. One remaining issue is because copper is lighter than lead, standard bullet weights include long-for-caliber profiles (and excellent ballistic coefficients) that can cause stabilization issues in older rifles with slower 1:14 to 1:12 rifling twists.

I've tried the scorching-hot .17 Rem. for predator hunting, but results remained too sporadic to remain a loyal fan. Loaded too hot, they frequently splattered on hide without penetration, and wind really does a number on them. Bullets designed for the hot .17s are typically made to turn smaller game such as ground squirrels and prairie dogs to mush, which is where these cartridges shine. For coyotes, not so much.

Even if you aren't paying bills by collecting predators with your rifle, fur prices are bound to climb again, and there's no reason to waste a prime pelt because you're just out to have some sport. Many buyers are happy to buy fur "on the carcass," though skinning and stretching fur — a fairly simple task for which there's a plethora of how-to information available — will typically fetch the highest prices and let you offset the cost of fuel while enjoying one of hunting's most exciting pastimes.

Calling in wide-open farm country where shots are generally longer and coyotes often running, the author choose a flat-shooting .204 Ruger and fast 32-grain bullets. Such rounds minimize holdover and leads on runners.

Don't Forget Scatterguns

Many predator hunters fail to consider magnum shotguns as deadly varmint tools, especially in brushy or wooded areas where range is generally limited or with cooperative coyotes desperate for a meal during cold winter months. In my predator calling tournament days, I regularly toted a shotgun and rifle into each calling stand, holding the shotgun in my lap to address close-range predators (especially winter coyotes arriving in packs), the rifle leaned against a tree or set within easy reach for those that refused to meet me halfway or escaped an opening fusillade of scattergun pellets. And of course, while calling predators at night and shooting with the aid of

In wooded or brushy habitats, using your favorite scattergun while calling predators is viable. Load up with 3- or 3 ½-inch magnum lead BBs (preferred) or Hevi-Shot T-shot, and keep shots less than 55 yards.

a handheld spotlight or weapons light (where legal, obviously), a magnum shotgun roughly correlates to the effective range of most light systems.

A 3- or 3 ½-inch chambered 12-gauge is obviously suggested (a 10-gauge not overkill, but appropriate shells are almost impossible to secure without handloading). The mistake most predator hunters make is choosing shot sizes that are too big — I suspect because many manufacturers push larger shot in coyote-labeled shotshells, obviously never

having conducted extensive testing on the real deal. The basic rule of thumb is to avoid anything that includes the word "buck" on the label. Believe me, I've had too many predators run right through shot patterns unscathed because of low pellet counts or, worse, rolled them up only to have them recover and escape wounded, likely gut shot and destined to suffer a lingering death. You want lead or heavier-than-lead Hevi-Shot in BB. End of list.

Even with 1970s-era 3-inch lead BBs (great strides have since been made in shotshell technology, mostly improved wads that produce tighter patterns), I regularly rolled even tough mountain coyotes at 50 to 55 yards with a full-choked Remington 1100. Custom screw-in choke tubes are another huge advancement, with smart engineering providing tighter patterns and extended ranges, often as much as 5 or 10 yards, which is substantial while shooting predators with scatterguns.

In the age of nontoxic shot, finding genuine predator shells filling this order isn't as simple as it once was. Winchester offers Varmint X 3-inch 12-gauge loaded with 1.5 ounces of lead BBs, Hornady Heavy Magnum Coyote comes in 3-inch 12-gauge with the same load of lead BBs pushed to 1,300 fps. If you need them, order a case, as this is becoming a rare commodity. Hevi-Shot gets close with Dead Coyote 12-gauge 3.5-inch 1.625-ounce T shot, the extra half-inch boosting pellet count and making it an acceptable alternative.

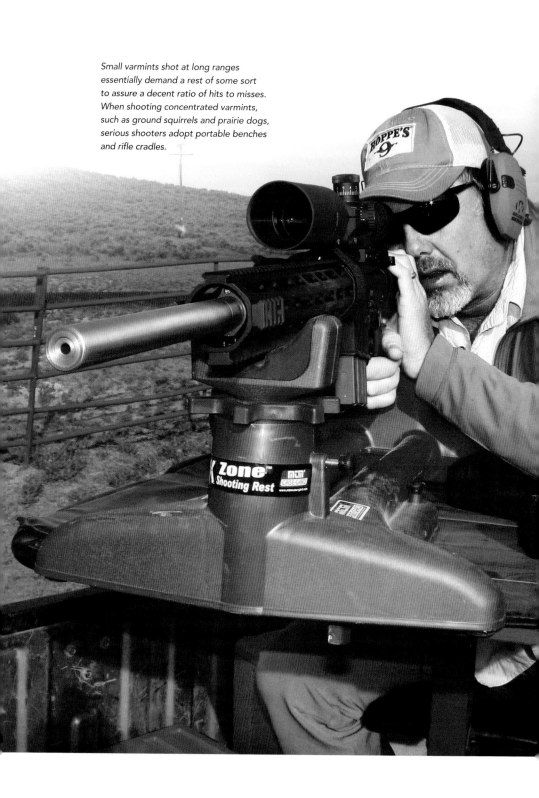

Small varmints shot at long ranges essentially demand a rest of some sort to assure a decent ratio of hits to misses. When shooting concentrated varmints, such as ground squirrels and prairie dogs, serious shooters adopt portable benches and rifle cradles.

⊕ Chapter 12
Give It A Rest

In certain circles, much is made of offhand shooting skills, but when it comes to actual nut cutting, only the foolhardy take important or long shots without a rest. Even the classic sling-wrap sitting position is better left to big-game hunters than targets in the small-varmint class. For our purposes, important shots are those directed at sometimes-valuable furbearing predators or maybe a hog for the freezer. Long indicates anything beyond the effective range of the .22 LR, which is commonly shot offhand, even while targeting small varmints. Admittedly, I have a blast burning .22 LR shells on running shots at small critters, shooting offhand within respective range limitations.

Still, serious varmint shooting and predator calling success requires your best effort, and that comes only by carefully steadying your weapon via a solid rest. If you're content taking only shots within 100 yards, shooting offhand is dandy. The rest of us likely want to shoot a bit farther — often a lot farther. And the longer ranges stretch, the smaller targets shrink and the more sophisticated rest systems generally become.

MOBILE RESTS

Any time I call predators, I'm typically carrying shooting sticks. While living in the Southwest, friends and I fashioned excellent shooting sticks from the straight, light-but-stout stocks of soltol cactus. Naturally, outdoors manufactures have developed better mousetraps in this arena; highly portable shooting sticks that prove more convenient, including rubber-padded V cradles to accept rifle forends. These might include simple monopods, which double as walking sticks in rough terrain, or bipod and tripod arrangements that allow increased steadiness. All include telescoping/collapsing designs for easier carrying and storage, but quick deployment and adjustable height for sitting, kneeling or standing shots. Primos' Trigger Sticks serve as the prototype example, with

Predator callers and roving varmint shooters can fashion viable shooting sticks easily with any straight sticks and a bit of twine. The author made his own shooting sticks from lightweight soltol cactus stalks and a leather thong.

models offered in various heights for sitting or standing, and locking/adjustable legs controlled by a spring-loaded trigger. They're available in a 33- to 65-inch-high monopod, a 24- to 61-inch bipod and an 18- to 38-inch tripod.

Other designs include simpler lever- or twist-lock mechanisms for height adjustment, with legs that manually pull to length or return to storage length. Such sticks are common, less costly and generally lighter. Examples include a dozen or more models from Bog-Pod. Quick examples include the mono Q-Stick, which extends 29.5 to 68 inches in three sections; bipod and tripod models in the RLD and CLD Series; the CLD-3S Short Tripod, which allows height adjustments from 42 inches for standing shots to a squat 6 inches for prone; plus the HD, TAC, SB and SB-2C Series. Common features include cushioned grips, padded V cradles to hold firearms securely, a 22-inch minimum length for shooting while sitting and a 68-inch maximum height for standing shots. Switch-E-Roo heads allow swapping out cushioned T rails, V cradles, camera mounts or compass heads when using monopods as walking sticks.

Caldwell takes this concept farther with its Deadshot FieldPods, including solid tripod bases with fully adjustable legs combined with a tubular T-top assembly holding front and rear rifle cradles. Standard, Max and Magnum models are offered, allowing standing, sitting or prone positions via 20- to 42-inch height adjustments and swiveling tops for fast target acquisition. They collapse to only 30 inches for easy storage and transport.

While predator calling, in particular, any of these portable products allow steadier shooting at the moment of truth and a way to hold your weapon at ready with less movement while getting into the gun before a shot.

GUN-MOUNTED BIPODS

Gun-mounted bipods are nifty. The best are light enough to hardly be noticed, and all fold parallel to the barrel when not in use or when shooting from a rest, locked into the shooting position by swiveling legs 90 degrees, an indent and stout springs or spring-loaded button holding them steady. They typically include individual height adjustments to accommodate uneven ground, and lengths permitting shooting prone or seated (with a small sandbag under the stock toe), or from a log, boulder or vehicle hood. Harris Bipods are the original and often imitated. They attach to standard front sling-swivel studs, the bipod base including

Commercial shooting sticks are common and a great asset to steadier shooting. Here, the author uses Primos'
Trigger Stiks while shooting prairie dogs in Wyoming. They aren't as steady as a bench, but they're highly portable.

Going prone while shooting off a rifle-attached bipod offers a high degree of stability — including enough precision for elite military snipers. Folding spring-loaded models like those from Harris are most practical in the field.

its own sling mount. All-steel construction and spring-loaded leg extensions with nonskid rubber feet make them the firebrand in this design. Knurled finger knobs allow locking single legs to length to accommodate uneven or sloping ground. Harris offers solid-mount or swiveling-head models.

Truglo offers the similar Tac-Pod in 6 to 9 inches for prone shooting and 9 to 13 inches for shooting while seated. They also mount to the front sling-swivel stud or, for AR-type rifles, the provided Picatinny rail sling-stud adaptor. The pivoting base allows leveling the rifle on uneven surfaces. Caldwell also offers XLA Bipods for standard and Picatinny rail AR attachment, the former with a swivel-head option.

The Swagger All-Terrain Bipod is a unique twist on the weapons-attached bipod. Crazy Legs Technology includes strong, flexible springs in leg bases that can be twisted to reasonable positions without sacrificing stability. The system can be used while sitting or from the prone position, and it self-adjusts while leaning forward, back, left or right, its three-section twist-lock legs extending to 29.25 inches. Swagger Bipods let you react more fluidly to developing shot opportunities without the need to adjust leg height. They can also be switched to a traditional rigid bipod with the push of a button. When not in use, the dual legs retract into the stock-mounted chassis for convenient, quiet transport.

These are just examples, and in many situations, they're an improvement on shooting-stick options, whether calling predators or picking off small varmints in remote locations. A couple of quick notes: When shooting off bipods, push forward into the bipod slightly to assure the steadiest rest possible, and when shooting at long range, always check zero while shooting off bipods, as they can alter rifle harmonics and impact slightly. Shooting prone off a short bipod is one of the steadiest shooting positions possible, but it can prove problematic in high grass or brushy areas.

MAKESHIFT FIELD RESTS

When I was guiding big-game hunters, finding a steady rest for my clients was just as important as how far a shot I could set up after locating trophy game. I would rather have a rattled client shoot 100 yards farther atop a solid natural rest than move closer and to a position where no rest was available. A varmint shooter or predator hunter often has the opportunity to take advantage of natural rests. In farm country typical of small-varmint settings, such as ground squirrels or woodchucks, parked or abandoned farm equipment sometimes provides that steady base. While predator calling, I try to set up beside a boulder or behind a low horizontal tree branch when possible, assuring a steady shooting base. In

Large, grounded objects are almost always steadier than legged props. When convenient, seek a large rock, stump, fence post or parked farm equipment, like shown here. A wadded jacket or sandbag makes these improvised rests even better.

prairie dog towns, an exceptionally tall mound or a line of fence posts provides welcome rests. Before I start shooting, I always look around to see if such an object is available. Rooted objects simply offer added stability.

Depending on the type of rest offered, I might toss a daypack of gear atop this object or place a rolled jacket, range bag, binocular case, pair of insulated gloves or just my hand. Firearms tend to push away from hard objects upon firing, often pulling shots off slightly. A little padding absorbs this bounce and assures shots stay on the mark. You'll likely encounter these improvised rests in predator shooting scenarios, where no two setups are alike and making do becomes standard operating procedure.

TRAVELING SHOOTING RANGES

In many cases, while tooling about varmint grounds in a vehicle, your truck or SUV provides an obvious shooting base, and these rules still apply. Though a truck hood (near-ideal chest height), truck roof (while standing in the bed for improved elevation), bed-box corner or even an opened tailgate provides the base, a simple gun rest serves as cushion for steadier holds. I'm thinking of products such as MTM Case-Gard's Quick Rest, a one-piece molded-plastic pylon with a padded top and nonmarring, nonskid bases, or Caldwell's molded-plastic Handy Rest NXT or heavier metal The Rock series rests with screw-adjustable height. Bog-Pod's Rapid Shooting Rest is another good one. It's a light, folding tripod offering 7 to 11 inches of height adjustment, rubberized feet and a swiveling rubber-padded V cradle. Simple sandbags are another standard in these situations and should always be kept on hand. I regularly use sandbags wedged into a rear-view mirror frame or atop a window edge while shooting pistols from the vehicle.

In many small-varmint settings, you'll likely park and stay a while, setting up for prolonged and often high-volume shooting. This allows transporting heavier or more sophisticated rest systems. Sandbags have long served as rock-solid bases, and that approach is as sound as it has ever been. Caldwell and Lyman are standard bearers, offering shooting bags large and small and for many specialized situations. I like a two-bag rifle system; larger up front to hold the stock forend (never rest a rifle on the barrel, as sporadic accuracy will result) and smaller behind to pad and level the stock. Standard, Medium and Magnum Rear Shooting Bags with rabbit-ear cradles are also offered for more versatility. Caldwell Deadshot Shooting Bags, for example, offer V center cradles up front, a smaller rabbit-eared bag supporting the stock from behind, with higher AR-specific models accommodating extended magazines and pistol grips.

Specialized bags include Caldwell's Tack Driver Shooting Rest, or Lyman Match, which are longer, heavier bags with H-like cross-sections, offering a degree of height adjustment or flattening against a solid base for wider support. The top channel better cradles a rifle for increased steadiness. The Caldwell Hunter's Blind Bag is made to drape over a blind or stand rail, even including laces to tie it in

Sandbags have been serving shooters well for decades. Set atop a solid object or even a pickup hood, this is an easy way to set up a rock-solid rest. Here, the author's father snipes Wyoming prairie dogs with his .17 Fireball from the pickup hood.

place, but it also serves well set over a partly opened vehicle window or door edge. Lyman's Bag Jack is another worthwhile investment; a compact, micro-adjustable scissor jack with a rubber-footed base and flattop designed to hold a Lyman Match Bag. Height is regulated precisely through an adjustment knob.

During the past couple of years, I've begun to rely more on portable rifle cradles for straighter rifle shooting. MTM Case-Gard's, MTM Predator and K-Zone Shooting Rests are models I'm most familiar with, including lightweight molded-plastic construction, a rear padded stock slot and star-nut/threaded-stem height adjustment of the padded front cradle. They're steady enough that I regularly use them atop my pickup hood to zero scopes and have produced one-hole groups from rifles nestled into them during load testing. There are a lot of other options in this area, some with built-in compartments to stash accumulating brass during high-volume shoots.

And though these highly portable models serve me well, companies such as Caldwell and Tipton take things to the next level. Caldwell offers its well-known Lead Sleds, with heavier metal construction and a closed-end rear cradle to contain the rifle butt. Sandbags (or bags of lead shot) are added to a lower tray to boost mass and help reduce felt recoil. Other hugely adjustable metal-construction shooting cradles include Caldwell's Stinger and Zeromax Shooting Rests, and a line of cutting-edge Hyskore options.

A cleverly designed rifle cradle, such as this Nitro Force-SR-1 SmartRest from LimbSaver, offers more control and comfortable shooting. It's at home on a portable bench or pickup tailgate, hood or roof while standing in the bed.

BENCHREST ACCURACY

In high-volume ground squirrel or prairie dog fields, I usually opt for the unsurpassed accuracy provided by a portable shooting bench, typically in conjunction with one of the rest options already discussed. My father regularly uses MTM's simple folding Predator Shooting Table, sitting behind it in a comfortable lawn chair. Newer to the scene, MTM introduced the High-Low Shooting Table in 2017. It's adjustable to allow shooting while standing or sitting. Caldwell offers the Stable Table Deluxe Shooting Bench, and Hyskore has the all-steel Portable Shooting Bench.

Muddy Outdoors' Swivel Action bench has become my favorite, as it accommodates the search-and-destroy approach I prefer, swiveling slowly, seeking targets through high-magnification scopes. It also allows quicker reaction to targets appearing on 360-degree fronts. The Muddy Swivel Action includes a flat seat and the Xtreme backrest seat, each including all-steel construction, weighing about 35 pounds. It has stable tripod legs and generous vinyl-covered top and side pockets to hold spent brass or water bottles. It's rock solid, folds flat for easy transport and assembles in seconds. Caldwell offers a similar bench, the BR Pivot Premium Shooting Bench, with a padded seat, independent or unified top/seat rotation, level-adjustable tripod legs and an offset school-desk hardwood top convertible for left- or right-hand shooters.

BenchMaster's Perfect Shot Shooting Chair is another interesting development in portable rests. It includes a comfortable powder-coated-steel, 360-degree-swiveling folding lounge chair holding a height-length adjustable swing-arm with a rubber V rest to support your rifle. The multi-position legs and large foot pads accommodate uneven terrain. It folds flat, reclines to 50 degrees and includes attached backpack straps for easy transport into off-road areas. Set on a rise or field corner or in an elevated pickup bed, any of these portable options provide comfortable and rock-steady shooting.

No matter what rest you use, a few basic fundamentals apply. Always position yourself directly behind your rifle, especially when shooting rifles with muzzle brakes. This assures your rifle moves the same each time during recoil for maximum accuracy and curtails muzzle-brake pull-off. Always work to maintain a natural point of aim — normally indicated by a crisp, edge-to-edge scope view — and minimize muscle involvement as much as possible, which decreases the affects of heartbeats and pulse surges. Finally, time trigger squeezes during respiratory pauses, between full inhale and full exhale, and follow through after every shot, waiting for impact before releasing concentration. Follow these rules and use a solid rest, and your hit-to-miss ratio will increase dramatically.

A folding/portable shooting bench in conjunction with a rifle cradle or large sandbag is the way to go while shooting at expansive colonies of small varmints such as ground squirrels or prairie dogs.

Serious Pistol Rests

Nowhere is the need for a steady rest more absolute than while shooting varmint pistols. This isn't a cowboy western, and even nasty little cannibalistic ground squirrels deserve your best shot. Long-range scoped pistols aren't designed for offhand shooting in any form. A large sandbag with a pair of leather gloves acting as a wrist rest makes a basic but suitable pistol rest. But be aware that high-pressure revolver cylinders, such as my Taurus Raging Hornet in .22 Hornet, can burn or blow holes through synthetic bags. A tough leather bag such as BenchMaster's American Bison shooting bag shrugs off cylinder leakage. Even while shooting a dot-scoped autoloader .22 LR, a V-top monopod or bipod shooting stick allows more effective marksmanship.

Better options come from MTM and Caldwell. Those MTM Predator and K-Zone and Caldwell Matrix shooting rests discussed in the main body of this chapter include removable rear assemblies, providing height-adjustable padded cradles with a comfortable wrist rest. The MTM Pistol Rest includes a forked top cradle and sliding block that can be positioned for 20 angles and heights, plus a padded wrist platform. The unit stores inside its own compact base. Caldwell offers a similar Pistolero rest, with oversized nut-and-bolt padded-cradle height adjustment (5 inches horizontal) and 3 inches of vertical adjustment, plus a raised/padded wrist/grip pad. Caldwell's height-adjustable, tripod-legged Handy Rest NXT also comes with a removable handgun wrist support.

While shooting from a portable bench, it's difficult to beat Hyskore's Parallax and Swivel Pistol Rests, the former including two-point level-ing, integral level and solid welded-steel construction, the latter with 120-degree movement and low profile for full arm extension. Another unique pistol-perfect rest is the LockedOn360, which in-cludes a channeled cradle with Velcro-strap lock-downs. Used in combination with Nikon's optics window-mount (or tripod), it pro-vides a rock-steady T/C Contender rest while shooting from the truck.

Long-range varmint pistols demand a solid rest. Many of MTM Case-Gard's rifle cradles can be converted into pistol rests by removing the rear section. Set atop MTM's High-Low Shooting Table, they allow comfortable, controlled handgun shooting.

⊕ Chapter 13
Long-Range Primer

Extreme long-range shooting is all the rage among many shooters today. Ask about a big-game season and you'll now get reports related in hundreds of yards or meters and not inches of antler. Long range meant something different when I was young and shooting out-of-the box rifles and standard big-game scopes. But modern technology and more readily available information have made longer shots well within reach of more shooters — and also more ethical. There's much more to long-range shooting than simply taking ridiculously long shots. Accumulated knowledge and careful attention to seemingly minor details is the name of the game.

LONG-RANGE REALITIES

Long is relative. For some, this means 400 to 500 yards on tiny ground squirrels. For others, this means much longer shots on larger game such as hogs. The 1,000-yard mark seems to represent the layman shooter's Holy Grail. This relativity also hinges on cartridge choice. I have a lot of fun with my .17s, in HMR and Hornet and equipped with high-power turret scopes. It seems customary in outdoor literature to minimize range capabilities of any cartridge. Based on such reports, you'd be inclined to believe the .17 HMR is a 150-yard rifle and the .17 Hornet is maybe good to 200 yards. In fact, I deliberately hit ground squirrels with my .17s at nearly double those ranges. I didn't say it was easy, any more than shooting big game at 1,000-plus yards with a .338 Lapua is easy.

CARTRIDGE CAPABILITIES

Cartridge choice really depends on how far you want to push things and the conditions in which you're generally shooting, as well as what you're shooting at (ground squirrels versus hogs). You don't need much of a hammer to thump ground squirrels, but a distant coyote requires some degree of oomph. You can see where this is going in regard to tougher hogs.

LEFT: *Long range is relative to target and conditions. The author shot this 10-pound Idaho rockchuck at 472 yards in a 12-mph crosswind and bullets with low ballistic coefficient — an impressive shot for the conditions.*

Long-range rounds and bullets, left to right, rear: .243 Win., 103-grain Hornady ELD-X; 6.5 Grendel, 130-grain Swift Scirocco; 6.5 Creedmoor, 120-grain Federal Trophy Copper; 6.5-284, 140-grain Sierra SBT; .270 Win., 150-grain Barnes TSX; 7mm-08 Rem., 169-grain Barnes TSX; 7mm Rem. Mag., 175-grain Hornady InterLock; 7mm STW, 175-grain ELD-X; and .338 Lapua, 285-grain Barnes TSX. Left to right, front: 6mm 110-grain Sierra MatchKing, 6.5mm Swift Scirocco, 6.5mm 142-grain Sierra MatchKing, .270 150-grain Barnes TSX, 7mm 168-grain Sierra MatchKing, 7mm 175-grain Sierra SBT and 285-grain Barnes TSX.

A general rule of thumb holds that a cartridge's maximum effective range is the distance at which bullets maintain supersonic velocities. When bullet velocities decrease to slower than about 1,100 fps, assuming subsonic (Mach 1) velocities, accuracy generally deteriorates. This varies according to muzzle velocity, but more important, a projectile's ballistic coefficient. Discovering these numbers requires consulting online ballistic charts, but here are some quick varmint-round examples: The .223 Rem. shooting a standard-issue 55-grain FMJ bullet has a BC of .250 and maintains 1,200 fps to about 600 yards, and a .223 68-grain Sierra MatchKing BTHP with a BC of .355 doesn't slow to Mach 1 until about 800 yards. By comparison, a .243 Win. shooting a 105-grain Hornady A-Max with a .500 BC doesn't go trans-sonic until about 1,100 yards.

BC is the index of how bullets decelerate in flight and also affects factors such as wind drift. Wind drift has everything to do with speed and nothing to do with mass, as light and heavy bullets are affected equally by wind push. High-BC bullets — whether a 40-grain .204-caliber or 200-grain .308 — drift less because they retain downrange velocity longer. BC changes with velocity, so it isn't a constant but rather more of an average during the entire flight path of a bullet at a given range. High BC should not be confused with inherent accuracy potential. High BC lets a bullet to slip through atmosphere more efficiently, but bullets with low BC can be quite accurate within respective range capabilities. They just won't carry velocity as well at extreme ranges.

Back to our earlier examples, at 500 yards and subjected to a 10 mph crosswind, that 55-grain .223 bullet drifts 17.1 inches, the 68-grain bullet only 5.6

inches and the 105-grain 6mm pill a scant 3.7 inches. In general terms, the best long-range projectiles possess BC numbers of .450 to .500 or higher. A BC of 1.00 is considered "perfect." Manufacturers generally supply BC numbers in catalogs or websites.

Another important factor: How long does your chosen cartridge/bullet retain energy sufficient to cleanly kill the targeted animal? This isn't important when shooting small varmints, but it's slightly more important when targeting tougher predators. However, it's vitally important with hog-sized game. With hogs, I'd call 500-foot pounds of retained energy minimal (at actual range).

Again, you'll need to study ballistics charts carefully. You'll likely encounter some surprises. That 68-grain BTHP .223 bullet that looked so good before produces only 437 foot-pounds of energy at 500 yards, nixing it for hogs at that range. Conversely, the 105-grain A-Max from the .243 Win. retains 942 foot-pounds at 500 yards. Now get this: The 7mm Rem. Mag. shooting a 162-grain A-Max with a BC of .625 retains 877 foot-pounds of energy at 1,700 yards. The more powerful .300 Win. Mag., shooting a heavier 180-grain A-Max with .495 BC, retains only 670 foot-pounds of energy at 1,300 yards. Who would have guessed, right?

I was also disappointed to discover almost all common .257-caliber bullets deliver pretty poor BCs, even the relatively long 117-grain bullets with which I've traditionally obtained my best .25-'06 groups. They give up a poor .410 BC, or only slightly better than .224 pills — and I always considered my .25-'06 a fine long-range choice. This is likely a product of most .257-caliber cartridges traditionally owning 1:10 rifling to accommodate 87-grain pills pushed early on for maximum advertising velocities, limiting the caliber to sub-120-grain bullets. Faster rifling and 125- to 130-grain bullets would likely improve the situation, though such bullets do not exist that I'm aware of. Some exceptions have arrived lately, such as Berger's 115-grain VLD Hunting (.483 BC) and Hornady's spanking-new 110-grain ELD-X (.465 BC) — bullets requiring 1:9 rifling twist many older rifles do not have. Check ballistic charts to see how your favorite round stacks up.

Here's an illustration of bullet shape and ballistic coefficient in .224-caliber, left to right: low-BC 50-grain generic soft- and hollow-points (BC about .214), and higher-BC 50-grain polymer-tipped and 52-grain Hornady Match and ELD Match (BC about .247 to .290).

Tye Lawrence used a venerable .30-'06 Springfield loaded with 180-grain Nosler AccuBond bullets with a ballistic coefficient of .507 to make a 400-plus-yard shot on this Texas hog.

BULLET DYNAMICS

Small-varmint shooters often fixate on terminal ballistics or bullets producing dramatic impacts, usually at the expense of BC. High-BC bullets include long, sharply pointed noses (versus blunt or steep ogives), and often boat-tail designs with hollow or polymer tips (versus soft points) to shift bullet weight into the bullet's center for greater spin stability. This relates to sectional density, which is the ratio of a bullet's weight to the square of its diameter. High BCs stack more weight into length than width, which also translates into pile-driving penetration.

The trouble with high-BC bullets is often poor terminal performance. High BC generally points to match bullets, often performing explosively at high velocities retained at close ranges (where superior BC is wasted) but acting like FMJs at longer ranges after velocity bleeds off. This isn't exactly a Greek tragedy on small varmints or even predators, as kills will result, though it becomes problematic on larger animals such as hogs. Penetration is adequate, but vital shock expansion is sometimes missing. Targeting bone (neck or shoulders) might be necessary to encourage fragmentation.

High-BC, long-range bullets now garner more engineering research and development than any other segment of the shooting sports. Some excellent examples include Hornady's ELD-X (suitable for big game, a 103-grain 6mm the lightest offering in this bullet), A-Max (match) and V-Max (varmint) in the heaviest-

Low- versus high-BC bullets in various calibers, left to right: .224 40-grain Sierra BlitzKing and 65-grain Cutting Edge MTH (Match/Target/Hunting); 6mm 100-grain HP flat-base and 110-grain Sierra MatchKing HPBT; .257 87-grain SP flat-base and 120-grain Nosler Solid Base; 7mm 100-grain Sierra Varminter and 168-grain Sierra MatchKing HPBT; .308 110-grain Hornady V-Max and 110-grain Barnes TAC-TX.

for-caliber offerings; Nosler's AccuBond LR (big game) and Ballistic Tip Varmint in its heaviest-for-caliber offerings; Sierra heavy-for-caliber Varminter HPs or GameKing SBTs and HPBT (big game) and venerable MatchKings (match); Barnes LRX (big game); Berger Long Range BT Varmint and VLD Hunting; and Cutting Edge's MTH (match/target/hunting) in heavy-for-caliber offerings.

LONG-RANGE RIFLES

In tandem with such bullets, long-range rifles must include barrels with faster rifling rates that provide greater gyroscopic stability, relative to caliber. Twist rates express the number of inches a bullet travels down the barrel before completing 360 degrees of rotation, and they're influenced not by bullet weight but overall length. Smaller calibers require faster twist rates than larger bullets of the same length (1:6 to 1:7 in .224 calibers, 1:8 in 6.5mm, 1:9 in 7mm or 1:10 in .308, for example). Pushing a bullet faster boosts stabilization a smidge, and although bullets subjected to marginal rifling twist might stabilize at higher elevations (thinner air), stability might deteriorate the closer to sea level you descend. In general terms, every 5,000 feet of elevation is the equivalent of an inch of rifling twist — meaning, as an example, a bullet that stabilizes with a 1:10 twist at 5,000 feet elevation might require a 1:9 twist at sea level. You can use formulas for determining required rifling twists, but the easy way is to visit websites such as bergerbullets.com or jbmballistics.com, inputting pertinent data and allowing their calculators to crunch the numbers.

Standard production rifling, especially in early rifles chambered in true .22-caliber varmint cartridges, was commonly 1:14 to 1:12, ideally suited to lighter, more explosive bullets. Slower rifling (larger numbers) will not properly stabilize heavier, longer projectiles. Savage Arms offers faster rifling-twist options in Model 12 Long Range Precision Varmint and 12 Varminter Low Profile (1:7 or 1:9 in .223 and 1:9 twist in .22-250). Mossberg offers faster twist options in its MVP Varmint series (1:9 in .223). Or, you can have your gunsmith install a precision aftermarket barrel on your favorite rifle, usually for around $500. The faster twist generally doesn't limit those rifles to longer, heavier bullets, within reason, allowing acceptable accuracy with lighter bullets.

I emphasize within reason because the fastest rifling (1:8 to 1:6 in .224-caliber rifles, for example) combined with the shortest-for-caliber bullets (35- to 45-grain normally) can overstabilize that projectile, causing it to wobble after leaving the muzzle (sometimes settling after 100 yards, grouping the same at 200 yards as 100) but in extreme cases spinning apart, given enough velocity. If you wish to use your varmint rifle for moderate-range small varmints with light, explosive bullets and long-range shooting with high-BC bullets, choose a middle-ground compromise of, say, 1:10 to 1:9 twists. Such rifling, in .223 Rem. for example, allows good accuracy with pills down to 40 grains (especially long-for-weight varmint designs such as Hornady V-Max, Sierra BlitzKing or Nosler Ballistic Tip) but also longer 60- to 65-grainers at the heavier end. To feed the light, fast craving with faster-twist rifles, you might also choose long-for-weight lead-free bullets with elongated cross-sections.

Before you proceed, the long-range rifle should print at least sub-1/2-inch 100-yard groups, as groups open exponentially with each 100 yards added. You'll normally pay more to guarantee this degree of precision, whether a factory rifle or custom creation. But you can pursue some avenues for making a rifle you already own more precise. Precision shooting is all about rifle harmonics. You tame these harmonics by first increasing rigidity to minimize barrel deflections.

The easiest solution is adding a heavier barrel. Shortening a longer, thinner barrel is also an option. My custom .223, for example, shot just average groups until my gunsmith cut away about 2 inches and recrowned that barrel. Groups improved instantly (reloading turned it into a one-holer). However, some cartridges need minimum barrel lengths for maximum performance, a matter of consuming all available powder before bullets exit muzzle — 26 inches for hot magnums, 24 inches for standard long-action rounds, 22 inches for 233-class rounds.

Many see fluted or triangular barrels as the solution. Hate to burst bubbles, but rifle barrels aren't load-bearing I-beams, instead flexing 360 degrees when fired. Any metal removed reduces rigidity but also

Rifling twist is important. For example, the three bullets to the left — Sierra's BlitzKing, Hornady's V-Max and Nosler's Ballistic Tip — shoot tight from the author's custom .22-250 Rem. The Barnes Varmint Grenade on the right keyholes. All weigh 50 grains, but the longer VG requires faster rifling twist to stabilize properly.

weight. Engineering calculus bears this out. But how about cooling? Recall that energy cannot be created or destroyed, only transferred from one form to another (the First Law of Thermodynamics). Expanding gases (burning powder), bullet friction and barrel flexing create heat during every shot. Heat seeks equilibrium, spreading first through highly conductive barrel steel, eventually dissipating into the atmosphere through convection. Increasing barrel mass helps spread and therefore dissipate heat. Fluting increases surface area to transfer heat through convection, but heat removal is minimized without steady air flow. Besides, barrel throats and crowns are most susceptible to heating, and flutes seldom extend into these areas. Overall, compared to the rigidity and steadying mass sacrificed, fluting is a dead-even tradeoff at best.

Larger-diameter barrels also reduce the effects of heat warp. Warping can result when a bore is slightly out of center inside the barrel blank. As that barrel warms, heat warp pulls the barrel unevenly by microscopic degrees. The heavier the barrel, the less it's affected. This is another good reason to invest in a premium custom barrel, as such bores are perfectly centered and usually provide superior precision.

Rifle rigidity also comes through proper rifle action and stock fit, as any shifting within this interface erodes accuracy tremendously. This problem is most pronounced with classic wood or cheap injection-molded plastic stocks. Glass bedding removes the slop and

Custom rifles long dominated the long-range scene, though new factory models have arrived, offering excellent long-range accuracy. Ruger's Precision Rifle is one of those, chambered in long-range rounds such as the 6mm and 6.5 Creedmoor.

generally strengthens a rifle's basic chassis. Any competent gunsmith can perform this task, normally for $75 to $100. In more extreme cases, aluminum pillars are added to bolster interface, another job for an experienced gunsmith. In my experience, bedding can turn even pencil-barreled rifles into tight shooters. And, of course, the barrel should be free-floated so impact isn't negatively affected by a hot barrel expanding into a stock to push it off center. A standard test involves wrapping a dollar bill around the barrel and sliding it between barrel and stock forend. It should slide beneath the barrel and to the action without binding.

Today, serious long-range shooters simply replace factory stocks with something more consistent and rigidly built, especially stocks built around full aluminum bedding. McMillan, Hogue and others offer many options. This also opens the opportunity for added features such as adjustable comb and length of pull, heavier bench-rest profiles and thumbhole designs, which add to cost but provide real-world benefits. Pure rigidity is why aluminum chassis rifles are a precision touchstone, eliminating all stock variability. A quality synthetic, laminated or chassis stock is also impervious to moisture, humidity and extreme temperature fluctuations.

Removing the factory wood or mold-plastic stock of your existing rifle and replacing it with a high-end custom stock, such as a McMillan A4, is one way to quickly wring a bit more accuracy from any rifle, as they offer a stiffer, more reliable base.

Added rigidity is also what makes top-quality one-piece scope bases valuable to long-range shooters, especially on rifles designed around open-top actions. A solid Picatinny-style rail increases scope-mounting options and anchoring security but also serves to stiffen the action, like a supporting crossbeam. To assure this truss remains secure, have your gunsmith retap mounting holes and add larger, stronger torx screws when necessary.

Many vintage military rifles included barrel tensioners, which are bolts mounted in the stock forend used to fine-tune barrel harmonics. You can accomplish this with modern rifles via LimbSaver's Sharpshooter X-Ring Barrel De-resonator. This is a NAVCOM-rubber donut that slides tightly onto the barrel. Its position is adjusted along the barrel length until discovering the vibration-wave sweet spot that tames muzzle movement during the shot, often allowing tweaking for sub-MOA groups with even factory ammo. They're offered in standard (½- to 7/8-inch barrels) and Bull Barrel (¾- to 1-1/8-inches). My custom .223 and Mossberg .204 wear them, and they definitely tightened groups. Interestingly, you might also find some rifles group better after several seasoning shots, as groups sometimes open with a squeaky-clean bore.

A huge factor in precision shooting is a crisp, clean trigger breaking at about 2 to 3 pounds and offering lightning-quick lock time. Quality triggers do nothing mechanically to make rifles shoot better, but they help the shooter, especially one prone to flinching. Adjustable triggers are best, though a good gunsmith can normally work any trigger for a lighter, crisper pull. Savage's AccuTriggers spoiled me, coaxing me to install drop-in models such as those from Timney or Velocity Triggers in my varmint rifles, typically for less than $200, including professional instillation.

TUNING THROUGH HANDLOADING

Another aspect of tuning rifles for better accuracy is careful handload development. What you are accomplishing, in essence, is harmonizing ammunition to a rifle. This is why I always caution that my pet loads might not produce duplicate results in your rifles. In long-range shooting, you must also choose a load and stick to it religiously so turret corrections remain constant.

My goal while handloading for long ranges is combining maximum velocity within standard working pressures with maximum accuracy, as speed equals elevation forgiveness and reduced wind drift. However, the emphasis always leans to accuracy. I generally begin by poring over load data and seeking a viable powder providing a high degree of efficiency, powders producing maximum speeds with minimum pressures and maximum speeds with less powder burned. I actually abandoned a speedy one-hole-group .223 Rem. load because it formed the highest pressures of any .223 load I've developed. I soon found a powder mirroring those velocities and group sizes, but with pressures almost 10,000 copper units of pressure lower.

Rifle harmonics affect accuracy, and handloading is a large part of this, creating ammo that agrees with a rifle's frequencies. LimbSaver's Barrel Deresonators also do an effective job of taming barrel harmonics and tightening groups.

Developing loads is often a matter of settling on something that's good enough but continually looking for a magic combination producing five touching bullet holes (I've owned rifles that shoot wonderful three-shot groups but begin opening on fourth and fifth shots). Starting loads are bracketed, loading five to 10 sets of five loads each in half-grain powder increments and shooting groups from the bench, the lightest loads upward, watching carefully for pressure signs such as flattened or cratered primers. I then take the tightest-grouping load from that batch and assemble more five- to 10-set, five-load test groups in one-tenth-grain powder increments. At that point, if it's not coming together, I move to another powder and/or bullet. If a load shows promise, I might load up various primer brands or types. From there, I began jockeying with seating depth, most rifles preferring bullets to sit just off the lands for minimal jump into the rifling (the reason so many factory loads fail to produce top-notch accuracy, as the bullets are seated deeply to accommodate the widest array of commercial rifles/magazines possible and require longer jumps into the rifling). Head-space gauges are available to determine seating-depth starting points. I might also audition various brass brands, seeing if a particular headstamp shrinks groups further. Tedious stuff, I know, and like I said, generally a continuing in-my-spare-time process.

Handloading also allows investing in the volume shooting necessary to become long-range proficient without breaking the bank. The larger varmint- or hog-suitable cartridges propelling best-quality high-BC bullets can ring up at $1.50 to $2 a shot in premium factory rounds, but reloading reduces costs to 50 to 75 cents per pull.

OUT-THERE OPTICS

You'll witness spirited campfire arguments about reticle styles, magnification indexes, fixed versus variable, MOA versus MRAD/mils, achromatic versus apochromatic glass, and even cost relative to quality. In extreme long-range shooting, those options are second in importance to turrets that track up and down, left and right, 100 percent reliably, 100 percent of the time. You'll be dialing turrets endlessly while long-range varmint shooting, and turrets — more correctly, interior erector-tube assemblies — that don't return to a precise zero after every shot only add to confusion and translate into more missed shots. If you plan to use MOA marks or mil-dots for elevation and windage estimations, that scope must also be a first focal plane configuration (see Chapter 9, "Varmint Scopes," "Focal-Plane Decisions" for detailed discussion).

In long-range shooting, fixed scopes are wholly viable, often letting you purchasing higher-quality optics and more reliability for less money. The variable-power fan might disagree, but understand that U.S. military snipers use straight 10X most of the time, including Chris Kyle, whose posthumous fame likely sparked the current long-range fascination. But military snipers are also shooting vertically oriented humans, a tad larger target than average prairie rodents or even horizontally oriented predators.

I prefer high-power variables to instantly adapt to changing conditions, but understand that lesser wares can actually lead to lower image quality at upper magnifications. I pay dearly for variable models with dead-reliable turret-tracking systems and top-quality glass. MOA (American system, ¼-inch clicks at 100 yards, one MOA about 1.05 inch) and MRAD (metric, 6,300 mils per 360 degrees, 1 MRAD equaling 3.438

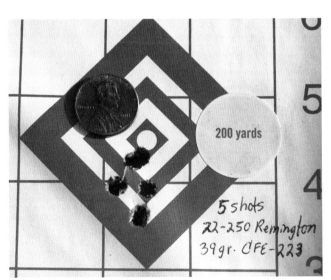

200 yards

5 shots
22-250 Remington
39 gr. CFE-223

If you are to achieve any degree of long-range accuracy, you must start with tight groups at shorter ranges. If a rifle is incapable of ½- to ¾-inch groups at 100 yards and sub-MOA groups at 200, it will generally relinquish poor accuracy at extreme ranges.

The needs of a long-range military sniper and small-varmint shooter vary greatly, mostly because of the smaller size of the latter targets. The author attached this Vortex Golden Eagle HD 15-60x52mm scope to his long-range rifle for that reason.

MOAs) are a matter of personal preference, so there's no wrong choice. Pick one, learn it and stick with it. Both systems are units of angular measurement, with increments compounding as distance increases. That is, ¼-inch clicks at 100 yards/meters translating into ½-inch at 200, 1-inch 400 and so on, which is why some serious long-range shooters choose 1/8-inch-click scope designs.

Requisite turret-travel parameters depend on cartridge and maximum effective range, a 1,000-yard shot with an average cartridge normally requiring at least 45 MOA of erector travel. This generally makes 1-inch-tubed scopes ill suited to extreme-range shooting, and 30mm most common (allowing about 60 to 70 MOA of travel) and perfectly suited to most varmint shooting ranges even when extreme. You'll need 32mm scopes for extreme long-range shooting past, say, 1,000-plus yards at larger targets. Should you find your erector-tube travel bottoms out before reticles reach required levels for the longest shots, scope rings can be set on tapered bases, normally

Turreted scopes, in the author's opinion, are vital to precision long-range shooting. They let you spin cross-hairs to exact ranges and dial away wind drift instead of applying Kentucky windage. This allows concentrating on spot-on aiming.

Modern laser range-finders make long-range shooting feasible. The author prefers laser-equipped binocular models, as they are more spot-on when ranging and can be used for spotting.

offset in 10, 20 or 30 MOA increments to tilt the scope downward. This means when you view targets through that scope, the barrel is pushed upward.

Units of elevation per rotation is also a consideration, as turrets with standard 15 minutes per turn requiring up to two full turns for, say, 750-yard shots, and 10-minute knobs maybe three at such ranges. The more turns required, the more confusing things become, especially when returning to zero on scopes without zero stop. In this case, remember to mark a horizontal hash mark with red Sharpie pen for instant verification of zero when returning turrets to zero after an extra-long shot.

I'm partial to Vortex Viper PSTs and Razors because they're familiar to me, but other worthwhile options include SWFA's Super Sniper (a quality fixed 10X for less than $300) and Bushnell Tactical Elite (another affordable option); U.S. Optics ST-10 (best-quality American-made fixed 10X) or Leupold Mark 4 (both running around $1,000); NightForce F-1 NXS and Schmidt & Bender Police Marksman in the $2,000 range; or NightForce ATACR, US Optics SN-3, Schmidt & Bender PM II or Zeiss Conquest for those who must have the best money can buy.

To make this come together, you must absolutely know the range, actual and compensated. I gave up on compact range-finder units long ago, as they're typically only useful at distant ranges when highly reflective objects — metal buildings or maybe a vertical cliff — are available. I prefer quality range-finding binoculars. They provide more precise aiming via increased magnification, include higher-quality microprocessors and are easier to hold steady for sure laser returns. Bushnell's Fusion 1 Mile binoculars are my choice, as they're Johnny-on-the-spot at 1,000-plus yards and the most affordable range-finder binocular offered at about a grand. Nikon's LaserForce series and Vortex's Fury HD are other relatively affordable choices. For the best available, look to Leica's Geovid HD-R, Zeiss' Victory RF or Swarvoski's EL Laser Rangefinding Binoculars, but know you'll pay dearly for them.

ELEVATION AND WINDAGE

Up front, I'm not an advocate of shooting big-game animals at extreme ranges. Deer and elk should not be treated as targets, as too much can go wrong. There's also a lot of difference between military snipers shooting enemy combatants at great distances and varmint shooters taking pokes at vermin to, say, 750 yards. The military sniper is under pressure to execute first-round hits. Shooting at a ground squirrel or prairie dog multiple times is pretty much par. A coyote or hog missed at plus-500 yards often has no idea what's happening when a bullet misses the mark. And long-range varmint shooting doesn't include the responsibilities carried by the big-game hunter or professional sniper, though enjoyment comes from doing it right. In reality, few varmint shooting scenarios exceed 500 to 700 yards, as varmints are too small to locate or discern beyond such ranges. Ethical issues usually arise on larger targets, namely the duty to produce clean, humane kills. Such ranges are still damned far, but details aren't as hyper-critical as shots taken at plus-1,000 yards/meters.

Accordingly, I'm going to weasel out of this just a bit, as I could pen an entire book on shooting at extreme ranges, and we don't have the space here for a detailed analysis. This is only a primer, after all. If you're interested, there's enough Internet content to keep you busy for weeks, including a lot of calculus and other mind-numbing minutiae. Most only think they want to get into extreme long-range shooting — until they become overwhelmed by the daunting finer points, including cosines and constants, graphing calculators, corialis (earth-rotation) and bullet spin-drift corrections, determined by several hundred dollars of equipment necessary to accurately measure atmospheric conditions, ammo temperature (IR thermometer), precise angle of fire and other considerations. Extreme ranges demand absolute precision, as the smallest errors become hugely compounded.

For our humble purposes, we'll rely heavily on assembled charts, as mundane details won't translate into more than a couple of inches here and there until about the 750-yard/meter mark. Basic forces at play on bullets traveling downrange include gravity, drag (BC) and wind. Gravity is constant, an element of trajectory. This is information provided by basic ballistic charts and more accurately by quality ballistics calculators. Calculators require humidity, air temperature and barometric pressure/altitude (standard altitude pressure charts generally suffice), which obviously change, sometimes daily. Relating to these, warm air is thinner than cool, low pressure, and higher altitude thinner than high pressure and low altitude, high humidity causing thinner air than low. Thinner, less-resistant air results in higher hits. Thicker, more-resistant air equals lower impacts.

The most practical approach is to record conditions typically encountered when and where you shoot most and create multiple compensation charts, extrapolating between five to 10 cards to fill in gaps. Print them on thicker stock, laminate them and carry them in your range bag. Ballistics calculators also require BC, or general bullet shape, represented by G1 (average pointed bullet) or G7 (high-BC designs), but the results are only approximations based on the three points of elevation, windage and distance traveled.

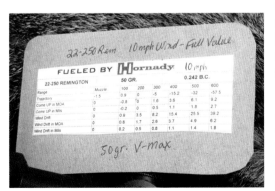

Ballistic charts help the long-range shooter make more educated range and windage corrections. At ranges less than 400 yards, basic charts are fine, but when stretching beyond that, information plugged into calculators must be more precise.

Hornady now offers its 4DOF (4 Degrees Of Freedom) ballistics calculator, established with Doppler radar to physically model projectiles in an extensive library. In addition to the standard "3 degrees of freedom" provided by most ballistics calculators, Hornady added movement (yaw and attack angle) in relation to a bullet's line of flight. Instead of a BC approximation, Hornady uses a drag coefficient specific to each bullet. In short, Hornady's 4DOF system is a more precise tool for long-range shooters, though it really comes into its own only at extreme ranges.

Now, ballistics calculators are only as good as the information supplied. Muzzle velocity is a big part of creating accurate ballistic charts. Yet muzzle velocity can vary according to ammunition temperature and especially barrel length. I encourage you to create ammo-temperature charts from your rifle, chronographing handloads (reloading manual numbers are not gospel) after allowing the ammunition and rifle to assume the same ambient temperatures they will be shot in. Don't, for example, leave your ammo and rifle inside a hot vehicle during warm, sunny days before shooting, or pull the ammo and rifle from an air-conditioned vehicle and immediately begin shooting on an especially hot day. Strive to compile this information during conditions closely matching those encountered during an average day afield. In a notebook, carefully record ambient temperatures and the chronographed velocities resulting, gathering enough information to extrapolate between gaps. Such charts help you plug more accurate data into ballistics calculators. How precise you shoot during actual field conditions is only as accurate as data inputted — garbage in, garbage out. When possible, confirm impacts at actual ranges, as your rifle might perform slightly differently than test guns used to establish computer constants.

You'll also need charts for wind drift for your specific cartridge/load/bullet from 90- and 45-degree angles (also 60 and 30 degrees, if available), headwind and tailwind. An angle-of-fire chart is also handy if regularly shooting in uneven terrain, letting you confirm laser range-finder drop-compensation numbers. Add these to your ring binder for quick reference.

EVIL WINDS

Plugging various wind velocities and headings into a ballistic calculator is one thing. The ability to actually read wind speed in the field is another matter. Wind drift increases at about four times the rate of range, and few shooters are truly proficient at reading true velocities. Some basic rules of thumb apply, but experience is the best teacher. When flags can be posted, say surveying ribbon on simple sticks, a flat-lined 24-inch piece of surveyor's tape indicates a 5- to 6-mph wind, and one drooping to 45 degrees indicates about 3 to 5 mph. The old-fashioned "feel method" is sometimes used but highly subjective: 1 to 3 mph moves dry, tall grass; 2 to 4 mph is barely felt, dust drifts slightly, large leaves

The shot on this Columbian ground squirrel was right at 400 yards, making it difficult enough. The bigger problem was variable wind between the shooter and target. The author spent 20 minutes studying and making corrections before making the one-shot kill.

Keeping tabs on the wind is the biggest challenge facing long-range shooters. Hanging ribbons, using wind meters and reading vegetation and heat shimmer help, but experience is the best teacher.

move; 4 to 8 mph is lightly felt on the face, smaller leaves move; 6 to 10 mph moves the tips of short-needled trees, with surrounding leaves or grass in constant motion; at 10-plus mph, small trees began swaying.

More sophisticated long-range shooters read wind velocity by noting mirage or heat-shimmer signatures through high-power rifle or spotting scopes. The object is to focus on the target before "de-focusing" back about 20 percent, tilting the optic up slightly and reading wave lengths. In simple terms, heat waves wiggling straight up indicate no wind (tail or headwind if boiling slightly); slight angles 1 to 3 mph; 45-degree angle 5 to 7 mph; sideways but squiggly 10 mph; and flat-line horizontal heat waves starting at about 12 mph. A wind meter — like those from Caldwell, Minox or Kestrel — is a sound investment but hardly foolproof, though a good tool for developing a feel for actual wind velocities.

Wind angle, determined by hanging a light thread or releasing puffs of light powder, also dictates correction values; 90 degrees, full value; 60 degrees, .85 value; 45 degrees, .70 value; and 30 degrees, .50 value. Wind speed is linear, so my advice is to create a chart for a full-value 10 mph wind (a round number most of us can wrap our heads around) and extrapolate for variations in velocity and angles using the established 10 mph values (list correction values on your wind card for quick reference). This is really the best you can do, as even 2- to 3-mph errors in wind-velocity judgment can mean 2- to 3-inch errors in impact, even while using precise calculus and graphing calculators. Remember, too, headwinds cause bullets to drop slightly, and tailwinds make bullets hit slightly higher.

And wind velocity is rarely consistent. It's important to remember bullets decelerate as they travel downrange. So, if a bullet is subjected by a 10-mph left-to-right wind on the first half of its journey and a 10-mph right-to-left wind on the second half, they don't cancel each other out, as ground is lost to the second wind column as the bullet slows. Averaging various wind speeds to the target requires a good deal of common sense. Let's say you're shooting marmots across a deep mountain canyon. Sitting on a cool north face, you feel thermals falling, while those marmots are sunning on a warmer south slope, where thermals are rising. Then, to make matters more confusing, a left-to-right atmospheric wind (which you might not be aware of) funnels down the canyon gap at still-higher velocities. Powerful optics focused on the open canyon gap and mirages might reveal this velocity difference, but not always.

One common-sense approach is to determine general wind direction and then basic parameters that will constitute an acceptable hit (the vitals of a hog, say) aiming at the windward edge of that vital area even after corrections have been made. Should wind drift prove greater than anticipated, you've created a wider margin for error. When shooting in gusty conditions, also attempt to time shots between spikes, minimizing corrections or hold-off. Luckily for the long-range varmint shooter, corrections can generally be made after a missed shot without ruining your day — another big plus of turreted scopes (and muzzle brakes allowing you to watch shots in). You might miss once, even twice or three times, but by noting impact, misses can simply be dialed away.

The author has developed a system that lets him carry about anything he could need while shooting in one rugged range bag. This allows grabbing one package and minimizes forgotten items.

⊕ Chapter 14
The Shooter's Field Bag

It doesn't matter whether I'm sighting scopes, testing handloads, simply plinking or seriously shooting varmints; if I'm shooting a firearm, my range bag accompanies me. This bag holds anything I might need while shooting; many of these not truly vital but included — you know, just in case. This is gear that makes common shooting-related tasks more streamlined. It includes necessary optics, gun-cleaning products, boxes to keep ammunition organized, my binder of long-range shooting charts, obvious hearing and eye protection, basic tools to get me out of simple (or not so simple) jams and many other odds and ends that only seem important when I don't have them.

I once used whatever cheapie bags were handed out at sports shows — usually thin nylon numbers with stenciled logos and holding zippers that failed in a season. When I finally decided it was time for a solid range bag, I hit the jackpot. Accompanying wifey into a box store while she filled a shopping cart with loot for the grandbaby, I naturally wandered into the sporting goods section. There, with a bright-red sales sticker attached, was a SOG Knives & Tools Take Point range bag — price, $35. Lucky day, as you can normally expect to pay $100 to $150 for a quality feature-packed range bag. This bag proved to be so perfect I'll use it as a prototype of features you should seek when purchasing your own.

This shooting bag includes a 9-by-9-by-16-inch main compartment — not too big, not too small. To each side of the interior are slip pockets to keep flat stuff neatly separated from bulky stuff. The main body is lightly padded, which is welcomed when packing valuable optics. The top zippered flap holds MOLLE loops if I need to bungee-cord an extra jacket or larger tripod in place. On one outside flat is a zippered pocket large enough to hold jags, brushes, cleaning rods, bagged oil rags, cleaning-fluid bottles and other related gear. An outboard flat-zippered pocket is perfect for slim notebooks and instruction manuals. Opposite is another large zippered pocket, this with an assortment of pistol-magazine slips ideal for small flashlights, writing instruments, compact multi-tools, lens cleaning and oil pens, caliber-specific laser-sighting cartridges and two torx drivers (scope ring and base specific, plus backup). The main compartment of this side pocket is also large enough to hold plastic organization boxes and a basic

Whether the author is running down the road to sight in a scope or test some handloads or departing for a long varmint-shooting road trip, his range bag and contained gear always go along.

gunsmith ¼-inch driver set. Clipped to one end is a cinch-top bag with a barrel lock, into which I drop spent brass while shooting, dumping them into the brass tumbler later. A wide removable shoulder strap and Velcro-secured carry handle are included, and all zippers, hardware and stitching are extra heavy-duty.

This bag gets me by, whether running down the road to quickly test fire new handloads or during a week-long road trip into the boonies. Dead Ringer offers a couple of range bags in medium and large, as well as a Tactical Backpack. Blackhawk! offers a good selection, and the company has a reputation for designing ruggedly dependable products. Uncle Mike's, Springfield Armory and Voodoo Tactical are other worthwhile choices.

Now here's what's contained within.

ESSENTIAL HEARING AND EYE PROTECTION

I've suffered from ringing tinnitus for as long as I can remember, the result of my tough-guy mule-headedness as a youngster and refusal to wear hearing protection. I also have a lot of guiding and duck blinds tossed into the mix. Because I now find it important to save what little hearing remains, I won't shoot even a .22 LR rifle without screwing at least foam earplugs into place or installing quality muffs. My range bag holds a plethora of foam plugs, pricey SureFire Sonic Defender plugs for tamer varmint rifles and two sets of top-quality earmuffs — low-profile Walker's Razor (the extra for guests). I've come to prefer the Walker's muffs, as they include volume-adjustable audio, allowing conversation or detecting whistling calls of nearby varmints. When I pull the trigger, they cut out to function like standard shooting muffs. Part of the fun of shooting varmints is spending time with my father, which is more enjoyable when we can converse without shouting or constantly pulling muffs aside.

The gel-like Sure-Fire Sonic Defenders are wonderful, offering all-day comfort and doing an amazing job muffling fairly raucous rifle reports. I plug these in while

An all-important part of the shooter's gear is quality hearing and OSHA-approved eye protection. Years of unprotected shooting have made the author determined to save what is left of his hearing, and it's pretty difficult to shoot when you can't see.

shooting alone or when temperatures are especially hot. Ear muffs can become awfully sweaty beneath a brassy sun. When I pull out my muzzle-braked .22-250, or while shooting bottle-neck-cartridge pistols (especially my break-equipped .223 Rem. T/C), I often wear earplugs and muffs.

There's a drop of vampire blood coursing through my veins, so I nearly always wear sunglasses, even when it's overcast or foggy. So I'm always wearing safety glasses. Muzzle blast, especially from rifles wearing breaks, can stir debris that irritates eyes. ARs and revolvers often spew hot gasses. In the unlikely event of a catastrophic firearms failure or returning bullet fragment, protecting eyes becomes most emphatic. Choose eyewear meeting ANSI and OSHA minimum standards to assure your eyes remain protected from flying objects. I kill two birds with one stone, choosing Wiley-X's Tobi, which provide sporty sun-shade style with industry-best eye protection. Its interchangeable lenses are nifty; clear for nighttime shooting, amber/orange for overcast or foggy conditions, and gray or brown in bright sunlight.

BINOCULARS AND SPOTTING SCOPE

Other than weapons scopes, optics are a large part of productive varmint shooting. In varmint shooting settings such as ground squirrel, prairie dog or chuck fields, binos help you locate your next victim or help another shooter mark their shots. While roving, I use optics to discover targets shaded up beneath cover. I've also adopted optics letting me kill two birds with one stone, using Bushnell's Fusion 1 Mile Laser Rangefinder Binoculars to find targets and get the range.

Years of living with binoculars around my neck while guiding made me fussy about how optics are carried. Split-shoulder harnesses with elastic straps, such as Crooked Horn Outfitters' original Bino Harness, are minimal, taking weight off your neck while keeping glasses handy. Still, I've come to prefer Rancho Safari's Binox Pouch, with a comfortable padded shoulder-harness holding a padded chest pouch. Open- and flap-top models keep expensive binos safe from hard knocks, dust or moisture.

Every varmint shooter should own a quality spotting scope. While sighting scopes, testing loads or confirming bullet-drop charts, they save a lot of back-and-forth walking to inspect shooting results. I insist on quality, as cheap scopes are worse than worthless. Spotters must possess the resolution necessary to clearly see bullet holes on paper at least 100 yards away, including tiny .17-caliber punches. For me, a spotting scope must also fit neatly in my range bag, as I have enough gear to wrangle and prefer to keep things in one grab-and-go package. My Nikon Fieldscope ED50 13-30x50mm works well for me. It's super compact but also gin clear. Stick with name brands, and remember with optics, you get what you pay for.

Spotting scopes are almost worthless without a tripod. Again, I prefer something that fits into my shooting bag. I choose a lightweight aluminum

Rifle and pistol scopes set well aside, optics are an important part of varmint and predator shooting. The author never leaves home without his Bushnell Fusion 1-Mile laser range-finder binoculars (killing two birds with one stone) and compact Nikon spotting scope.

(fiberglass or carbon are excellent) camera tripod with lever-lock adjustment extending to about waist height. It works well placed on a truck hood or on the roof while watching over a shooter's shoulder while standing in a pickup bed. This is my shooting-bag tripod. When sighting, testing loads or spotting long-range shots for other shooters, I'll sometimes use my big professional-grade photography tripod, as it allows me to comfortably stand behind the scope. Tripods must be highly adjustable (preferably with two to three telescoping segments) to allow leveling on uneven ground or surfaces, and include a swiveling/tilting head to pan onto targets with minimal effort. You don't have to break the bank, but don't buy junk, either.

GUN-CLEANING GEAR

High-volume varmint shooting requires occasionally pausing to brush out a barrel, most notably with the .17s. I can usually tell when I've waited 25 or 50 rounds too many, as accuracy begins to deteriorate sharply. In the field, I generally use a bore snake, which is a brass weight on a string fished down the barrel and used to pull a brush-impregnated rope through with a couple of drops of bore cleaner applied to scrub the bore quickly. A quart zip-top bag holds color-coded snakes for multiple calibers. At day's end, after 300 to 500 rounds, obviously a more thorough scrubbing with a classic cleaning rod is indicated. My shooting bag always holds take-down cleaning rods in various diameters, as you never know what you'll encounter, including a muzzle stuffed with snow or mud while predator calling — a dangerous situation. Whether bore snake or rod, always remove the

When space is tight during long varmint shooting road trips, the author gets along with a compact camera tripod. But when there's room, he prefers his professional-grade tripod, as it allows viewing while standing.

bolt/action, and feed from the breech (something obviously not possible with auto-loading .22 LRs). Real Avid offers super-compact cleaning kits such as the Gun Boss Pro Universal and AR15.

I keep a separate supply of various cleaning fluids in camp, but my shooting bag holds smaller sample or compact bottles of the same products, including bore cleaner, gun oil and action grease. Oil pens are quite convenient, as well as smaller aerosol cans that let you spray down dirty parts and flush contaminates away. A Zip-Lok bag of assorted patches and another filled with shop rags can always be found in my range bag in case I must wipe away grit and accumulated carbon. I also stash a couple of compact travel toothbrushes from Lethal for tougher jobs, such as cleaning AR gas systems after a couple of days of shooting.

As a quick aside, I prefer one-piece, bearing-handled fiber or ceramic-coated rods such as Montana X-Treme or Tipton Deluxe Carbon Fiber Cleaning Rods for serious cleaning. MTM's Gun Cleaning Rod Case allows storing four such rods and a bore guide, and keeping them safe and grime-free when tossed behind a pickup seat.

A super-soft cleaning cloth, stored in a clean zip-top bag, is standard for addressing optics. A LensPen (a brand name) is a must. These inexpensive tools include retractable soft-bristle paintbrush for brushing away visible dust and grit, with a cap-protected, felt-covered dish at the opposite end providing more thorough cleaning. These are the size of an AAA-battery flashlight but keep fine optics scratch free and bright. I also keep individually packaged moistened lens wipes on hand for thoroughly cleaning the nooks and crannies of eyepieces and lenses at the end of each day. I purchased a case of Zeiss lens clothes affordably at a local warehouse store, which is enough for many years of shooting.

BASIC GUN AND SCOPE TOOLS

Because of the high-volume nature of many varmint-shooting settings, "stuff," as they say, happens to even the best firearms and optics. I recall my father's customized 10/22 scope rail coming loose in the middle of a hot shoot. The scope had to come completely off, the base removed (turns out taps were stripped), a thin bead of high-temp Loc-Tite added to the underside of the rail, globs squirted into the taps, and the works reassembled carefully, left to cure and resighted. This temporary patch got him through the weekend. Scopes and mounts seem to present the most persistent problems, so any screwdrivers, box-end wrenches or hex or torx wrenches necessary to deal with every part of the ring and base assembly should be part of your kit. Super glue, JB Weld and Loc-Tite are always in my bag. You never know when these adhesives will come in handy and get you through a weekend until parts or a gunsmith can be summoned.

My shooting bag holds a basic Pachmayr gunsmith driver kit assembled in a hinge-topped plastic case, and a rolled-up Real Avid Pistol Smart Mat, which includes small trays to keep small parts and screws from becoming lost, and a neoprene pad to lay parts on if I must work on something in camp or at the truck.

Into the voids of the driver set, I've added a selection of common scope-ring and base screws (ask any gun-store owner or gunsmith, as they'll generally have plenty lying around), an eye-glass screwdriver, manufacturer-supplied scope-ring torx wrenches, turret set-screw Allens and spare set-screw sets, and spares of the torx or Allen drivers compatible with my guns in case of

Varmint shooting can involve high-volume powder burning. Firearms sometimes require daily cleaning. Your range bag should contain everything needed to keep your rifles and pistols in good working order.

accidental stripping. I also own a couple of Real Avid multi-tools: the Gun Tool Pro and AR-specific sets. Gun-wise, I've never had to deal with anything more severe than a loosened action, stock screw or scope bases, but I'm prepared, just in case. Xtreme Hardcore Gear's Action and Tank Crosshair Levels are also handy if a scope needs to be removed to, say, tighten a base before remounting.

AMMUNITION STORAGE AND ORGANIZATION

I'm admittedly pretty anal about my centerfire ammunition. One friend tosses completed handloads into Zip-Lok bags, fishing them out while shooting. Watching this makes me cringe. I want my lovingly assembled handloads protected, neatly labeled and at my fingertips. Stacks of MTM Case-Gard Ammo Cases make me happy, and they're so much easier to slip into a range bag for a day of shooting, or into larger MTM Ammo Crates or military .50-caliber or 20mm ammo cans for prolonged expeditions. Basic Case-Gard Rifle Ammo Boxes come in 50- and 100-round models, with crosshatched dividers keeping cartridges from rattling together, and including snap-lock lids to seal out dust and moisture. Deluxe Ammo Cases, in 50- and 100-round versions, include top carry handles and cartridge-specific interior trays with two height positions and drop-in holes to hold ammo securely. Fingers molded into the base protect bullet tips from hard impact. They're offered for 200 cartridge

sizes. There are other ammo-case manufacturers but few with as many options. Berry's Manufacturing, Midsouth Reloading, RCBS, Plano and Cabela's are but a few.

On longer trips, when large quantities of various rounds must be stored and organized, my shooting bag obviously won't hold it all. I use MTM Ammo Crates and/or the aforementioned steel military latch-lid ammo

. . . .

Stuff, as they say, happens, even to the most solid and well-maintained firearms. The farther from home and a gunsmith you are, the more likely this seems. An assortment of basic tools can leave you ready for minor scope-mounting and gun issues and save your weekend.

cans, letting me stack 500 to 800 rounds of varmint ammo inside 100-round MTM cases, latching lids tight and keeping ammo secure even should it's subjected to dust or rain while riding in the back of on open pickup bed or left stacked in camp.

The range bag might also hold magazine speed loaders if I'm shooting my 10/22 in high volume, and spare clips for that rifle.

OVERLOOKED ITEMS

The object of the shooter's bag is to keep you prepared for whatever might occur. After many years of hard lessons, I've discovered some seemingly innocent items can be important when far from home or even just sighting a gun. Sighting targets are obviously needed. I keep a pack of 14-by-18-inch gridded sight-in targets in my bag, folded neatly and stashed in a side pocket. These really came in handy when dealing with my father's scope-base issue and another time when my .17 HMR lost zero for no logical reason. It's not uncommon when traveling to find a riflescope must be rezeroed after a large elevation change. I also have a pad of small Hornady Post-It Note targets in my bag, which are compact and great for confirming impact or seeing how a load is grouping. I always keep a roll of masking tape in my bag to tack targets onto flat backstops (normally a cardboard box).

I always keep a roll of toilet paper in my shooting bag, for reasons beyond the obvious. In a pinch, toilet paper also makes a good lens cleaning wipe or oil rag. A hand towel is also a handy addition, especially on hot days when hands and brows turn sweaty. I pack a couple of promotional hand towels picked up at sports shows with a ringed corner and shower-curtain clip-ring, letting it hang from a belt loop or portable bench. I always keep a compact flashlight on hand, as you never know what you might need it for, including getting a better look while working on a rifle or scope. Mine is a SureFire E1L-L1 Digital Lumamax, because it's indestructible and holds lithium batteries with decade-long shelf life, so I don't worry about it sitting for years without use. It will be working when I need it — guaranteed. It includes a clip, allowing it to be attached to a ball-cap brim if I'm working on something and need both hands, and a neck lanyard so it doesn't become misplaced. Light gloves — Sitka Gear's Shooter's Gloves, in my case — are nice to have on hand in many situations.

And, of course, you'll have stowed your ballistics charts; bullet-drop, wind deflections, standard-unit conversion tables, angle-of-fire and so forth, organized in a small ring binder or mini accordion file. Even when not engaged in long-range shooting, with its need to add and subtract correction values, I always carry a notebook and ballpoint pens. You never know when you'll want to make notes on load, bullet or firearm performance, or problems or what-have-you in real time. Maybe cartridges are sticking slightly, indicating the need for case trimming or backing off a tad on your powder charge. Perhaps a rifle that shot only OK suddenly begins drilling after the barrel becomes a tad dirty. Maybe a bullet isn't opening on small varmints like you'd hoped, or your AR loads need to be seated slightly deeper to prevent tight extraction. Don't trust memory. Take notes. It's often these kinds of notes that help lead you to better shooting or give you deeper insight into how to wring more accuracy from a firearm.

Shooting well comes with experience, and the learning curve is often flattened by poring over notes in the relaxed comfort of home, away from the frenzied fun and excitement experienced while shooting varmints and predators far from daily responsibilities, work and telephones. A carefully assembled range or shooter's bag is all about being prepared. Half the stuff in my bag never gets used, but it's there should I need it, and that provides peace of mind.

The well-made shooters or range bag is all about keeping you ready for whatever might occur, keeping all that gear on hand and well organized to minimize rooting and maximizing the good times while shooting.

 Chapter 15

Author's Gear Picks

Benjamin

Crosman.com

Benjamin's Trail Hunting Air Rifle uses Nitro Piston 2 to drive .177-caliber alloy pellets to 1,400 fps (lead to 1,150). The break-barrel air rifle comes with CenterPoint 3-9x32mm scope set in an integral Picatinny rail. Other features include a two-stage adjustable Clean Break Trigger, a synthetic pistol-grip stock, friction/vibration-reducing tail guides, a precision-machined piston for smooth cocking and firing, a recoil arrest system and a rifled steel barrel with an integrated sound-suppression system.

Gamo Outdoor USA

Gamooutdoorsusa.com

Gamo's Swarm Maxxim pushes pellets to 975 fps in .22 caliber, with repeating capabilities via a 10-shot magazine. It uses a powerful and consistent Inert Gas Technology gas-piston system, and also sports a synthetic stock, a smooth Custom Action Trigger, an SWA recoil pad, a Recoil Reducing Rail to prolong scope life, integrated Whisper sound suppression technology and a GAMO 3-9x40mm AO scope.

Savage Arms
Savagearms.com

Savage's A-Series is now available in .22 LR. It remains available in A17 .17 HMR and A-Mag .22 WMR. Its semi-auto rimfire system is designed for reliable operation via a hard-chrome bolt, case-hardened receiver, 10-round rotary magazine and button-rifled barrel. Its user-adjustable AccuTrigger is an industry touchstone. The A17 is offered in Heavy Barrel, Target Sporter Laminate, XP (Bushnell Rimfire scope package) and Target Thumbhole.

Remington Arms Co.
Remington.com

Remington's Model 700 Varmint-Tactical Rifle, or VTR, offers long-range precision without excess weight because of its triangular-contour barrel. This provides sporter-barrel weight with heavy-contour rigidity and promotes faster heat dissipation. The 22-inch barrel includes an integral brake to tame muzzle jump and sits in a vented tactical stock. Its excellent trigger and proven 700 action produce tight groups right out of the box.

Mossberg

Mossberg.com

Mossberg's MVP Varmint rifle includes a laminated benchrest-style, pillar-bedded stock with a wide, flat forend perfect for shooting from a sandbag or bipod. Plus, it has a 24-inch medium fluted and threaded bull barrel with twist rates suited to longer/heavier bullets. Other features include the LBA (Lightening Bolt Action) trigger, adjustable from 3 to 7 pounds; factory-installed Weaver bases; and a fluted bolt with a checkered knob. They're chambered in .204 Ruger, 5.56mm/.223 Rem. and .308 Win., fed from AR-style magazines.

Alexander Arms

Alexanderarms.com

The Advantage Series from Alexander Arms, chambered in 6.5 Grendel, is serious hog medicine, providing the knockdown power needed during a recent Texas foray. The AWS is offered with 20- and 24-inch Shilen Match-Grade 416R stainless steel barrels with a 1:9 twist to handle pile-driving, long-for-caliber bullets and Midwest Industries rifle-length quad rails to hold a wide array of accessories. The classic A2 stock and ergo pistol grip are comfortable and easy handling, and the trigger is a standard single stage.

Browning

Browning.com

Browning's X-Bolt Varmint Stalker includes a heavy-contour blued barrel and a Mossy Oak Brush camouflage composite X-Bolt stock. The Varmint Stalker I shot in .204 Ruger was a tack-driver without being burdensome to carry. They're available in .204 Ruger (24-inch barrel, 1:12 twist), .223 Rem. (24-inch barrel, 1:12 twist), .22-250 Rem. (26-inch, 1:14 barrel) and .243 Win. (24-inch, 1:10 twist) and include five-round detachable magazines.

Rock River Arms

Rockriverarms.com

Rock River's 24-inch LAR-15 Varmint A4 is accurate, with a forged A4 upper receiver holding a stainless-steel .920-inch bull barrel with a TRO-STD free-float forend with three Picatinny rails and a fixed A2 butt-stock. Order a 16-, 18-, 20- or 24-inch barrel, all with .223 Wylde Chamber for 5.56mm/.223 Rem., 1:8 twist and guaranteed ¾ MOA at 100 yards. They include a low-profile gas block and an RRA two-stage trigger with the Winter Trigger Guard. They come with a 20-round magazine and hard case and weigh 8 to 10.2 pounds.

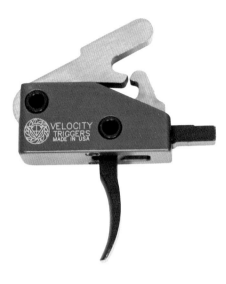

Velocity Triggers

Velocitytriggers.com

Velocity Triggers' AR Platform Triggers give AR rifles a bolt-action feel. These ultra-precise trigger groups include Diamond Like Carbon Coating, or DLC, for low-friction bearing surfaces and smoother operation, and high micro hardness for greater wear resistance and extreme rust resistance. They're compatible with .22 LR, .223 Rem./5.56mm and .30-caliber ARs, sold with 3-, 4- and 4.5-pound pulls, including a steel-cased version, and with standard, straight and large-pin triggers — retailing for only $150. A Remington Model 700 model is also sold.

Timney Triggers

Timneytriggers.com

Timney Triggers, in business since 1946, got its start designing single-stage triggers for common military rifles. Timney set the standard in aftermarket triggers, and 70 years later, it manufactures 170 trigger models, each hand assembled, tested and calibrated. Available models include five AR styles, four Mausers, seven Rugers, 12 Remingtons and three each for Savage and CZ, as well as triggers for Browning's A-Bolt, Howa, Mossberg, Sako, Weatherby, Winchester and others.

Hogue

Hogueinc.com

Hogue's Ruger 10/22 Tactical Thumbhole Stock is available for standard or .920-contour barrels, and in seven colors. They eliminate the forend band to produce free-floated barrels and greater accuracy. The pistol grip includes ambidextrous palm swells, and the forend includes a raise for steadier offhand shooting. The comb has an integrated cheek platform optimized for scope use. The anti-snag heel/recoil pad allows quick shouldering, and its built-in bench rest hook promotes stabilized, accurate shooting. The stock sports OverMold soft-touch rubber.

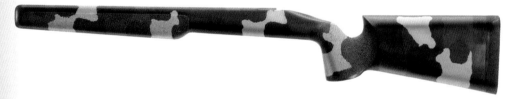

McMillan Stocks

McMillanusa.com

McMillan's A-2 Tactical is the stock worn by my one-hole-group Savage .223 Rem. It was designed with input from U.S. Marine Corps and FBI snipers and includes a vertical pistol grip and a straight-line, extra-high comb accommodating prone or bench shooting. The tapered forend allows elevation adjustments over rests by moving the stock forward or back. It comes with a three-way adjustable butt assembly, and an adjustable spacer system or with fixed length. They fit most popular rifle actions, and are offered in left- or right-handed versions in 35 color and camouflage options.

Taurus International Manufacturing

Taurususa.com

Taurus' 991 Tracker .22 Mag. nine-shot revolver combined with a pistol scope provides fun small-varmint pistoleroing. The stainless-steel revolver is inherently accurate via a 6.5-inch barrel. An extended ejector rod offers positive cartridge extraction, and Taurus' Ribber grip provides comfort. The Taurus Security System allows locking the firing mechanism for safety, and a transfer-bar design prevents discharge without pulling the trigger fully rearward. Scope mounts are available.

Sturm, Ruger & Co.

Ruger.com

Ruger's 22 Charger pistol is based on the proven 10/22. The semi-auto .22 LR includes a 10-inch hammer-forged barrel with ½-inch-28 end threads (with a thread protector). The A2-style grip is interchangeable with aftermarket MSR grips. An integral Picatinny rail allows mounting cross-hair or dot scopes, and the BX-15 magazine provides a 15-round capacity. It includes an adjustable bipod, models offered with synthetic or laminated-wood stock, and comes in one-piece or takedown versions.

Bushnell

Bushnell.com

Bushnell's Rimfire Optics are ideal for .22 LR or .17 HMR rifles. Five versions are offered, from 3-9x40mm with interchangeable .22 LR/.17 HMR turrets, to compact 6-18x40mm for extended-range shooting. They're sleek and waterproof, with multi-coated glass delivering bright, clear images. Three include side parallax, and two have adjustable objective rings for sharp images at any range. The 4-12x40mm AO model includes BMag350 bullet-drop compensation reticles for the 20-grain .17 WSM to 350 yards. They're affordably priced but big on performance.

Trijicon

Trijicon.com

Trijicon's Electro-Optics IR-Hunter Thermal Imaging Riflescope provides best-in-class thermal imaging for precision nighttime shooting. The IR-Hunter includes a 640x480 thermal image sensor and digital image processing. Digital focus and contrast controls adjust for maximum clarity and sharpness. Four models are offered, including Enhanced Target Recognition (ETR) for best-quality images; an 8X digital zoom that maintains bore sight; MicroIR 12 Micron Technology, with 42 percent greater magnification; crisp, detailed reticles; ergonomic turret knobs; digital image/video capture; and multiple reticle options.

FLIR Systems

Flir.com

FLIR's new ThermoSight Pro Series provide the latest thermal-imaging technology for nighttime predator or hog hunting. New 12-micron Boson thermal camera core produces smaller, lighter units with improved performance and range. On-chip video processing and uncompressed signal feed directly to an HD 1280x960 display, providing cleaner target imaging. They're offered in three configurations, each offering 320x256 thermal resolution, Bluetooth 4.0 and USB-C connectivity and a wide array of user options. The unit records up to two hours of video or 1,000 images, and includes an internal compass and inclinometer. They're offered with 19mm/12-degree, 50mm/4.5-degree and 75mm/3-degree lenses and 4X zoom, starting at an affordable $2,199.

SIG Sauer

Sigsauer.com

Sig's ECHO1 Digital Thermal Imaging Reflex Sight offers direct view and targeting via five default reticles (and you can download others). The design includes a top-mount peep sight, and captures single or burst-mode downloadable images. LCD display allows faster day/night direct-view targeting and multiple temperature settings. The unit has M1913 Picatinny rail mounting. The 1-2X electronic zoom allows 1,000-yard detection and 300-plus yard targeting via ½ MOA adjustments. Other features include white-hot/black-hot settings, a 206x156 uncooled VOx Bolometer Array, PX-6 waterproofing, a 30 Hz frame rate and 12 micron HD pixel size. It runs eight hours on two CR123 batteries.

Leica

Us.leica-camera.com

Leica's ER 6.5-26x56 LRS provides high-end magnification, 90 percent light transmission and excellent contrast. Best-quality glass and coatings, including water-shedding AquaDura, assure no color fringing and clear, sharp images, combined with exceptional scratch resistance. Its finely tuned tracking system assures precision turret adjustments, and a side focus knob allows instant clarity. It's available with lighted 4a (ultra-fine cross-hairs), Ballistic and LRS reticles (with multiple range cross-hairs). The 30mm scope weighs 21.5 ounces.

Vortex Optics

Vortexoptics.com

Vortex's Gen II Viper PST 30mm turreted scope provides affordable performance. RZR Zero stop assures accurate zero returns after elevated correction, and its fiber-optic turret indicator helps mark turret rotations.

Combined illumination/side parallax dials create cleaner lines, with illumination including 10 intensity levels with off positions between clicks. The reticles are highly functional without clutter. First focal plane reticles are offered in select models, with matching MOA or MRAD turrets. XD lenses assure excellent resolution and color fidelity, and ArmorTek coating protects them from grime and scratches. The 5-25x50mm makes a fine long-range option.

Meopta USA

Meoptasportsoptics.com

Meopta's MeoPro 6.5-20x50mm HTR (Hunt/Tactical/Range) offers precision, European-designed/American-assembled excellence in an exposed-turret scope. It includes TO2 (Twilight Optimized Optics) MeoBright coating for 99.7 percent light transmission; accurate, repeatable MeoTrak RZ ¼ MOA hunting or target turrets (adjustable zero, posi-click); a MeoQuick fast-focus eyepiece; and a 1-inch, nitrogen-purged, fog- and shockproof one-piece aluminum tube. It is designed to provide long-long confidence and extreme reliability. Four reticle styles are offered, and the scope includes lifetime transferable warranty.

Styrka

Styrkastrong.com

Styrka's S5-Series 4.5-14x44mm SH-BDC riflescope offers affordable quality. This fully multi-coated scope includes the SH-BDC reticle with holdover marks from 100 to 600 yards and an oversized side-focus knob adjustable from 20 yards to infinity. Adjustments are ¼-inch MOA, with 50

MOA adjustment range for elevation and windage, in a 1-inch, one-piece aluminum tube. Adjustments include zero reset. The scope is waterproof and nitrogen purged, weighing 19.1 ounces. A web-based ballistic calculator app can be loaded on IOS or Android devices.

Leupold & Stevens

Leupold.com

Leupold's VX-3i 8.5-25x50mm CDS Target gives budget-minded long-range shooters quality in a 30mm tube with excellent color fidelity, resolution and exceptional light-gathering abilities — including Twilight Max Light Management System. Easy-dialing zero-stop turrets are covered with caps when not in use, and a Custom Dial System is included. CDS dials are matched to your exact load, velocity and bullet drop and can be ordered for various loads and conditions. The lightweight scope includes generous eye relief, a side focus knob and super-fine cross-hairs.

Xtreme Hardcore Gear

Xtremehardcoregear.com

Xtreme Hardcore Gear makes my favorite scope-mounting systems. The TRU Level Long Range Picatinny Base includes an integral level visible while shooting, milled from 7075 T-6 aluminum and including Mil-Spec Class III hardcoat anodizing. It's anchored by 6-48 torx screws, for Remington 700, Ruger 10/22 and American, Savage, T/C, Tikka and Winchester actions in 0 and 20 MOA. Ranger Rings include a secure .875-inch mounting platform with two cross bolts and twin stainless-steel guide rails for perfect alignment. Six torx screws assure that scopes remain anchored. They include .030-inch radiused edges, in 30mm or 34mm.

Hornady Mfg. Co.

Hornady.com

Hornady's Superformance Varmint, loaded with NTX, V-Max bullets and proprietary powders, offers velocities often unmatched by handloading without undue pressures. This ammo is also exceptionally accurate, producing sub-½-inch groups in a couple of my rifles. It's offered in .17 Hornet (15.5-grain NTX, 20-grain V-Max), .204 Ruger (24-grain NTX, 32- and 40-grain V-Max), .222 Rem. (35-grain NTX, 50-grain V-Max), .223 Rem. (35-grain NTX, 53-grain V-Max), .22-250 (35-grain NTX, 50-grain V-Max) and .243 Win. (58- and 75-grain V-Max).

Federal Premium Ammunition

Federalpremium.com

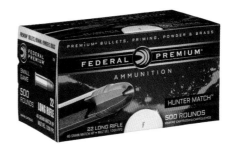

Federal's Hunter Match .22 LR shells offer exceptional accuracy plus devastating terminal performance. Lead 40-grain Hunter Match hollow-point bullets are tuned for optimum penetration and expansion to 100 yards, with high-velocity (1,200 fps) loading assuring flat trajectories and maximum energy delivery. Bullets are held in nickel-plated cases and launched by reliable Federal priming and a specially formulated propellant.

American Eagle

Federalpremium.com

American Eagle Varmint offers those depending on factory-loaded ammunition for high-volume varmint shooting an affordable alternative with terminal impact. Look for it in 50-grain .223 and .22-250 Rem. 20-packs; 90-grain 6.5 Grendel, 20-grain .17 Hornet, 35-grain .22 Hornet, 50-grain .223 and .22-250 Rem., and 75-grain .243 Win. 40-packs; and 6.5 Grendel, 6.8 SPC and 130-grain .308 Win. 50-packs. Hornets include poly-tipped bullets, and others have JHPs.

ELEY

Eley.co.uk

ELEY is synonymous with accuracy, as its .22 LR shells are used by the world's top competitive shooters. You also get that accuracy in ELEY's hunting loads, including Subsonic Hollow (1,040 fps) and High Velocity Hollow (1,250 fps), both shooting 40-grain, rapid-expanding hollow-points. The loads provide exceptional accuracy, and the HV includes an oxidized case that helps control bullet-ejection force to better regulate velocity and accuracy.

Aguila Ammunition

Aguilaammo.com

Aguila is a reliable source for quality .22 LR ammo, delivering even during previous shortages. It makes some of the fastest .22 LR ammo, including the .22 SuperMaximum (in brass or nickel cases) at 1,700 fps, and .22 Interceptor at 1,470 fps. The SuperMaximum shoots 30-grain flat-points, and the Interceptor shoots a 40-grain flat-point. Both include copper plating for cleaner barrels.

CCI Ammunition

Cci-ammunition.com

CCI is the industry's most reliable source for rimfire ammunition, including .17 HMR, .22 LR and .22 Mag. loaded with quality polymer-tipped and hollow-point bullets. For .22 Mag. fans, this is great news, as CCI has kept sporting goods shelves stocked while other companies have come up short. CCI .22 WRM ammo is offered in Maxi Mag and Maxi Mag +V, including Maxi Mag 40-grain JHP, +V 30-grain JHP, 30-grain TNT JHP and Signature Maxi Mag 40-grain JHP.

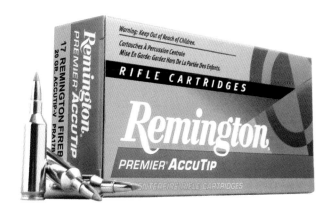

Remington

Remington.com/ammunition

Looking for match-grade accuracy and explosive results on varmints? Remington has your answer. Remington Premier AccuTip-V offers ultra-tight groups and dynamite impacts in several classic and even hard-to-find varmint cartridges. These include .17 Fireball (20-grain); .17 Rem. (20-grain); .204 Ruger (32- and 40-grain); .22 Hornet (35-grain); .221 Rem. Fireball (50-grain); .222, .223 and .22-250 Rem. (50 grains); and .243 Win. (75-grain).

Hodgdon Powder Co.

Hodgdon.com

Hodgdon's CFE BLK is spherical powder specifically formulated for the .300 Blackout. CFE stands for Copper Fouling Eraser. CFE BLK also performs beautifully in varmint cartridges such as the .17 Hornet, .218 Bee, .22 Hornet, .221 Fireball and many more. While working up .22 Hornet loads, I found CFE BLK meters like water and burns quite cleanly. Free loading data is available at hodgdonreloading.com, an excellent overall resource for all handloading needs.

Vihtavuori Powder

Hodgdon.com

Vihtavuori is all about accuracy, and N140 has emerged as one of my most versatile varmint-round propellants (equivalent to Alliant Reloader 15 or Hodgdon H380). N140 provides sub-¼-inch groups from my .204 and .22-250, but it's also useful for the .223 Rem. with heavier bullets and .243 Win. with lighter pills. The clean-burning powder is at its best in the .22-250 to .220 Swift.

Western Powders

Westernpowders.com

Ramshot TAC is another of my favorite powders because of its extreme versatility. This double-based spherical propellant burns clean and meters flawlessly. TAC produces one-hole groups with 40-grain bullets from my .223 Rem., and is also suitable for .17 Rem. and Fireball, .204 Ruger, .222 Rem., .22-250 Rem., 6.5 Grendel and low-capacity .257-caliber rounds. Other Western Powders favorites include A1680 (Hornets), A2230 (.204 Ruger, .223 Rem.), Ramshot X-Terminator (.17 Fireball to .22-250 Rem.) and A2700 (.22-250 and 6mm Rem.).

Alliant Powder

Alliantpowder.com

If you're loading varmint and predator cartridges, odds are you'll eventually turn to Reloder 15. This medium burn-speed powder provides excellent results in varmint rounds from .223 Rem. to .243 Win. and more. RL-15 isn't affected by temperature fluctuations and produces higher velocities and tight groups in most varmint rounds. Other Alliant favorites include RL-10x (.223 to .22-250 Rem.) and RL-7 (a .221 Fireball ideal).

Speer Bullets

Speerbullets.com

Speer TNT bullets have gained a following among high-volume varmint shooters because of supreme accuracy, rapid expansion and reasonable prices. These flat-base bullets include thin, precision jackets with internal fluting and dead-soft lead core for explosive impacts. Long ogives and a small hollow point provide improved ballistic coefficients. They are offered in 39-grain .204; 50- and 55-grain .224; 70-grain 6mm; 87-grain .257 and larger calibers.

Midsouth Shooters

Midsouthshooters.com

Midsouth Shooters has the answer for those seeking affordable, quality bullets for high-volume varmint shooting. Varmint Nightmare X-Treme bullets are top-quality and accurate bullets made to Midsouth specs by a big-name bullet manufacturer. They're offered in .172 (20-grain HP flat base), .204 (34-grain HP flat base) and .224 calibers (50- and 55-grain soft-point and 55-grain hollow-point), priced at about $45 per 500, giving you more shooting for your money.

Cutting Edge Bullets

Cuttingedgebullets.com

Cutting Edge's lead-free Copper Raptors expand lethally at speeds down to 1,600 fps. These milled monolithic pills include aggressive hollow points that hold large, BC-boosting polymer tips. On-impact internal scoring encourages the tip to break off into six controlled blades, cutting and ripping while the BTB (Blunt Trauma Base) exits like a wadcutter. Slightly oversized SealTite Band means the bullets aren't critical of groove diameters. They're offered in .224, .243, .257 and larger calibers.

Sierra Bullets

Sierrabulles.com

Sierra made its name with extreme accuracy, and BlitzKing expands that tradition. BlitzKings share MatchKing accuracy characteristics but with proprietary-formula polymer tips and thin jackets to produce dramatic terminal performance. The .204- and .224-caliber BlitzKings can be safely driven to 4,400 fps, and the lightest 6mm offerings to 4,000 fps. They're offered in 32- and 39-grain .204; 40-, 50- and 55-grain .224; 55- and 70-grain .243/6mm; and 70- and 90-grain .257.

Barnes Bullets

Barnesbullets.com

Barnes' aptly named Varmint Grenades provide a lead-free, long-for-caliber bullet that pulverizes small varmints. The hollow-cavity, flat-based bullet holds a powdered copper-tin core surrounded by a gilded metal jacket. VGs remain intact at high velocities and from fast-twist barrels but produce instant fragmentation on impact. Look for them in 26-grain .20-caliber; 30- (Hornet), 36- and 50-grain (one of my favorite AR bullets) .22-caliber; and 62-grain 6mm.

Rocky Mountain Reloading

Shop-rmrbullets.com

The .224-caliber 3-Gun Hunter (3GH) from Rocky Mountain Reloading was designed for ARs but work in other gun designs. The 3GH mirrors the profile and ballistic characteristics of Sierra's proven .224-caliber, 69-grain MatchKing but expands on game. The HPBT design includes a tapered jacket and jacket crimp, which lets the nose peel away for maximum shock, with expansion checked at the crimp to assure ample weight retention. What you get is match-grade accuracy combined with killing terminal performance.

MTM
Molded Products

Mtmcase-gard.com

MTM Case-Gard cases keep ammo safe and organized. The RS-50 and RS-100 hold 50 and 100 rounds of .223 Rem. (and similar-sized cartridges), and the RM-50, RM-100, R-50 and R-100 (with top carry handles) hold 50 or 100 .22-250 Rem. Cases stack neatly and are made for 200 cartridges sizes. Store in larger Ammo Crates, with the 7.25-by-13.5-by-14-inch ARC8-72 easily holding eight each of the RS-100 and RS-50, or 1,200 rounds of .223 Rem., keeping them safe from dust and moisture.

Real Avid

Realavid.com

Real Avid's Gun Tool Pro-X covers most in-field firearms needs. The compact, nylon-sheathed multi-tool holds a removable magnetic LED

light for peeking into dark spots, plus 14 firearm-specific Torx, Allen, Phillips and flat bits. It also has a 2.5-inch claw-point knife, a choke wrench, a ¼-inch bit driver and wrench for high torque, a scope-turret tool, two metal files, a lanyard loop, a tap hammer and a punch.

GSM Outdoors

Gsmoutdoors.com

Walker's Razor electronic muffs include slim ear cups and a rubberized coating for easy handling. Two high-gain omni-directional microphones enhance hearing but cut out within .02 second when decibels spike. Advanced electronics are frequency tuned for natural sound clarity and include an audio input jack. The recessed side volume control is easily adjusted by feel, and the muffs fold compactly for easy storage. The comfort headband includes a metal wire frame and muffs sound dampening composite. They operate on two AAA batteries and cost less than $75.

Wiley-X

Wileyx.com

Wiley-X's Tobi POL Silver Flash/ Gloss Black Frame sunglasses look stylish and include shatterproof Selenite Polycarbonate Lenses that meet ANSI high velocity and high-mass impact and OSHA standards. They're designed to fit medium to large heads, and come with a black zippered hard case, a leash cord with rubber temple grips and a microfiber cleaning cloth. Multi-coated Z-Oxide lenses include 100 percent UVA/UVB protection with distortion-free clarity, and T-Shell lens coatings resist scratching.

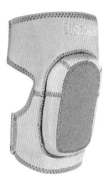

Blackhawk!

Blackhawk.com

Blackhawk!'s Neoprene Elbow Pads are a lifesaver while shooting off a rough portable bench or lying on the ground prone. Layered construction makes them comfortable, and textured contact points increase durability and improve grip on slippery surfaces such as pickup hoods. A high-density, closed-cell foam core provides padding with minimal moisture retention. Its contoured interior cradles your elbows and prevents slippage and movement. The slip-on design is available in black, Coyote Tan, Foliage Green and Olive Drab.

PREDATOR GEAR

Primos Hunting

Primos.com

Primos makes many practical predator calls, my favorites including the Raspy Coaxer, Still Jackrabbit and Hog Grunter. Raspy Coaxer imitates jackrabbit screams and is a good long-range call, plus it produces rodent squeal to coax hung-up predators closer. The Still Jackrabbit produces realistic distress calls and can be used hands-free. The Hog Grunter is excellent for coaxing nearby hogs out of thick brush for a clean shot or stopping them for standing shots.

Flextone Game Calls

Flextonegamecalls.com

Flextone's Dog Soldier K9 Killer Long Range and Mouse Trap have become company favorites. The K9 Killer is a long-range rabbit distress call including Lip Band to reduce lip and mouth fatigue when calling long hours. The rubber body bends to impart instant inflection. The mouse-shaped Mouse Trap produces loud or soft squeaks to lure smaller predator in tight cover or coax a hesitant predator closer. It straps to your gun or hand for one-handed operation.

FOXPRO

Gofoxpro.com

FOXPRO's mid-priced Banshee is a compact electronic caller with big sound. It holds 100 preloaded MP3-format calls, including predator and distress vocalizations. It runs on 10 AA batteries, and the remote uses three. Its bullhorn design allows extreme volume for big reach, and FoxBang technology automatically changes calls after rifle reports to confuse remaining predators. Its remote includes longer range, a larger screen and an elapsed timer with an alarm, programmable calling routines and more. External jacks accommodate accessories such as the FoxJack 3 electronic decoy.

Tenzing Outdoors

Tenzingoutdoors.com

Tenzing's Predator Pack provides comfort and organization while calling. It has fully adjustable spring-loaded legs, an internal aluminum frame and a fold-down seat with a padded comfort backrest. It weighs 7.5 pounds and includes 2,200 cubic inches of storage space, including 23 pockets for calls, optics, ammo and other critical gear. Other features include hardwarmer/hip pockets, 17 rifle cartridge and six shot-shells loops, three mesh pockets for small items and a rifle tote system. Thick shoulder and waist straps assure comfort, and the pack/seat is covered in A-TACS AU camo.

Streamlight

Streamlight.com

Streamlight's TLR-1 Game Spotter Pic-rail light includes a shockproof green LED invisible to game. C4 LED technology and a parabolic reflector produce 150 lumens while optimizing peripheral illumination. It's offered with standard or remote switches. It runs on two 3-volt CR123A lithium batteries for 1.75 continuous hours. It also has an O-ring seal, a rugged black-anodized 6000-series aluminum body, and an unbreakable, scratch-resistant polycarbonate lens.

TRUGLO

Truglo.com

TRUGLO's TRU-Point Laser/Light Combo allows choosing constant laser or flashlight, or a flashlight-laser combination. Its quick-detach lever quickly mounts to Picatinny rails. The light generates 250 lumens, and the 520nm green or 650nm red laser can sighted for fast nighttime bullet placement through micro elevation and windage adjustments. It operates on two CR123A batteries. A remote pressure switch is included. It's milled from aluminum and water and shock resistant.

Cyclops

Cyclopssolution.com

Cyclops' REVO 1100 LED Handheld Spotlight is compact but provides 1,100 lumens of nocturnal illumination. The rechargeable unit comes with A/C and cigarette-lighter plugs, providing 68 minutes of nonstop burn time on a full charge, powered by an integrated 6-volt battery. Two Luxeon LED lights can be covered with a detachable red lens. It includes an LED power meter (green/ yellow/red), alerting you when recharging is necessary. The ergonomic handle/grip includes a trigger pulse switch or can be switched to continuous operation.

Plano Molding

Planomolding.com

Plano offers two gear boxes perfect for varmint shooters. The XL Shooter's Case includes a lift-out tray, a roomy interior and a yolk system to cradle rifles while cleaning. The Hunting Stool Field Box includes a removable tray atop a roomy interior, plus side mesh and side zippered pockets for additional storage, and an integral seat cushion and carry strap. Lift-out lids are excellent for organizing cleaning gear, and latch-top lids and interiors are perfect for keeping ammo safe from dust and moisture.

Benchmaster USA

Benchmasterusa.com

BenchMaster's Perfect Shot Shooting Chair allows you steady shooting in maximum comfort. The web-style chair includes full 360-degree rotation and an adjustable-tilt back reclining to 50 degrees. Four multi-position/locking legs with large, solid foot pads allow leveling on uneven ground for added stability, and all steel parts are powder-coated to resist rust. The gun-rest extension adjusts for height and length to accommodate all sizes of shooters and weapons. I set a cooler full of cold drinks beside mine to hold boxes of ammo and binos and shoot in comfort.

Swagger

Swaggerbipods.com

Swagger's Bipod is ideal for dynamic situations such as predator calling. Legs extend to 29¼ inches and include Crazy Legs Technology. Spring bases allow twisting, pushing or pulling rifles to address targets at various angles. Legs lock to act like standard rigid bipods. Each leg includes a shock cord to retract into the base when not in use, the base then acting as a second forend.

LimbSaver

Limbsaver.com

The Nitro Force-SR-1 SmartRest from LimbSaver includes a side-to-side swiveling center bracket set on bearings, fully adjustable front and rear rifle-cradling V brackets, and vertical rails attached to Dyna Pneumatics Nitro Pistons. It allows pivoting rifles smoothly left, right, up and down while controlling tension, its pistons dampening sudden movements for improved accuracy. It includes a lightweight anodized alloy frame and nonskid rubber feet (magnetic feet optional).

SKB Cases

Skbcases.com

SKB i-Series cases are dust- and waterproof, indestructible but lightweight. They include sturdy latches and handles and transport wheels on larger models. SKB offers 46 options to fit everything from handguns to the longest rifles. My ATA-300-rated, military-approved i-Series Custom AR Case holds ARs up to 41 inches long, includes foam inserts cut to perfectly cradle rifles/scopes to prevent jostling during transport, and has cut compartments for gear, extra magazines and ammo boxes. They include an unconditional lifetime warranty.

Uncle Mike's Tactical

Unclemikes.com

Uncle Mike's 10-by-43-inch (large) Tactical Rifle Case is perfect for AR-style rifles with scopes, shorter rimfires or longer single-shot handguns. A full-length zipper offers instant access, and an adjustable web shoulder strap is included. A zippered accessory pouch allows carrying cleaning gear or spare ammo, and five vertical pouches with Velcro closures hold AR magazines. Another Velcro-top center pocket is perfect for shooting muffs.

Lakewood Products

Lakewoodproducts.com

Lakewood's Double Scoped Rifle case is a godsend when traveling with pickup beds full of gear. The top-loading/drop-in design, with 8-1/8-by-11-by-49-inch dimensions, holds two scoped rifles safely while offering quick access via zippered, locking top. Rifles/scopes are separated in contoured slots by extra-thick foam. Cases include four metal D-rings for tie down and a shoulder strap. They come in black or TrueTimber camo. Personalized logos/name can be added for $20.

Hoppe's

Hopes.com

Hoppe's Black offers premium care for modern rifles, with new formulas designed for intense cleaning. These high-performance gun-care cleaners and lubes are designed to deliver maximum performance in high-volume, gas-operated AR firearms but are suitable to all firearms. They're formulated to withstand temperatures from minus 65 to 540 degrees. The line is comprised of Gun Cleaner, Precision Oil, Copper Cleaner, Grease Syringe and Lubricating Cloth. The molecular composition of each provides maximum performance and excellent cleaning action.